In the autumn of 1950 Graham Jones joinec
Grammar School, and for the next five years th
educate him. He wishes now that he had been

In an attempt to divert a young master
lesson a cheeky boy might enquire, 'And what d

The response was usually very short. However, this was not a pointless question because this was the decade of National Service when every able-bodied lad was expected to spend two years in uniform. Graham chose blue and served for three years in the Royal Air Force.

The Korean War and the Suez Crisis were over, but there were still 'trouble spots' – Malaya, Kenya, Aden, and for Senior Aircraftsman Jones, Cyprus. This overseas experience gave him a touch of wanderlust, and over a lifetime he has been twice round the world. He has visited historic sites of conflict as far as Pearl Harbour in Hawaii, Rorke's Drift in South Africa, the Crimea, My Lai in Vietnam, Scapa Flow in the Orkneys, and numerous battlefields in Europe.

Graham has a particular interest in the Great War because his father served as a gunner in the Royal Artillery. He lost friends, one of them an Old Boy of Bridgnorth Grammar School.

OLD BOYS
YOUNG
LIVES

GRAHAM JONES

Published in 2018 by the author

Copyright © Graham Jones 2018

The right of Graham Jones to be identified as the author of this work
has been asserted in accordance with the Copyright, Designs
and Patents Act 1988 Sections 77 and 78.

ISBN 978-1-78132-727-2

British Library Cataloguing in Publication Data
A CIP catalogue record for this book is available from
the British Library

Page design and typesetting by SilverWood Books
Printed by TJ International on responsibly sourced paper

This book is dedicated to those students of Bridgnorth Grammar School and Bridgnorth Endowed School who served their country in conflicts world-wide and upheld a centuries-old tradition.

Contents

An Inspiration

Some of the most dramatic images of the battlefields of the Great War came from the valley of the Somme. In 1916 a battle raged here for over four months. It began on the 1st of July and came to an end in mid-November. An early report in the Daily Mirror was upbeat, *'Allies' Losses Slight – A Very Satisfactory First Day'*.

The British Army lost 57,000 men on the 1st of July, it was the most disastrous day in British military history and the day George and Isabella Wightman lost their son, Charlie. He was reported missing, he was never found. His name is one of those inscribed on the panels of the Thiepval Memorial among the 72,000 who died on the Somme.

Richard Findon also died in July – in August Fred Head died – September Frank Findon and Alfie Stokes – October Tom Robins. All had been boys together and all are remembered on the Thiepval Memorial and in their old school, Bridgnorth Grammar School.

Private Charlie Wightman's brother, James, survived the war. He was a schoolmaster by profession but turned his hand to carpentry in his spare time to build an honour board to be hung in the school hall. He assembled it from odd pieces of oak. He carved a wreath and cut gilded letters to left and right, HONOUR – VICTORY. He found mouldings to surround the three panels on which he carefully painted in black the names of the men he had known and that of his younger brother.

Nearly a century passed by. To commemorate the anniversary of the outbreak of the Great War Wightman's work was restored. Waiting for a final polish it lay on a table near the library window. July sunshine streamed in and warmed the oak panels to body temperature. Rebecca felt no

© Graham Jones

chill as she leaned forward and rested her palms on the surface. The oak had once had life as had the lads whose names she read. The girl hadn't broken any hearts yet but soon she surely would – so pretty, so charming she was. Who would be the lucky man, none of those before her now?

If the honour board had been a 'touch screen' a head and shoulders picture of the boy would have popped up as she ran her fingers over the names. There would be a brief note of his achievements, interests, hobbies. Which one would she choose?

"Not him definitely, his hair's parted down the middle, nor him, he's got a tickly little moustache. He looks a bit wild, I wouldn't trust him."

"He's nice."

"Horace Price, old fashioned name, and he's got glasses but he's still nice, I like him."

After school she paused in the High Street, to look at the brightly lit display of watches and trinkets in the jeweller's shop. The door to the right of the window was once the Price's door. She turned away and passed the door that closed behind Horace Price on his last home leave, before he left for France to die.

The next time Rebecca visited the school library the Honour Board

Left to right Jesse Marston, Richard Findon, Horace Price

had been firmly fixed to the wall. Some names stood out – Schoolcraft, what an odd name, McMichael, sounds Scottish, Boucher MC, what's that about? Who were these men? What of the families and homes they left behind? Their classmates that did return, what became of them? There must be a story behind every name she thought.

I am most grateful to Rebecca and Phoebe, sixth-form girls of Bridgnorth Endowed School, for their help in drafting this introduction.

Author's Notes – Not to Be Missed

I apologise. I have failed. Failed to do justice to the memory of the Old Boys of Bridgnorth Grammar School, who served in the Great War.

After two years of war the editors of the School Magazine compiled a list of one hundred and twenty 'Old Bridgnorthians with the Colours'. By the end of the war more than two hundred and fifty had served 'King and Country' and forty-three had given their lives. I have included the service and family histories of less than half of these men.

I hope my readers will be forgiving, and accept the many imperfections in this book. There are no doubt inaccuracies and certainly omissions. I have attempted to set out the events in chronological order. A few of the Old Boys stories do not fit into any particular event during the war so, in this introduction, I will offer the histories of a handful of them, in the same format that I have used throughout the book.

Searching service records is made easier, of course, if the surname is uncommon. Only twenty-one Hockenhulls served in the Great War, whereas there were twenty-one thousand Joneses.

PRIVATE (42165) LATER CAPTAIN ALFRED WILLIAM HOCKENHULL – 3RD SOUTH STAFFORDSHIRE REGIMENT

A Sergeant of the South Staffordshire Regiment filled in most of the form for Alf Hockenhull. He was a boot-boy at the Victoria Hotel in Wolverhampton. Alf added his signature to the document. His faultless copper-plate handwriting was far superior to that of the recruiting sergeant. This seventeen year-old lad, cleaning shoes for visitors to the town, was no ordinary boot-boy.

The second son of William and Emily Hockenhull, Alfred's first memories were of the family farm at Chelmarsh and the games he played with his brother John and sister Mabel. The family grew, and when Alf was twelve he filled in the census form for the whole family in his own distinctive handwriting. Family circumstances had changed, father was no longer a farmer at Chelmarsh, he was a farm labourer at Barnsley. Alf, the bright boy of the family, had moved from the village school at Worfield to Bridgnorth Grammar School, this would not have been possible without a County Council Scholarship.

Alfred began his military training with the 5th Graduate Battalion of the Leicestershire Regiment, exactly what was expected of a Grammar School boy. Training complete, a number of recruits went on to be commissioned officers, Alf went to the South Staffordshire Regiment as a Private soldier. He had the wit but not the background to be an officer.

Private Hockenhull joined the Battalion in France just before Christmas 1917. There wasn't much to celebrate although the childish banter between the North Staffs and the South Staffs did help to keep the lads cheerful through the winter months. They shared the dangers, taking turns to man the front line trenches near St Quentin. In March there were signs of spring, green shoots appeared in the cold mud of no man's land, the earth began to stir. The enemy also began to stir, they had been planning a series of operations that they hoped would lead to victory.

On the 21st of March 'Operation Michael' was launched with brutal efficiency. A heavy bombardment signalled the start of the advance towards the British lines. All along the battlefront infantry battalions buckled under the onslaught and were forced to retreat. Alf Hockenhull's battalion was virtually wiped out in the attack and the withdrawal that followed, they lost 19 officers and 662 men, killed, wounded or missing.

Some of the wounded limped back to the reserve trenches, helped by comrades. Alf was one of the wounded, shot through the chest, he needed treatment. He lay in no man's-land and waited. German shock troops had swept past him. At last he was picked up and given first aid. He was in good hands even if they were enemy hands, Alf was a prisoner of war.

The Spring Offensive was the last throw of the dice for the Germans.

They were held, and then pushed back during the summer months. Fresh drafts arrived to fill gaps in the ranks of the Staffordshire Regiment. In October they were on the attack. After the Battle of Selle two hundred more keen young lads were added to the casualty list.

Private Hockenhull's wounds had healed. He was safe and had only a month to wait before his release. Prisoners of war were on short rations but everyone was on short rations. He may have complained about the grub dished out by the British Army but no doubt he was grateful for the hot meal he was offered on the 30th of November.

At home in Barnsley, he soon caught up with local news, of lads he had known, 'killed, wounded and missing'. They swopped stories, Alf had battle scars, his mates said, 'You ought to get something for that.'

The medical board agreed, the bullet holes were clear enough but they also accepted that he was suffering from neurasthenia, mental exhaustion. Alf was given a pension, five shillings and six pence a week. His father was earning about sixty shillings a week at the time.

Alf was discharged in June 1919 and shortly afterwards a large envelope was delivered to Rowdale House. It contained something to hang

King's Certificate

on the wall, the King's Certificate – 'Served with honour and was disabled in the Great War' it said. Above this, carefully written, but no better than Alf could have done himself was, '42165 Private Alfred William Hockenhull 3rd South Staffordshire Regiment'.

Used to cover a damp patch

That was all he had to show for his efforts. The time had come to get on with life, to shake off his neurasthenia and 'pull himself together'. Meeting Ellen Mackerness helped.

Alfred and Ellen were married at Cleobury Mortimer in 1922. They were the roving kind. They moved to Faversham in Kent where 'little Alfred' was born and then to Maidenhead, where Gwen was born. Alfred it seems was willing to try his hand at anything, and when the possibility of owning land presented itself Alf was ready to take up the offer.

The Canadian government offered assisted passages to families willing to work the land. This Farm Settlement Scheme had the blessing of the British Government, they offered cheap loans for the purchase of land, stock and machinery. The Hockenhulls made their way to Southampton and boarded the *SS Minnedosa*, they were eight days at sea before they docked at St John, Newfoundland. There was still a long way to go, to Alberta, one of the Prairie Provinces. They crossed the Cabot Strait by ferry and then began the train journey along the banks of the St Lawrence to Quebec. There was so much French spoken there that Alf thought he was back in France. There was still two thousand miles to go, but plenty of stops along the way, Sioux Lookout, Moose Jaw, and Medicine Hat. What an adventure, this was Indian country!

The family settled north of Calgary, good land, wheatland prairie, and they prospered. Hard work 'breaking the sod' on the prairie must have taken a toll on Alf's health, and the old gunshot wound didn't help. He was only fifty-four when he died.

Following Alf's death in 1952, Ellen visited family in England. It wasn't entirely a social visit, she was looking for youthful labour to help out on the farm. Aunty Mac, as she was known, tried to persuade her nephew, Michael, to try his hand at farming. She described the wide open spaces, waving corn as far as the eye could see, and rich pasture for the cattle. This was fine in the summer time but she did admit that farming could be hard in the winter. Stock had to be fed and watered.

By the time you've crossed the yard the water in your bucket is frozen.

That was enough for the lad to make up his mind, Michael stayed at home, his aunt returned to Alberta, and the farm. It was rich land, and beneath it was something really valuable. They struck oil on 'Aunty Mac's' Land. It was part of the Joffre Oil Field.

King George had sent a certificate to acknowledge that Private Hockenhull had been disabled in the Great War. That was not enough, his children held him in higher regard. In 1973 they put up a headstone to both parents and promoted Private Hockenhull to Captain.

Peace at Last

With permission from the Hockenhull Family

Alfred died young, and life had been hard for Ellen but there had been some rewards. For others a promising start in life was cut short. There were lucky ones who faced danger many times and survived without a scratch. Others spent a fortnight on the battlefield were wounded and never fully recovered. Young men came from far-off lands to join the fight, local farm boys, and the sons of High Street shopkeepers all played a part.

Surgeon Lieutenant Thrusfield and Sub Lieutenant Peck were already at sea when war was declared. The news of war spread worldwide in min-

16

utes, signals were sent to ships of the Royal Navy, and regimental outposts throughout the British Empire.

Old Boys heard the call. Percy Nevett left a dusty gold-mine town in Western Australia. Leslie Smith took the train from Medicine Hat and with other Old Boys crossed Canada to join in. Ralph Bourne was ranching in Argentina, and did not want to be left out. He travelled to the United States and sailed to England to join the fight, all were 'brothers in arms'.

There were also many examples of true brothers in arms, where families had sons of a similar age.

LIEUTENANTS CONRAD & GEORGE PAYLING WRIGHT – ROYAL GARRISON ARTILLERY

Conrad Payling Wright was two years older than his brother George. The Wrights were not native to Bridgnorth, they moved to the town from Middlesbrough. William Wright was a Congregational minister. Neither of sons had the same commitment to the church, Conrad became an economist and George a pathologist. Completing their education at the Grammar School set them on the road to success.

These were studious boys, unfortunately the war interrupted their studies. Both were commissioned in the Royal Garrison Artillery, both served in France, and both returned safely to North London. William and Mary Wright had moved on again to a more permanent residence in Golders Green.

George continued his studies at Exeter College, Oxford and completed them at University College Hospital in 1923. He was awarded a travelling scholarship to study at Washington University and did further research at Harvard University. He returned to London to lecture in 'morbid anatomy', the study of the structure of diseased organs and tissues. This was not the sort of thing to talk about at a dinner party. Service on the battlefield may have prepared George Wright for this gruesome work.

Conrad Payling Wright had also applied himself to his studies during the decade following the war. His studies took him well away from the world of morbid anatomy, perhaps he had seen enough of it in France in 1916. Like his brother he too completed his studies in America. He was an economist, and the only anatomy he was interested in was that of Esther Isabella Clark, they married in 1924. She was an academic, a lecturer at Harvard. The couple moved to Wolfville Nova Scotia. Conrad's career progressed from instructor, to lecturer, to professor.

By the outbreak of the Second World War the Wright brothers were leaders in their chosen specialisms. Conrad served with the RAF in North Africa during the war, he wasn't a flyer, more likely a strategist.

Studying, moving around the country, travelling abroad, this did not appeal to everyone. Certainly the Ridley family could see no reason to move away from Bridgnorth. They had been farming and trading in the town since before the Civil War. They set up a business to supply seed to farmers in the surrounding area in the year of Shakespeare's death, 1616.

Ridley's Seeds

Old Established

Although the Ridley brothers both served in the Great War, this had little effect on the course of their lives. Evan Ridley volunteered to serve in October 1914, and his name was added to the list of Old Boys serving with the Shropshire Yeomanry. His brother John, two years younger, volunteered in March 1917 when he was just eighteen.

PRIVATE (2140) EVAN PAUL RIDLEY –
RESERVE REGIMENT, SHROPSHIRE YEOMANRY

Both Evan and John were educated at home before attending the Grammar School. Evan suffered from rheumatic fever and was advised to leave school to be taught by a governess at home. He was the eldest boy and expected to farm, like his father. The farmhouse at Oldington must have been a busy place, there were the parents, five children, two housemaids, the governess and the farm bailiff, all under one roof.

Evan rode into Bridgnorth to sign the attestation form. He was given a medical examination the same day, 23rd of October 1914, a month short of his eighteenth birthday. He was passed fit, 'good physical development'.

Evan served with The Yeomanry for just ninety-two days. Then he was discharged, 'medically unfit for further service'. The superficial medical examination on the day he joined had not revealed 'a 'valvular disease of the heart'. Evan returned to the farm.

The condition that resulted in his early discharged from the army did not seem to affect him greatly. He farmed very successfully, and he was seventy-five when he died at High Trees. Evan Ridley married twice, Dorothy Barrett in 1923 and Daisy Jones in 1954. He certainly had a heart condition, he loved them both.

PRIVATE (139171) JOHN BROUGHALL RIDLEY –
ROYAL ARMY MEDICAL CORPS

Compared to that of his brother, John Ridley's experience with the British Army seems to have been equally frustrating.

When he went before the medical board in March 1917, although he was taller than Evan and apparently more robust, he was classified as B1 and not A1. He was training as a motor engineer and had volunteered for the Royal Flying Corps. The best the army could offer was the Royal Army Medical Corps.

Serving with a Reserve Battalion in Lancashire, Private Ridley seems to have spent his time either at Preston or Blackpool. There was no record of any medical training although he was awarded a Certificate of Education. John's contribution to the war effort was not going to be great. He had his own problems, optical, dental and behavioural.

He appeared on the Regimental Conduct Sheet in April 1918 – he lost a day's pay and was 'confined to barracks' for seven days. John had been granted special leave, probably to help with farm work – this was not uncommon. He was late returning to camp. In May he was in more trouble, 'being in possession of a comrade's belt', and confined to barracks for a further seven days.

It was the last year of the war, and in preparation for transfer to France, John made one last visit to the dentist in Blackpool. This was a painful experience – two extractions, ten fillings and two root fillings.

Private Ridley was waiting at Chatham when the war ended. Three months later he reported to Prees Heath and joined the queue of lads picking up their 'demob' papers, then back to Oldington. At least the army had solved his dental problems.

Evan and John Ridley were not posted abroad, they never set foot on a battlefield, they did not qualify for any war medals. Not everyone could be a hero, and no one set out to be a hero, but heroes there were.

Eleven Old Boys were awarded the Military Cross, two airmen were honoured for their bravery, and others were decorated by foreign governments. The highest award went to Sydney Westrop who received the Distinguished Service Order.

Tom Wilson, a Lieutenant in the Tank Corps, died leading his men at the Battle of Cambrai, in November 1917. His commanding officer recommended him for a Victoria Cross. The award went to a senior officer who died in the same action. The only Old Boy to receive Britain's the highest award for valour was Hugh Rowlands, he died in 1909.

It would be surprising if the generation that went to battle in France had not heard the story of this Old Boy who fought at the Battle of Inkerman sixty years earlier.

THINGS ARE LOOKING GRIM

Among the boarders at the Grammar School in 1843 was nine year old Hugh Rowlands from Llanrug, a village in North Wales. Within a year he had left and continued his studies at Beumaris Grammar School. This was nearer home – he loved Llanrug, this was his final resting place.

© BES Library

The rest was well earned. For over forty years he served Queen Victoria in every corner of her empire. Eventually she appointed him Lieutenant of the Tower of London.

His reputation was made during the Crimean War, at the Battle of Inkerman. Private John McDermond and Captain Hugh Rowlands went forward to the rescue of Colonel Haly. He lay wounded, surrounded by Russian soldiers. Rowlands and McDermond fought them off and brought the Colonel back to safety. They both received the Victoria Cross for their bravery.

Did this story inspire any of the Old Boys who went to war in 1914? Probably not. Lads of every generation suffer from the arrogance of youth, they are not interested in the past deeds of old men. Wearing the grammar school uniform would also have given some of them an extra level of arrogance. The majority the families bought their privileged education, although some were there on merit. War was the leveller. A fine example of the levelling was that of Southwell and Sherry.

The early years for George Sherry and Arthur Southwell were very different. George's father was a council labourer, Arthur's father was the manging director of H & M Southwell's Carpet Manufacturing Company, and chairman of governors of the Grammar School

The homes of the folk in Cartway and Friar's Street were modest and their trades various. The Hollands were chimney sweeps and the Bowens hawkers and scrap dealers. Mr Badick was a tinman, Mrs Rowe took in lodgers and did their 'mending', and Ted Jennings was a soldier and Jesse Green a marine. 'Tinker, tailor, soldier sailor', they were all there.

Also, to ensure that William Southwell's business was profitable, there were the setters and tuners, dyers and weavers, yarn winders and threaders, creelers and bobbin boys.

William Southwell came down to his office daily from 'Fairfield', more than a mile away, and far removed from the clatter of the weaving sheds of his carpet factory. The family house was very grand and very suitable for the owner of the company that was the biggest employer in the town.

At the turn of the century when Arthur Southwell was completing his education at Hillside School, Malvern. George Sherry was a creeler in Southwell's carpet works, a monotonous job in an atmosphere of noise and dust. Southwell's company was well established and William must have hoped to hand it on to his son one day, although at the time Arthur Southwell seemed more interested in agriculture.

Lord Kitchener called for volunteers in 1914 and all over the town lads changed their trades, blacksmith and clerk, carpenters and carters all dressed in khaki. Walter Sherry, George's brother, was on the battlefield within a month of the outbreak of war. By Christmas 1914 the Bridgnorth Journal could report that from Cartway and Friar's Street alone over seventy young men had joined the colours, all but twenty joined the county regiment.

Arthur Southwell had joined the 6th Battalion Shropshire Light Infantry, at the outbreak of war. He had been given an education that would have qualified him to be an officer but he enlisted as a Private soldier. The Battalion trained throughout the winter months. Newly promoted Corporal Arthur Southwell and 'C' Company first set foot on

French soil in July 1915 and were soon in the thick of it.

In a letter home in September he reported, "We made an attack here last Saturday morning...we were in a communication trench just behind the firing line...shells of every kind were falling around us, 'Jack Johnson's', huge shrapnel".

The object of the attack was to draw the German fire and enable the French to advance. The Black Watch and Gurkas led the way.

> *After three hours we were moved into the firing line... Dead men were lying all over the place and shells bursting in every direction. A 'Jack Johnson' killed a number of our wounded men, and a doctor at the first dressing station in the lines. The next night we had to go and hold a trench some little way off. It had been raining on and off since the attack began, with the trenches a foot deep in mud and there were still dead men all over the place – it was an awfully gruesome sight.*

With only rainwater to drink and biscuits and bully beef to eat Arthur and his company 'stuck it out' for a week.

"However, I am alright, only tired and done up." He must have been in a state of shock, his senses numbed by the cold and wet and the scene around him. "We can see any amount of dead men in front but cannot get out to them."

Over 150 men of the KSLI died on the 25th of September 1915.

Arthur Southwell was promoted to sergeant and sent home to England for further training. He had shown himself to be a good leader and steady under fire. By midsummer 1916 he had been commissioned as a 2nd Lieutenant. From Prees Heath Camp he travelled to France to join the 7th Battalion on The Somme. He soon made a name for himself. Lieutenant Southwell and ten of his men carried out a bombing raid, it was later described in Battalion Orders as being carried out 'with great daring and resolution'.

The Battle of the Somme, begun on the First of July, ground on through August, September, October. As winter approached the days grew shorter, the weather more gloomy. The generals planned a 'last big push' in November. The county regiment prepared for the Battle of the Ancre. The Ancre was a muddy stream no wider than the Worfe Brook.

© Imperial War Museum

In preparation for any attack inexperienced young officers were given guidance on Army Form SS415, 'the Duties of an Officer'. The text was taken from an address by a Senior Officer,

Drop hard on any slackness, disobedience and slovenliness. Never stand any rot or nonsense. I don't want you to go away, however, with the idea that the men must be treated like dogs – very far from it. Remember that although we are officers and the men are privates, still we are all comrades.

Lieutenant Southwell had served as a Private soldier and did not need this sort of advice.

Private George Sherry and Lieutenant Arthur Southwell prepared to do battle. The artillery began pounding the German positions early on a Saturday morning, the bombardment continued the next day. Soldiers in the front line got very little sleep. Ahead of the 7th Battalion, leading the assault, were Royal Scots. They were old friends, Salopians and Scots had fought together before. The aim was to capture a chain of fortified villages, Serre, Beaumont Hamel, Thiepval.

When the whistle blew, just before six o'clock on the Monday morning the troops began to go 'over the top'. It was pitch dark, 'thick fog was spread over the ground and the morning was as black as the darkest midnight'.

The ground was so sodden that tanks could not be used and the infantry went forward without support. So deep was the mud in places that the ration parties took four hours to cover a thousand yards. Conditions did not improve. At daybreak, the fog was as thick as ever. When it began to clear at about eleven o'clock it was found that all units were hopelessly mixed. With the chain of command broken young officers acted on their own initiative.

Arthur Southwell was 'dangerously wounded' last seen sheltering in a shell hole, he was reported 'missing'. His death was not confirmed for over a month.

The action at the Battle of the Ancre had cost the battalion dear. Over two hundred men were reported killed, wounded or missing. George Sherry died the same day that Arthur Southwell lost his life. They had fought well and deserved to live on and enjoy life to the full.

George Sherry might have returned to Southwell's factory and picked up where he left off as a creeler, a job with little prospect. Had Arthur Southwell survived and inherited the company, he would surely have helped his old comrade in arms. William Southwell was generous, and did provide a living for many men who did return.

The Great War was not won by Old Boys of the Grammar School, with families living in fine houses in East Castle Street or Victoria Road. Boys with little schooling, from crumbling cottages on Bernard's Hill, were just as willing to fight for freedom. Joining the army at eighteen they were already mature, they had been in the world of work since they were twelve years old.

No matter the school or the street, Bridgnorth town can be proud. Every generation has produced young folk with a gift for learning, excellent athletes, the brave and adventurous, and the steady and stalwart. So it is today.

Graham Jones, Bridgnorth 2018

Chapter 1

The Call to Arms

The Great War might have started earlier, in 1905 or 1911, but the rival nations of Europe drew back from the brink. Gavrilo Princip, a Serbian student, may have held back if he had known that his actions, on a Sunday afternoon at end of June in 1914, would trigger the catastrophic Great War.

Crowds lined the streets of Sarajevo to watch the Archduke Franz-Ferdinand of Austria pass by. Serbians wanted independence from Austrian rule. Gavrilo looked upon the archduke as the most powerful symbol of an oppressive regime and he planned to kill him. The archduke and his wife acknowledged the applause of those in the crowd who were clearly pleased to see them. Princip might have just jeered as they passed by. Instead he stepped forward, drew his pistol and fired three shots at point blank range. Within twenty minutes the heir to the Austrian throne and his wife were both dead.

The assassination gave the Austrians the pretext to humiliate their troublesome neighbour, Serbia. A man who could have prevented this was Wilhelm II of Germany, Kaiser 'Bill', a vain, neurotic little man with a withered arm. He encouraged the Austrians in their squabble with Serbia and the whole of Europe was plunged into war.

The nations took sides. Austria had Germany's backing, Serbia was assured of Russian support. France and Russia were allies. A month after the shooting in Sarajevo the nations began to mobilise. It was clear that Britain and her Empire would soon be drawn in.

The Germans put the Schlieffen Plan into action. Drawn up by Count Schlieffen in 1905, he believed that if his plan was followed the French would be brought to their knees within six weeks and then

German troops could be swiftly transferred to the Russian front on a rail network built for that purpose.

To cross the border into France the invaders must pass through Belgium. On the 2nd of August 1914 the Germans demanded free passage, it was refused. Britain had been a guarantor of Belgium neutrality for seventy years and was ready to honour that agreement.

The War began on a Bank Holiday when well-to-do families might have taken a hamper into the countryside and enjoyed a picnic. On August 4th Great Britain declared war on Germany – that would be no picnic.

This was truly a World War involving not only the European nations but also their colonies and overseas territories. Africa had been carved up by the British and French to create some of their colonies and comparatively little was left for the Germans: Togo and Kamerun in West Africa, Namibia in the South, and Burundi, Rwanda and Tanganyika in East Africa.

Richard Thursfield must have been the first Old Bridgnorthian to see action in this part of the world.

Surgeon Lieutenant Richard Thursfield – Royal Navy

He joined the crew of *Astraea* in 1912. She patrolled the coast of Africa from a secure anchorage near Cape Town. From her moorings at Simonstown *Astraea* could sail west into the South Atlantic or east into the Indian Ocean.

Under Table Mountain

NAVY LEAGUE OF SOUTH AFRICA. CAPE TOWN BRANCH.
Our British Navy protecting our Nationality, our Commerce, our Produce.
Ons Britse Vloot beskermende ons Nasionaliteit, ons Handel, ons Produkte.

BALMORAL DUNLUCE BRITON   H.M.S.   GUILDFORD GOORKHA KENILWORTH   H.M.S.
CASTLE CASTLE   HYACINTH   CASTLE   CASTLE   ASTREA
Warships escorting steamers from Table Bay, 27th August, 1914.
Vertrek van Stoombote uit Tafelbaai op 27 Augustus 1914 onder beskerming van Oorlogskepe.

As tensions grew in the months before the war the gunners practised their skills along the coast of South Africa. They let fly at floating targets with mortars, six-inch guns and torpedoes. *Astraea* steamed on along the coast of Mozambique.

At the time Winston Churchill was the government minister responsible for the Royal Navy. He recalled the scene in the briefing room at the Admiralty on that fateful day.

It was a warm evening and the windows were thrown open wide. Cheering and singing could be heard from the direction of Buckingham Palace.

Big Ben struck eleven, it was midnight in Germany – the ultimatum expired. Admirals and Captains, splendid in uniform, and clerks in dark suits with pencils in hand stirred themselves. The telegram, prepared earlier, was flashed out to all His Majesty's Ships on the high seas – COMMENCE HOSTILITIES AGAINST GERMANY.

Astraea was patrolling the seas off German East Africa, present-day Tanzania, when she received the signal confirming that Britain was at war with Germany. Within four hours the captain took action. Two dhows bobbing about in the ocean off the coast of Zanzibar were flying the German flag. They were boarded and the bewildered African fishermen made prisoners. Three days later Astraea's guns were brought to bear on a wireless station at 07.05. At 07.12 white flags appeared on all the surrounding flagpoles.

Patrolling the coast of East Africa was the German light cruiser *Konigsberg*. She was short of coal and in need of repairs but still a danger to shipping. *HMS Pegasus* was moored at Zanzibar, taking on coal, when she was attacked by *Konigberg*. *Pegasus* was outgunned and sunk, *Konigsberg* returned to the Rufiji River Delta and surrounded herself with camouflage. The captain planned to complete the necessary repairs to the ship's engines there. All available Royal Navy ships in the area, including *Astraea*, were tasked with finding the *Konigsberg*. Her hiding place was discovered, a blockade set up, she was scuttled the following year.

In land, German forces held out until the end of the war. Another equally stubborn enemy were the Turks, either defending their homeland or invading Mesopotamia. Among the first to take them on were Australians and New Zealanders, at Gallipoli. Percy Nevett was one of the Anzacs.

SERGEANT WILLIAM PERCY NEVETT – 12TH BATTALION AUSTRALIAN IMPERIAL FORCE

Day Dawn

Old Boy, and once the head boy of the Grammar School, Percy Nevett had done well. He had qualified as a civil engineer and gone out to Australia to practise his skills at Day Dawn, a gold-mining town in the outback of Western Australia.

Scores of miners downed tools when they heard that the Germans had started a war. Percy Nevett would not be left behind. When the miners left he packed away his books and instruments and went with them to the camp at Black Boy Hill outside Perth, where miners, ranchers, bank clerks and men of every trade were turned into soldiers. These men were a special breed of adventurer, full of good cheer and grit, they formed the backbone of the 12th Battalion of the Australian Imperial Force. Their first battle would be fought, not against the Germans, but against the Turks at Gallipoli.

It is difficult now to understand why there was so much enthusiasm for war – cheering crowds, brass bands thumping out patriotic tunes, girls dashing forward with flowers for grinning boys marching down the street.

Back in Britain there was a truce in the class war, labourers and landed gentry, factory hands and stockbrokers were united. They all marched off, shoulder to shoulder, behind their regimental banner.

Territorials like Selby Piper and Victor Westcott marched down St Mary's Street and took the train from Bridgnorth Station. There was no smoke and steam for The Yeomanry, they rode to war in style.

PRIVATE (265620) JESSE MARSTON – SHROPSHIRE YEOMANRY AND 6TH KSLI

Smart Lad

© BES Library

On the front page of the Bridgnorth Journal on 15th of August 1914 there was a 'Call to Arms'. It was too late, the Shropshire Yeomanry mobilised on the 4th of August, the day war was declared.

Four squadrons from around the county assembled and made their way to Shrewsbury to enjoy the hospitality of the publicans and drink to victory in battle. The regiment moved on, serious training began at Brogyntyn Park, near Oswestry before the end of August.

There was no shortage of men, the regiment was above strength and some volunteers were turned away – they didn't clear the first hurdle, they couldn't ride! All the specialist vacancies such as shoeing-smiths, saddlers and cooks, were soon filled.

These weekend soldiers now had to be turned into professionals, although one or two had served in the Boer War. Discipline was something that had to be improved. The sergeants and corporals were 'too kind', giving friendly advice instead of orders.

Initial training consisted of mounted drill in the morning, and dismounted drill in the afternoon. Reveille was at 5.30 am, and the troopers were kept busy until 7.00 pm, and still found time for a game of football after that.

Fresh horses, harness and equipment were issued. Bundles of new tunics arrived at the camp, this did not suit everyone. The Yeomanry were better fed and stockier than the average soldier, some troopers had difficulty squeezing into their new uniform.

Volunteers for overseas service were called for and, hoping they would stay together as a regiment, most were prepared to go. According to their commanding officer, Colonel Lloyd, 'The troops are enjoying very good health and they are exceedingly happy and cheerful.'

The Yeomanry were cavalry, men at home in the saddle, where they could look down on the infantry. Now, if they wanted to see some action they had to swallow their pride. It was all very well charging about on horseback waving lances and sabres but a more effective way to deal with the enemy was with the rifle.

Those who agreed to serve as foot soldiers were rewarded with the Imperial Service Badge.

Jesse Marston was dismounted and went to France to serve with the 6th Battalion King's Shropshire Light Infantry. In August 1917 Jesse Marston was killed in action.

He was a country boy, Herbert Ormerod was a town boy. They had not been friends at school.

'Rusty' Ormerod was six years his senior. He served throughout the war. He might have claimed to be the first Old Boy to see action on a battlefield in Europe.

The Ormerods had a bakery at 12 St Mary's Street. It was a prosperous business. The Ormerods had every reason to be proud, they had worked hard for half a century and given good service to the community. This was recognised in 1907 when Herbert Ormerod's father, was elected Mayor of Bridgnorth. His lady wife, Hannah, certainly dressed the part.

Now Let Me Think

Hannah looked slightly pensive when she posed for the studio portrait, thinking of the future perhaps. Her husband had been a Grammar School boy and their eldest son was given the same opportunity, and to add to the confusion, he was given the same name. It was decided that Herbert Ormerod junior would train as a chemist, this turned out to be a wise decision.

The family moved to the Rectory at Glazeley in 1910 and Herbert senior was the organist at Chetton Church. They were not going up in the world, far from it. They were bankrupt. This was made public in the Bridgnorth Journal. A temporary setback, Herbert was soon back in business, as a corn merchant, the family moved to Wolverhampton.

Meanwhile 'Rusty' Ormerod was practising as a pharmacist in London and must have been already in uniform. A part-time soldier with the Territorials at the outbreak of war, he sailed from Southampton to Le Havre, and first set foot on French soil just three weeks after war was declared, which meant he probably did have the distinction of being the first Old Boy to serve on the Western Front. He began his military career as a Private soldier, in the Royal Army Medical Corps.

The church bells of Mons were ringing to summon the worshipers to prayer on that sunny Sunday morning of August 23rd 1914 when Royal Fusiliers and other British marksmen opened fire on the advancing Germans, cutting them down in swathes. The gaps in the ranks of the enemy were soon filled and by late afternoon it was clear that the Germans had the upper hand and the 'Retreat from Mons' began. It was a messy affair, the Battle of Le Cateau held up the advance but at a cost – 8000 British casualties. After days of skirmishing the retreat came to an end on the 6th of September and weary soldiers could rest and lick their wounds.

Within the racetrack at Rouen, Royal Engineers set up a thousand-bed hospital, No 12 General Hospital. 'Rusty' Ormerod was standing by in this tented camp. Anyone arriving at this Base Hospital had a good chance of survival, the medical staff here were the very best. Patients often arrived from the Casualty Clearing Stations, where their condition was assessed. Some were returned to their regiment after treatment, serious cases taken to the coast and shipped home.

Corporal Ormerod kept in touch with the school and he was given a mention in the School Magazine of 1916.

Corporal H J Ormerod, now promoted to Sergeant, is stationed at 12 General Hospital where he is kept very busy but fretting at not being in the firing line.

He got his wish in the final year of the war. He was given a battlefield commission in the Lincolnshire Regiment in August 1918 at a time when the Germans were in retreat.

However, there were still battles to be fought and the Lincolns went into action on the St Quentin Canal. Here the Hindenberg Line was broken by a combined force of British, Australian and American troops at the end of September. They pressed on and in the second week of October took the town of Cambrai. The advance continued across the Selle and Sambre rivers. Valenciennes was recaptured and finally the town of Mons where it had all begun for the British Expeditionary Force, and Private 'Rusty' Ormerod more than four years earlier.

In the New Year the victorious troops came home. Back in England Lieutenant Ormerod reverted to Private Ormerod. After home leave he crossed the Channel once again and regained his commissioned rank – 2nd Lieutenant, this time with 4th Battalion Essex Regiment. The Army thrived on paperwork and this was a fine example.

Herbert Ormerod, pharmacist, returned to a sensible life in Acton Vale. Time to settle down. He had found a bride, the bans were read, and on the 10th of June 1919 he married Edith Annie Minter, at St Dunstan's Church. There was even an announcement in 'The Times'. The young couple set up home in Willesden. This was where, eventually, his war medals arrived, including the 'Mon's Star'. This medal was awarded only to those who had served with the Expeditionary Force between August and November 1914.

The men who sailed to France at the outbreak of war were the best trained soldiers of the British Empire. They were led by men with experience of earlier campaigns in South Africa and on North West Frontier of India. No one had experienced anything like the conflict that began in August 1914 and became known as The Great War.

By comparison the War of the Roses was a garden party, the Crimean War a skirmish, and the South African War a sunny affair. Great War, there was no other way to describe it. Close to a million men of Britain and her Empire lost their lives, at least three times that number were scarred by war.

The Germans had expected a 'walk over'. They had a plan, the Schlieffen Plan, designed to knock France out of the war within six weeks. The British Expeditionary Force, commanded by Sir John French, was an obstruction. These professional soldiers were highly trained but small in number. They succeeded in holding up the German advance. Kaiser 'Bill' (Wilhelm II) was not pleased, in a stern letter to his army commander he wrote...

Address your skill and all the valour of my soldiers to exterminate the treacherous English and walk over French's contemptible little army.

The Old Contemptibles' Association was formed after the war by men who would not be walked over. Old Boy of the Grammar School, 'Rusty' Ormerod was one of the Old Contemptibles.

Chapter 2

The County Regiment

Anyone who had served in the county regiment had every reason to feel proud. They had earned a fine reputation. Duty done the 7th Battalion rapidly faded away in 1919, the colours were laid up in St Chad's Church, Shrewsbury. A reunion dinner was held the following year. Afterwards General Deverell, who had commanded the 3rd Division during the final two years of the war commented:

> *This was a battalion with a fine soldier-like spirit, upon whose gallantry, steadiness and cheerful willingness I was able to rely upon at all times and in all circumstances.*

Always on Target

With permission from Pat Debes

It wasn't only the 7th Battalion that had shown soldier-like spirit. Battle Honours were awarded to eight battalions of the King's Shropshire Light Infantry.

Local lads with a sense of duty and fondness for khaki tunics joined the Territorial Force. Old Boys who served with the 4th Battalion King's Shropshire Light Infantry, as part-time soldiers, were Roger Haslewood, Bill Westcott, Selby Piper, Ernie Gardiner, Tom Hawkins and Frank Cooksey.

CRACK SHOTS

The marksmen of 'F' Company (Bridgnorth) were consistent winners of the county shooting competition. The Territorials met at the Drill Hall in St Mary's Street where they could perfect their martial arts, before retiring to The Swan or the Golden Lion for refreshment.

A social event they all looked forward to was the annual camp. In August 1914 they had hardly settled in at Glan Rheidol, near Aberystwyth, when they were ordered to break camp, return to the Drill Hall and 'await orders'. No one complained, this was what they had been training for.

They did not have to wait long for orders. The prearranged duty of the 4th Battalion was to defend the Barry Docks at Cardiff.

Mobilised on the 4th of August, they boarded two special trains at Shrewsbury and steamed south. There was a certain amount of confusion, eager to get on with the job they forgot to take blankets and the 'camp kettles'. They were saved by local inhabitants who fed and housed them for five days.

In early September 'F' Company retreated to Bridgnorth for some home cooking and home leave. In mid-October the town prepared to give them a real send-off. The towns' bandsmen tuned up at the bottom of St Mary's Street, and a hundred lads from Bridgnorth and Highley lined up behind them – 'a fine body of men'.

The Mayor of Bridgnorth, Captain G C Wolryche-Whitmore was absent, an officer in the Yeomanry, he was charging about Belgium with the Household Cavalry at the time.

The farewell address was given by Alderman Whitefoot. He made the most of the occasion, talking at length about 'our Mayor at the front'…'hundreds of years of faithful service to the Crown by Bridgnorth men'…and given the size of the town the large number of young men who had now answered the call. He reminded them of the words to 'It's a Long Way to Tipperary', but by then the troops were getting restless. It was understandable that he should 'go on a bit'. His son, Tom Whitefoot, a signaller with the Canadian Expeditionary Force, was on his way to England to join the fray.

The band struck up, Colour Sergeant Foxall barked, and the parade strode off down Squirrel Bank to the Railway Yard, cheered on by well-wishers. After a certain amount of fumbling on the platform 'F' Company boarded the train, and the Station Master signalled the departure. A large crowd had gathered on the Castle Walk overlooking the railway station. Lining the railings, family and friends, neighbours and lovers waved goodbye. They would soon be back, it would be 'over by Christmas' they were told. That did not seem likely but no one could imagine then how dreadful the next four years would be.

With a whistle and a burst of steam the train set off for Bewdley, first stage of the journey to Sittingbourne in Kent where the whole of the 4th Battalion were reunited.

Lads from all over the county were about to share the unforgettable experience of being billeted with hordes of rats in a deserted jam factory. This was the sort of place they would find 'comfortable' in the days ahead.

Volunteers for overseas service were called for, and eighty per cent of the battalion stepped forward. Fred Head hesitated, he later transferred to the Staffordshire Regiment and served in France, and died there. Lieutenant Cooksey had served in the Boer War, he was too old, and several others were also in their thirties.

The Commanding Officer of 'F' Company, William Westcott, was fifty-two and definitely 'time expired'. His son, Lieutenant William Horace Westcott, represented the family. Commanding 'E' Company (Shifnal) was another Old Boy, Lieutenant Roger Haslewood, and there were several 'Old Grammarians' in the ranks – Bill Breakwell from Gatacre Park, Corporal Bernard Turner, a machine gunner, Bert Ward from 58 St Mary's Street and Corporal Selby Piper, from Victoria Road. They were all given their 'marching orders'.

At midnight on 28th of October they piled onto trains to Southampton, boarded His Majesty's Troopship *Deseado* and 'set sail'. Ferries crossed the Channel in a matter of hours. They were going a voyage that took weeks. The 4th Battalion were off to the Far East, to replace the regulars manning the garrisons at Hong Kong and Singapore.

Within a week they were sailing through the Straits of Gibraltar and out across the blue Mediterranean, a whole new experience. Lads who had been brought up on the green banks of the Severn sailed on, through the Suez Canal with desert on both sides, and marvelled.

Ships of the Desert

© Piper Collection, Shropshire Archives

After a month at sea they arrived in Bombay and immediately began the journey across India, by train, to Calcutta. They were not at journey's end. The battalion marched straight to the docks and boarded *SS City of Marseilles* bound for Rangoon. While in Rangoon the first casualty occurred, Sergeant Tudor died of a heart attack just before Christmas.

They were a very long way from the fighting in France but that didn't mean they were out of trouble.

They had no sooner arrived when the commanding officer of the Shropshires was sent an urgent message. Companies of Native Infantry (129th Baluchi Regiment) were on the verge of mutiny. The 4th Battalion were sent out to disarm them and they managed to do so without a shot being fired. To demonstrate who was in charge two hundred and fifty men of the KSLI were sent 'up country' on a eighteen day route, march visiting forts on the Irrawaddy manned by local troops.

Meanwhile there was more unrest in Singapore. Six hundred men were rushed to the docks, boarded *HMT Edavana,* and arrived in Singapore in record time.

The mutiny by the 5th Bengali Light Infantry was an altogether more serious affair. Seventy Europeans had been killed, including the wives of government officials. Shore parties from warships in the harbour confronted the mutineers and took control.

The KSLI occupied Tanglin Barracks and completed the round-up of the rebels. Courts martial and executions followed, forty faced the firing squad outside the jail, and others were hanged. Selby Piper kept a souvenir, a particularly gruesome photograph of the beheading of one of the ringleaders.

Rough Justice

© Shropshire Archives

There were minor incidents from time to time which were dealt with promptly. The Battalion began a training programme, aware that sooner or later they would return to the battlefields of Europe.

Captain Haslewood, Corporal Piper and some forty lucky lads, were dispatched to Hong Kong to pick up passengers and sail on to Sydney. On the voyage British troops were outnumbered two-to-one by German sailors but there was no conflict. The sailors were the survivors of the *Emden*, a light cruiser of the Imperial German Navy.

Emden had been making a nuisance of herself. In two months she captured two dozen ships, attacked a shore base at Penang, and sank a Russian cruiser and a French destroyer. Then she made the mistake of attacking the Cocos Islands. The Australian cruiser, *HMAS Sydney*, arrived and inflicted such damage on the *Emden* that the captain ran her aground. Over a hundred German sailors were killed in battle, the survivors made prisoners of war. The KSLI were escorting them to Australia, and there they would stay until the end of the war.

During the course of the next eighteen months the battalion lost about eighty men, a few expired in the heat of the tropics suffering from malaria and dysentery, most were 'time expired'. Too old to serve longer, they returned to England.

Lieutenant William Horace Westcott – 4th King's Shropshire Light Infantry

Like Father – Like Son

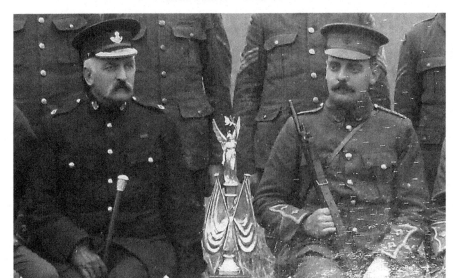

With permission from Pat Debes

William Westcott, commanding 'F' Company, was thirty-seven years old when the battalion was mobilised at the outbreak of war. He was nearing the age limit for active service but nevertheless sailed with the 4th Battalion when they were dispatched to the Far East. A number of others, who did not want to be left behind were in a similar position.

In May 1915 the battalion was reorganised, 'F' Company (Bridgnorth) disappeared, merging with 'E' Company (Shifnal), commanded by Lieutenant Roger Haslewood.

It was time for Will Westcott to retire, to return to Rose Lane, to his wife Dorothy, and their little boy. Faced with retirement Ern Gardiner made a different decision.

WARRANT OFFICER (511) ERNEST WILLIAM GARDINER – 4TH KSLI

Ern Gardiner was an enterprising man, not exactly tinker, tailor soldier, sailor – but he was, at one time or another, tailor, soldier, harbour master, and miner.

Born in 1876, his early life was spent in Friar's Street. His father was landlord of the Old Friar's Inn and a coal merchant. Richard Gardiner died young, his widow, Sarah took on the licence of the pub and remarried.

Ernest's step-father was a fireman, in charge of the engine at the station in the High Street.

Coal merchant, publican, fireman, none of these trades appealed to Ern Gardiner, he was apprenticed to a tailor in the town. He liked to dress smartly, he was six feet tall, and in the uniform of the Shropshire Rifle Volunteers he must have looked every inch a soldier.

To gain more experience as a tailor he moved to London, took lodgings in Islington and worked as a 'cutter'. Returning to Bridgnorth, he set up business as a Master Tailor in West Castle Street, and married.

In the outside world there was disquiet, rivalry between the European nations grew. The Royal Navy launched more Dreadnought battleships to match those of the German High Seas Fleet.

Volunteer soldiers began training to a more professional standard, in Britain the Territorial Force was created and Major William Westcott welcomed him back in 1908. By the outbreak of war he was ready for action, although he was by then thirty-eight years old.

Marian Gardiner and her baby boy, James, waved goodbye as Ernest marched away with the 4th Battalion to take ship to the Far East. When and where would they meet again?

Arriving in Singapore Sergeant Gardiner played a part in supressing the mutiny of a local infantry regiment before 'A' and 'D' Company sailed on the Hong Kong to take up garrison duties. No one would describe life in Hong Kong as dull it was vibrant, full of enterprising business men. Ernest Gardiner understood this, he was now a man with authority, the senior non-commissioned officer, a Warrant Officer. There were married quarters for the privileged few.

In January 1917 the War Office decided that the 25th Middlesex Regiment would take over the duties of 4th KSLI in Singapore and Hong Kong. After some delay, half the regiment arrived in Hong Kong to replace two Companies of the KSLI.

The Shropshire lads said their farewells, and boarded the *Ingoma,* happy that they were on their way home, at last. The voyage back, to home waters, took over three months, nervous times for the waiting families. Mrs Charlie Smith wrote to the regimental depot at Shrewsbury – where were her brothers, Dick and Ernie Gardiner, both of 'D' Company? Dick was on his way home, Ernie had decided to stay in Hong Kong.

Ernest Gardiner had celebrated his fortieth birthday in the Far East, he was therefore too old for active service. A year earlier he had been offered a position with the China Mining and Smelting Company. They were mining lead and silver at Lin-Ma Hang, a village in the New Territories.

The family had moved on. When medals were sent out to those who had served in the Great War Ernest's were posted to Holt's Wharf, Shanghai.

TAKES SOME HANDLING COPY – JOHN SWIRE AND SONS LTD

Marian and her children, James, Winifred and Joyce would have enjoyed a privileged life- style, Ernest was a Wharfinger – an outdated title for the Harbour Master.

Ernest's age had prevented him from leading men in battle, he left others to finish the job. Tom Hawkins had arrived in Singapore with a draft of 460 fresh troops in May 1916.

PRIVATE (201389) THOMAS JAMES HAWKINS –
1/4TH KING'S SHROPSHIRE LIGHT INFANTRY

Tom Hawkins was a Private soldier, and unlike many Grammar School boys, he did not seek promotion, content to sit out the war and return 'in one piece' to the family home on Albion Terrace. After two years of 'easy life' in the Far East the boys of the Fourth Battalion were going home, or so they believed.

The Hong Kong garrison boarded the '*Ingoma*' and sailed for Singapore, where they made room for the rest of the Battalion. Equipped to carry eight hundred men an extra three hundred were packed in.

Escorted by a Japanese cruiser, they sailed for Ceylon. They stretched their legs at Colombo before steaming south to Durban and on to Cape Town where they were forced to wait for a second escort vessel.

The passage across the Indian Ocean was not an experience anyone wanted to repeat, and neither was the month spent at the Wynberg Rest camp. The weather was not what they were used to after two years in the tropics. At Wynberg there was torrential rain, hail and sleet, something even 'the locals' were not used to. One hundred and fifty men reported sick with 'fever', probably hoping for a warm bed.

At last, on the 25th of June they boarded the *Walmer Castle* bound for England. The troopship spent a week in Freetown Harbour, Sierra Leone, this was described as 'a torrid stay'. The boys were in high spirits anticipating the welcome home and perhaps some real action in France.

Arriving at Plymouth on the 27th of July, still in tropical kit, and carrying souvenirs of the Far East, they boarded a train to Southampton, not Shropshire. Waiting at the docks was another troopship to take them to France. After another night at sea they landed at Le Havre. They surely had every reason to feel disgruntled.

Lord Derby complemented the Battalion on the way they had accepted the situation.

It was unfortunately impossible to grant leave owing to shipping arrangements after two and a half years abroad, and when the decision came the whole battalion accepted it without a murmur of disappointment.

New uniforms, rifles, horses and equipment were issued and training given in 'wiring', 'bombing' and 'gas'. In August they were ready for the service on the front line near Arras. Here special leave allotment was granted for twenty men at a time.

Private Tommy Hawkins came home at the end of September. It must have taken a week for him to relate, to the family, all that had happened to him over the past year.

He re-joined the Battalion on the 3rd of October just in time to join a route march from Hardifort to Houtkerque. They camped on a canal bank near Ypres. Conditions there were impossible, flood waters filled their dugouts and much vital equipment was lost. Preparations for battle went ahead, they moved from Irish Farm to Albatross Farm. Shrapnel from shells bursting overhead caused some thirty casualties.

There were those in the High Command who expressed concern that a Territorial battalion straight from the Far East might be unreliable under fire for the first time. They were proved wrong. On the 30th of October, when the order to advance in attack formation was given, the lines moved forward as on a parade ground. Wem and Whitchuch Company suffered most in the battle. The Battalion lost over a hundred men, killed, wounded and missing.

Among the casualties was Private Tom Hawkins. A sick man before the battle he fought on, finally succumbed to Trench Fever and was admitted to 63 Casualty Clearing Station on the 4th of November. His symptoms were typical, fever, head ache, pains in shins and shoulders.

Tom though that this was due to exposure to cold and damp conditions in the trenches and so did the medical experts of the time. Lice were the real villains. Some patients recovered quickly only to suffer a relapse, treatment might have to continue for months. After a week Tom was put on an Ambulance Train and taken to the 11th Stationary Hospital, Rouen. A week later he was lying in the 2nd Western Hospital in Manchester. It was three months before Tom returned to duty, he was posted to the Reserve Battalion at Heaton Park.

Home on sick leave he would have noticed a change, not in the shops and houses but in the population. Children still played in the streets, young maids, domestic servants were running errands, old men, carters and draymen were struggling with kegs of beer and baskets of vegetables. It was business as usual. There were familiar faces, the lads from school, the cheeky boys, now in their twenties. A few stood out wearing uniform, chatting to friends, and 'telling the tale' to anyone who could spare the time.

Heads went down when they heard bad news. "Walter Brown, he's gone I hear, at Passchendaele."

Walter Brown had been one of Tom's Company. He was thirty-seven, near the age limit for service on the front line. His had been a hard life. Brought up by his grandmother in the Alms-houses in Church Street he worked as a jobbing labourer. Powerfully built, with perfect vision he was declared fit. Six months later he was discharged, 'unlikely to become an efficient soldier'. Undeterred he volunteered again a year later and joined the 4th Battalion. Killed in action during the Second Battle of Passchendaele, his persistence had cost him his life.

It was the final year of the war, Tom Hawkins never returned to France.

At Pembroke Dock the details of his service were set out on Army Form Z 22. He was still troubled with pains in shins and shoulders, the medical officer advised a review of his case after three months. Tom could not wait, he made no claim for any disability, caused by the prolonged bout of Trench Fever. In January 1919 he came home to 6 Albion Terrace, a civilian once more.

He had served in France for just over a hundred days and seen enough to understand the appalling nature of war. The challenge now for young men out of uniform was to find employment, anywhere. Victor Westcott returned to Argentina, to the Buenos Aires Western Railway Company.

CAPTAIN VICTOR REGINALD WESTCOTT, MC, 3RD KSLI

Victor's father, Major William Westcott, who commanded the Territorials in Bridgnorth was too old for 'active service'. Victor's brother, nine years his senior, was also retired after service in the Far East.

Victor Westcott was exactly what the army were looking for, mature capable men.

As a schoolboy, he shared the headmaster's enthusiasm for mathematics, and went on to study applied mathematics and engineering at Birmingham University. He went on to put theory into practice at the Railway Wagon Works. There were opportunities worldwide for railway engineers.

At the outbreak of war Victor was a superintendent with the Buenos Aries Western Railways in 'The Argentine'. When duty called he did not hesitate, he travelled halfway round the world to join the fight – crossed the Pacific to board the *Turakina* of the New Zealand Shipping Company at Wellington. Travelling with him was another engineer, a railway clerk, and a loco fireman, all willing volunteers.

Victor Westcott disembarked at Plymouth early in September 1914 and by the middle of the month he had enlisted in Birmingham with the 21st Service Battalion Royal Fusiliers, formed from the Public Schools and University Men's Force.

Mr Westcott was now Lance Corporal (3384) Westcott with No 3 Company, and training to be an infantryman at Woodcote Camp, Epsom.

Training complete, Royal Fusiliers paraded for Lord Kitchener in dire weather in, January 1915, in February, they landed in France. They were a select contingent, the majority expected to become officer. Victor Westcott was commissioned in the King's Shropshire Light Infantry in May 1915. A character reference was provided by the Secretary of the Buenos Aires Western Railways.

Details of Victor's service over the next four years were 'sketchy'. He certainly distinguished himself on the battlefield because he was awarded a Military Cross. At a later stage in the war he was attached to the Royal Engineers, Signals Section and promoted to Captain. His name appears on the crew list of *Cable Ship Colonia* belonging to the Western Union Telegraph Company. Cables were laid on the sea bed all over the world, one of them between Ascension Island in the South Atlantic and Montevideo at the mouth of the River Plate, an area Captain Westcott knew well.

He was still in uniform in March 1919 when he married Leonora Barlow in Stourbridge, he was finally discharged in August of the same year. Victor returned to Argentina and the Western Railway Company. He crossed the Atlantic several times, in May 1922 on the *Desna*, to Liverpool, returning in August on the *Royal Mail Steam Packet Deseado*. This was the same ship that had carried his brother to Singapore at the outbreak of war.

Victor was still resident in Buenos Aires in 1923 when his medals were sent in a packet addressed to Ferro Carril Oeste, Estacion Once,

(Western Railways, Station 11). Life in 'The Argentine' may not have suited his young wife because Victor Westcott returned to England and applied his engineering skills to the manufacture of fire bricks in Stourbridge, near to Leonora's family home.

Victor had survived the war, he had seen the world and may have expected a long life and happy retirement – he was only fifty-four when he died. Many who had served alongside him during the Great War would have been grateful to have lived that long. Tom Robins and Jesse Marston, comrades in the Shropshire Yeomanry died on the battlefield, Charlie Jones died in bed at Aldershot. Frank Cooksey made the arrangements for his funeral.

LIEUTENANT FRANK REGINALD COOKSEY – KING'S SHROPSHIRE LIGHT INFANTRY AND SPECIAL RESERVE

Looking the Part

With permission from Pat Debes

49

Frank's father, James, was Town Clerk, his younger brother, Tom, a solicitor. The family lived in the High Street and this is where Frank served throughout the Great War. This did not mean that Frank had no experience of war, he had served with the 2nd Battalion KSLI during the Boer War.

The county regiment fought in South Africa throughout this conflict. They were praised for 'excellent work' at Paardeberg and Thoba Mountain. Men of Bridgnorth were lost, Sam Gittoes and Tom Jones killed in action, Chas Langford and Trooper Hill of the 13th Hussars died of enteric fever. Sergeant (7550) Frank Cooksey survived and came home in 1902.

Two years later he was commissioned in the 1st Volunteer Battalion KSLI and promoted to Lieutenant in 1908.

At the outbreak of war, a recruiting office was set up in the Agricultural Hall in the High Street, Frank was the officer in charge. Young men came in to 'attest', many he knew well. They signed the Attestation Form that committed them to 'Serve the King, for the duration'. From his own experience of war he knew that this document would seal the fate of some.

Not all died in battle. Charlie Jones, son of the landlord of The Shakespeare, died of pneumonia during training at Aldershot. His body arrived in an oak coffin with brass fittings at Bridgnorth Railway Station and was conveyed to the family home. Lieutenant Frank Cooksey made arrangements for the funeral service. He marched with a guard of honour escorting the flag-draped coffin along the High Street to Saint Leonard's Church. It was a tragic scene.

There was worse to come. In the final year of the war George and Sarah Jones lost two more sons in France, both died of wounds, Mark in May and Alfred in October 1918. Within a month peace was declared, Dick Page wrote home to tell the family.

Private (43761) Richard Wyre Page – 7th Battalion KSLI

Neither Richard Page nor his brother Bill showed much enthusiasm for the war. Without them and Fred Jones, one of the farmhands, running Manor Farm at Middleton Scriven was practically impossible. They were 'deferred' for over two years, but as the casualty lists grew, they were finally claimed by the army.

Privates Jones and Page joined the 7th Battalion in France in 1918, there were a few familiar faces, 'Edgy' Piper was now a Lieutenant.

The first taste of battle for Private Dick Page was at Albert on the 21st of August. The objective was the railway line between Bapaume and Albert and the orders for the battalion were simple, 'to reach and hold the railway at all costs'. They made their way forward through heavy mist at 5 o'clock in the morning. Two hours later they were on the railway embankment and fighting hand-to-hand with the demoralised defenders. The Germans fell back. The following day they launched counter-attacks but were repulsed.

The battalion withdrew to Moyenneville to 'reorganise and clean up', and count the cost. Over two hundred Germans had been captured together with their field guns, machine guns and trench mortars. The 7th Battalion were sent a number of congratulatory telegrams, no mention was made of the 250 killed or wounded during the month of August. Reinforcements arrived in preparation for the Second Battle of Bapaume.

It was another early start on the 2nd of September. Whippet tanks arrived to help out. The Germans held the high ground. The Shropshires forged ahead and reached their objective ahead of the Scottish regiments to left and right, and ahead of the tanks that faltered, most suffering mechanical failure. Forty men died, two hundred were wounded, eight gassed and a number were missing. Private Dick Page was unharmed. More telegrams of congratulation arrived from Brigade Headquarters.

Newspaper reports at home were full of optimism, the Germans were certainly 'on the back foot'. For troops in trenches there was still death and danger from shells, bullets, bayonets and gas. Another forty men died and many more were wounded at Canal du Nord.

Lieutenant William Edgell Piper was hospitalised. The Page boys knew him well, he had been a lively sportsman at school and had a lively time in the trenches for two years, first with the 'Warwicks' and then with the Royal Berkshire Regiment. He joined the 7th KSLI early in 1918 when he was promoted from the ranks. 'Edgy' Piper returned from hospital in time for one last battle at Selle.

It was a brief affair. The Royal Scots Fusiliers set off ahead of the Shropshires in the early morning of the 23rd of October, in mid-afternoon Private Page, Lieutenant Piper and the 7th Battalion passed through the Fusiliers and continued the advance. Dick and 'C' Company were back in billets at Escarmain.

The next morning, 'Edgy' Piper was back in hospital. They were all ready for a rest, after ten days of continuous marching, fighting, and 'holding the line'.

They didn't rest for long, just long enough to refit and practice musketry and the use of the bayonet, as if extra training was necessary. On the 10th of November they were treated to a route march, to billets at Romeries near Cambrai. The next day they set off for the battlefront. As they formed up Dick spotted a familiar face, Fred Jones. This young cowman, more at home in the pastures surrounding Manor Farm, was now making his way across unfamiliar fields.

As the head of the column arrived at the starting point for the battle they were ordered to 'about turn' and return to billets at Frasnoy.

Dick put aside his rifle and pack, sharpened a pencil and on note paper from the YMCA began a letter to his sister.

Something to Write Home About

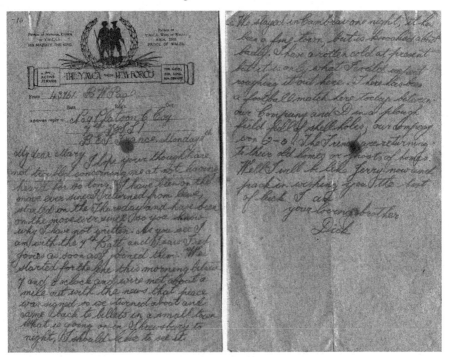

© Margaret Crawford-Clarke

My Dear Mary

I hope your thoughts are not troubled concerning me at not having heard for so long, I have been on the move ever since I returned from leave, so you know why I have not written. We started for the line this morning between 7 and 8 o'clock and were met about a mile out with the news that peace was signed so we turned about and came back to billets in a small town.

What is going on in Shrewsbury tonight, I should like to see it?

We stayed in Cambrai one night, it has been a fine town but is knocked about badly.

I have another cold at present but it is only what I could expect roughing it out here.

There has been a football match here today between our Company and 'D' in a ploughed field full of shell holes, our company won 2-0.

The French were returning to their old homes or ghosts of homes.

Well I will be like Jerry now and pack in.

Wishing you the best of luck, I am your loving brother, Dick

It was all over, now they could all go home. The first to be sent home and demobilised were the coal miners, then farmworkers. Within a fortnight Dick was back at Manor Farm. The Page family rejoiced – a whole generation mourned.

Things would never be the same for thousands of families, but life went on. William Westcott, company secretary at Southwell's Carpet Factory, went back to his desk – Selby Piper returned to the design department. The lucky ones picked up where they left off, many found themselves out of work or forced to accept work of any sort.

Four years after the war Tom Hawkins was working as a 'road foreman', still unmarried, a man with limited prospects. He decided to try his luck on the other side of the Atlantic. Many young men were encouraged by the Canadian Government to emigrate, to replace all the lads lost in the war. Tom paid for a 3rd Class passage on *SS Pitzberg*, sailing from Liverpool to Quebec, arriving on the 23rd of August 1922. He made his way to Winnipeg, with just five pounds in his pocket, his intended occupation, 'harvesting'. Anyone willing to work on the land was especially welcome.

When Tom completed the immigration form he was asked how long he intended to stay in Canada –'I cannot say at the present time' was his response. In October, when the harvest was over, he sailed home, returned to Albion Terrace. This move had changed his luck, the Council recognised his enterprising spirit and he was given a new appointment, road surveyor.

The war had disrupted the lives of tens of thousands, it certainly seemed to unsettle Roger Haslewood. A solicitor, in partnership with his father, returning to a secure living in his home town should have been easy.

Captain Roger John Rodwell Haslewood MC – 1/4th KSLI

At 'The Croft' in Mill Street R F Haslewood and R J R Haslewood, father and son were both solicitors. At 2 Castle Hill, (another 'Croft') Edward and Guy Haslewood, father and son were also solicitors. The 'senior partners' had to carry on alone when war came, the boys were in uniform.

This was nothing new for Roger Haslewood; he transferred from the Bridgnorth Cadet Company to 1st Volunteer Battalion and in 1908 was commissioned in the 4th KSLI.

Roger Haslewood must have been a versatile man, at ease behind a desk in a suit, starched collar and tie, or wearing khaki uniform behind sandbags in a trench of mud, or going out to bat for the town in immaculate 'cricket whites'. For two years he was batting for England in the tropics, then returned to Europe for a 'second innings'.

Arriving in France in July 1917 the 4th Battalion were sent straight to the front. In billets near Arras they heard, for the first time, the sound of guns in action and saw the results of shell holes in the walls. By the end of October they were hardened fighters. Following the Second Battle of Passchendaele they counted the cost, twenty-two comrades were dead and over a hundred wounded.

With permission from Pat Debes

They were on the battlefield again at Bapaume in March 1918 and at Messines in April. This was all part of the German 'Spring Offensive' of 1918. The enemy overran many front line positions, along a wide front the Allies were in retreat. 4th Battalion were defending a small village, Neuve Eglise. Several minor attacks were driven off with rifle fire, at nightfall they withdrew to a more secure position, heavy shelling the following morning forced them to retreat further. Among the wounded on the day was Captain Haslewood. Fortunately he recovered quickly and was back with his Company in June and preparing for battle at Bligny where the 4th Battalion made regimental history.

The Shropshires found themselves on unfavourable ground at the foot of Bligny Hill, on the 5th of June, with only hastily dug slit trenches and little cover except for growing corn, virtually no protection from the barrage of gas shell that rained down on them in the morning and high explosive shells after mid-day. They watched with dismay as wounded men, North Staffs and Cheshire's trickled back down the slopes. They were in retreat, the Shropshire's were ordered to counter attack, and 2nd Lieutenant Bright was the officer who led the charge.

He marshalled his forces, less than 200 men, and led them in four waves uphill for nearly a mile over open country. Despite taking least 80 casualties they pressed on, without artillery support, to take Bligny Hill at the point of the bayonet. For his bravery and leadership the French awarded Lieutenant Bright the Croix de Guerre. In September the Battalion as a whole received the same honour for what General Berthelot described as 'magnificent dash'.

Captain Roger Haslewood had been in reserve at Bligny but had distinguished himself in a separate action.

> *For conspicuous gallantry and devotion to duty. When the enemy had nearly succeeded in cutting off some of our troops he was one of the first to respond to the order to advance, and by his example and courage led forward a number of men, first stopping and them forcing the enemy to retreat in disorder. Throughout he has shown great courage and self-sacrifice.*

This was the citation for the award of the Military Cross.

The war ended, it had disrupted the lives of tens of thousands. Many would never be able to settle completely and enjoy the peace. Roger Haslewood seems to have found the return to 'normal' life difficult. He was not out of work. There was plenty of work for solicitors many families needed to put their 'affairs in order' after the war and this applied to the Haslewoods.

Roger's father died on Christmas Day 1921, and six months later his mother, Gertrude, also died. Roger and his sister Gladys were left 'comfortably off' but this was no consolation. They were both of marrying age but neither had found a partner at this stage in their lives.

Roger applied for his war medals in 1922 and gave three possible contact addresses, the Croft in Mill Street, his office in the New Market Buildings or Hammersmith Town Hall. He was certainly not settled. His voyages to and from the Far East seem to have given him a taste for the sea.

In 1926 he cruised the Atlantic, with his sister, from Liverpool to Madeira and the Canary Islands, and home again. The following year he sailed from London to Gibraltar on P&O *Naldera*. He was off to Tangiers in 1930 and returning from Calcutta the same year. His last recorded voyage was on the *Matiana* from Beira, in Mozambique, to London in 1931.

*

Roger finally found romance, in 1937, when he married Joan D'Arcy. She was thirty-three and he was forty-nine, better late than never. At last he could settle down to work, in a modest office in Bank Street. He was even given one last chance to wear the King's uniform and the ribbon of his Military Cross, as a Captain in the Home Guard.

Roger Haslewood died in 1955. He left a valuable legacy for local historians. In the Shropshire Archives there is a collection of letters, deeds and wills that he accumulated during a lifetime of practice as a solicitor in Bridgnorth. The collections fills twenty-three boxes, many stories dating back to 1750 are yet to be told. There are even earlier references to the Hasleswoods as far back as the thirteenth century.

For the Hasleswoods and every family in the land the most significant event in history was, without doubt, The Great War.

Chapter 3

Return to the Old Country

Canada was the land of opportunity for enterprising young men. More than a handful of Bridgnorth 'Old Boys' went out before the war to try their luck. Europe was rumbling to the edge of war. The British Government asked the Canadians for 20,000 men, twice that number volunteered. They came from every corner of the land. The journey from the Pacific coast of British Columbia to Quebec was the best part of two thousand miles. The first stage for any traveller was to get to the nearest railhead, board the train, settle in a window seat and watch mountain, forest, prairie, river and lake roll by, time to consider what might lie ahead. The end of the line was Valcartier, where an enormous tented camp was set up.

The first troops arrived on the 24th of August, within three weeks of the outbreak of war. The trains travelled slowly, carrying 600 men at a time accompanied by scores of horses. Stops were frequent, all along the line well-wishers cheered the volunteers on their way. The line had been extended to carry them right into the camp at Valcartier, by the end of September over thirty thousand had arrived.

Among the first to volunteer for the Expeditionary Force were Eric Burton, Leslie Smith and Tom Whitefoot. Tom boarded the train at Calgary on August 21st, two days later he arrived in Winnipeg, he was halfway there.

SERGEANT THOMAS WEDGEWOOD WHITEFOOT MSM – CANADIAN MEDICAL CORPS

Tom already had two years military experience with the British Columbian Light Horse. He gave his profession as 'photographer'. Perhaps it was his knowledge of chemistry that meant he was drafted into the Medical Corps and first assigned to No 2 Field Ambulance.

Next of the trio to arrive at Vacartier was Leslie Smith.

PRIVATE LESLIE CHARLES SMITH – BRITISH COLUMBIA REGIMENT

Tom Whitefoot remembered him as a slight, athletic lad. He could cover the ground, door to door, from school to 64 High Street, in less than a minute. Nobody used the house numbers, this was where Richard Smith, Leslie's father, welcomed customers in need of groceries and something to quench their thirst at the Cross Keys Vaults. Elected mayor of Bridgnorth, a well-respected man with a profitable business, providing a secure future for his family, he died aged 33.

Leslie could hardly remember his father, he was four years old at the time. Marion Smith moved with her two young boys to more modest premises in Salop Street. With the help of her brother-in-law, she brought up the boys. At school Leslie was a popular lad, with a 'cheerful irrepressible temperament'. He left the Grammar School in 1905 when he was 16, and three years later he took ship to Canada to try his hand at farming, on the prairie lands of Alberta. Mechanically minded he changed his trade from rancher to civil engineer, working on the Canadian Pacific Railway and moved west to British Columbia. His mother joined him in Canada, and found a husband. Mrs Brooks settled in Winnipeg.

For all recruits to the military the first part of the process was the 'medical'. Although Les Smith didn't have 'much meat on him' he was still a very fit man. Posing for the camera Leslie appeared reserved and aloof but when he was stripped to the waist 'distinctive marks' were revealed. He had a girl on his right forearm and a snake and a bird on the left. There was no tattoo parlour on Bridgnorth. He may have picked up the girl and the snake in Medicine Hat where ranchers, lumberjacks and railwaymen came to part with their money in the bars and brothels. This was a long way from his mother in Winnipeg, who might have frowned on this decoration.

Leslie Smith was on his way to Valcartier with his pals of 9 Platoon, 1st British Columbia Regiment. They boarded the train at Nelson on the shores of Lake Kootenay, travelled east, through the Rocky Mountains across the familiar lands of Alberta to call at Calgary, stretch their legs and travel on. Eric Burton began his journey at Calgary.

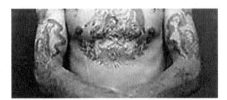

© BES Library

LANCE CORPORAL ERIC BURTON – PRINCESS PATRICIA'S LIGHT INFANTRY (EAST ONTARIO REGIMENT)

The Captain at the Fire Hall in Calgary, and the rest of the firefighters, shook hands with Eric, slapped him on the shoulder and sent him on his way. A popular man in the town, everyone was sorry to see him go, but they knew he was just the man to take on the Germans. For Burton, Smith and Whitefoot there was no turning back now.

Kitted out in khaki, drilled and given instruction on the rifle range the First Army of Canada was ready for battle. The Duke of Connaught took the salute at the final parade at Valcartier. The camp was only sixteen miles from the docks at Quebec, a short step for infantrymen.

The weather was so foul on the night of the 23rd of September that they were taken by train. The gun carriages of the field artillery, supply wagons and hundreds of horses trekked down the valley through the rain and mud. The whole operation took three days. An armada of 33 liners, escorted by warships of the Royal Navy set sail on the 3rd of October, the largest contingent of troops to cross the Atlantic at the time. They were vulnerable to attack by German U-boats.

The crossing was slow, they were at sea for ten nervous days. Troop transports, cruisers and battleships carrying over eighty thousand men edged their way into Plymouth Sound and anchored at Devonport. The 1st Division of the New Canadian Army had arrived.

Such was the secrecy surrounding the operation that they arrived at Devonport unannounced. The news of their arrival soon spread and the townsfolk of Plymouth flocked to the waterfront to give the lads a rousing welcome.

You cannot imagine how good the old country looks to me after so long away.

These were the words of Tom Whitefoot standing on the deck of *SS Tunisian*.

It was three days before Signaller Whitefoot came ashore, the artillery and horses disembarked ahead of the infantry. Somewhere in the sea of khaki trooping down the gangplanks and assembling on the quayside were Eric Burton and Leslie Smith. No contact had been made so far between the Grammar School Old Boys.

Marching from the dock to the rail depot the troops were showered with gifts of sweets and cigarettes – back-slapping and handshakes all round.

The whole Canadian Division set up camp on Salisbury Plain, Tom called it 'The Prairie'. He set himself the task of finding Eric Burton's camp. He was not successful but he did meet up with Les Smith one evening in the YMCA. He looked well but 'as thin as ever'. They must have talked about the 'good old days' at school, friends and family in the town, and of course, the War. Both were eager to get over to France.

Tom asked for a transfer from the Medical Corp to the Infantry. His request was refused, he was a trained specialist and could not be spared. This decision probably saved his life.

Before Christmas there was a month of miserable weather, there was much sickness in the camp. A new issue of stronger boots seemed to help matters.

Tom came home for Christmas. The scene in the High Street must have changed since he left three years earlier. The customers at the Cross Keys were as lively as ever. A few doors away, at number 33, Eric Burton's parents Ed and Annie were doing a good trade in groceries, wines and spirits. The war was supposed to be 'over by Christmas'. It was not, but the townsfolk seemed determined to make it a merry Christmas. McMichael's 'Fancy Warehouse', next to the Town Hall, had knick-knacks and novelties to entertain the children and Ryders 'Friendly House' on Waterloo Terrace had muffs, mufflers and winter woollies to keep out the cold.

On the dark side, this Christmas was different, there were men in uniform all over the town. Some were bearing the wounds of battle and a few had sad tales to tell of lost comrades. Even so the mood in the town and throughout the nation was one of optimism. In the New Year there would be more battles but surely the British Empire and her allies would be victorious.

There was sobering news from France. Princess Patricia's Canadian Light Infantry were the only regiment of fully trained regular soldiers. They had left for France before Christmas to fight alongside the 2nd Battalion of the King's Shropshire Light Infantry. They went straight into the front line. Within weeks Princess Pat's suffered 300 casualties.

Christmas leave over, Tom Whitefoot returned to Bulford Camp. He was nineteen hours late and at least a dozen more were also late. Their commanding officer was in festive mood and let them off with the loss of a day's pay. In January one more casualty was added to the list. The papers reported the death of a young officer, shot accidentally on the rifle range on Salisbury Plain. Tom watched the burial party carry him away. This would become a familiar scene.

The weather was bright for the final parade on the 4th of February. King George and Queen Mary and the 'top brass', Kitchener and Roberts, came down to congratulate the Canadians. Twenty-four thousand men were on parade. The inspection took over an hour, the King had to walk at least two miles through the ranks. Tom Whitefoot had a front row view. The King seemed pleased, smiling and joking with his generals. No sooner was the parade over than preparations were made for the Division to be shipped to France.

It took a few days for Les Smith and the British Columbia Regiment to arrive at the front line near Ypres. The Great Western Railway took them to Avonmouth to board a troopship. They sailed across the Bay of Biscay to St. Nazaire, here they piled onto a freight train to begin the 500 mile rail journey to Steenwerk. It took three days.

We came across France in box cars about ten feet by twenty-five, sixteen men to a car and straw on the bottom to lie on, awfully bumpy ride but it could have been worse.

Despite all this spirits were high. They arrived at Steenwerk a quiet village near Bailleul and Tom Whitefoot was happy enough. A hospital was set up and he could begin his work.

Preparations were made for the Second Battle of Ypres. On the 22nd of April 1915 the Germans released chlorine gas from 5000 cylinders causing panic and confusion. Within minutes French troops in the path of the gas cloud suffered 6000 casualties, a four mile gap was left in the front line. The Canadians were ordered in to fill the gap. There were no photographs to capture the real horror of the event. There was no official photographer and the British Army had confiscated all cameras. Magazine illustrators used their skill and imagination to record the scene.

The Canadians managed to halt the German advance. Two days later another cloud of gas swept over the trenches. The troops defending the village of St. Julien were told to urinate on their handkerchiefs and place them over their noses and mouths. This was helpful but there were still many casualties.

The 'medics' worked night and day to cope with the enormous number of casualties following the gas attack at St Julien. Tom Whitefoot serving with the 3rd Field Ambulance wrote home to describe his own experiences.

Tuesday evening we were shelled out and had to evacuate our wounded under shell fire, quite exciting I can tell you. A shell burst twenty feet from me when we were carrying a stretcher, wounding a dispatch rider and one of our men but I did not get scratched, only knocked over and covered with earth. We lost ten men wounded and five missing. Eight people were killed in a house close by, dead horses were lying about all over the place. I have seen quite enough slaughter. Some of the wounds are simply awful but we soon get hardened to the sights.

The Field Ambulances moved back with the Canadian Division as they withdrew from the front line to regroup.

The weather is just perfect here and the country looks lovely, altogether too peaceful for the conflict that is going on nearby. This is certainly the most senseless slaughter that civilised nations ever devised

A man was brought into Tom's dressing station suffering from shell shock. He carried bad news – Leslie Smith had been killed on the 24th of April 1915, the first of the Old Boys to fall in the Great War.

PRIVATE LESLIE CHARLES SMITH – 7TH BATTALION
BRITISH COLUMBIA REGIMENT

Les Smith and Charlie Krempeaux were mates, they had been together from the day they joined the regiment. From his hospital bed in North Staffordshire, Charlie wrote to Les's uncle in Bridgnorth.

I might say that the Ypres salient was in the shape of a very narrow horseshoe and we were in the toe, so that our left flank was bent back and we were practically surrounded.

The situation being desperate we were ordered to the aid of the Highlanders advancing under heavy shell and rifle fire over open country and it fell to our lot to occupy one of these gaps. Leslie was about fifty feet away on my left when we reach our position. We had got separated in the rush, but during a lull in the attack he waved his hand to me.

A short while after this the German Artillery opened up and got our exact range, point blank… It was bad enough to be shelled in the trenches but in the open with just a little soil scratched up to shelter our heads! What the Germans could not do with their infantry they tried to do with artillery, but none gave way except the wounded who crawled away on hands and knees. And here word was passed to me that Leslie was killed by shrapnel. A few moments later I was blown up.

Les Smith's body was never recovered, he is remembered on the Menin Gate at Ypres and on the Honour Board in his old school. Tom Whitefoot also learned that Eric Burton had died. He appears to have died a happy man.

LCPL (1553) Eric Burton – Princess Patricia's Light Infantry

In a letter to the Bridgnorth Journal Eric described life in the trenches and reassured the readers.

…you have no need to worry about my comfort, as I have got quite used to life now, and know how to make myself comfortable under any conditions, and I feel just as happy as I ever felt in my life…

Some complained about the food, not Eric. He described the menu.

At 6 am I had hot tea and buttered toast; and at 11 am. Welsh rarebit with an onion sliced in an Oxo. At 2 pm I had tinned ration, meat and vegetables, just like good Irish stew. Then for supper, brown bread and marmalade and tea. Agree with me, that this is feeding fit for a king.

In addition there were two things that made Eric's life more comfortable: rubber boots, to protect against 'trench foot' and Keating's powder to ward off 'vermin'. The advertisement claimed the Keating's was harmless to animals but unrivalled in destroying fleas, bugs, beetles, cockroaches and moths. Eric recommended it particularly for fleas.

I have managed to keep clear the last three weeks with the aid of Keating's.

Cockroaches are said to be able to withstand heavy doses of atomic radiation so Keating's must have been powerful stuff.

Lance Corporal Burton was happy enough, but even he must have hoped for a quick victory and he believed he knew how this could be achieved. The way to shorten the war was to double the rum ration.

The rum ration is given to us only in the trenches and it seems to put new life into a man; there is a regular transformation after a man has taken it. Beforehand, everyone is cold and feeling out of sorts with everyone around; afterwards everyone is on the best of terms and all trying to talk at once. It would only take two tots instead of one, and no German would be able to stop us until we got to Berlin.

The Germans moved their artillery and brought their guns to bear on Frezenberg Ridge. Following the bombardment that began on the 8th of May German infantry made repeated assaults and threated to break through. A two mile gap opened up, Princess Patricia's were ordered in to 'hold the line'. They did so but at a terrible cost. A fighting force of 700 soldiers was whittled down to 150 who were in any shape to fight.

Eric Burton was wounded, he made light of his injuries as he lay in the trench joking with his comrades. The 92nd Field Ambulance gathered him up and moved him to a safer place. He died the next day, the 9th of May.

The sad news did not reach his old friends in Calgary for weeks. In June he appeared on the casualty list of the Calgary Herald, and his old Fire Chief said,

*His many friends will hope that his injuries are not of
a serious nature.*

When Eric's death was confirmed 'Cappy Smart' hung a framed
photograph of Eric Burton in his office alongside other Calgary firemen
who had recently died in France.

Cool Under Fire

PTE. E. F. BURTON

In Bridgnoth his old headmaster remembered him well,

> *He did not distinguish himself by his scholarship... Where
> mischief was afoot Eric sure to be... He was of the adven-
> turous type, fighting fires in Calgary he could always be
> trusted in a tight corner. In the trenches the story was told
> that loaded himself with bombs and crept out one night on
> his own to bombard the Germans. No one was surprised,
> Eric was of the adventurous type.*

Eric was buried along with many others in the Lijssenthoek Military Cemetery, still within range of German artillery.

For two more years Tom Whitefoot was witness to this 'senseless slaughter'. He was promoted to Sergeant. In 1917 he was mentioned in dispatches. In 1918 he was awarded the Meritorious Service Medal for repeated acts of bravery.

FOR MERITORIOUS SERVICE

Tom returned to Canada when peace was declared but for many brave men their final resting place was far from the land of their dreams.

The Whitefoots carried on their trade in wines and spirits in the High Street (Tanner's today). Tom sailed back to Canada and took up his trade as photographer, he visited England from time to time. Crossing the Atlantic he must have thought back to the ten anxious days he spent at sea with the first contingent of the Expeditionary Force as they sailed to Devonport in 1914.

Years passed and Tom became well known as a photographer and film maker. As the Second World War drew to a close he filmed a parade in Vancouver. Canadian and American troops strode by. There were bands, airmen with bomb trolleys, tanks and jeeps. The onlookers waved and cheered as ambulances and artillery pieces drove by. Trailers carried huge portraits of Churchill and Roosevelt, the American president. Girls in uniform threw out their chests and stepped out confidently, the crowd cheered them on. Then at the end of the procession The Whitefoots carried on their trade in wines and spirits in the High Street (Tanner's today). Tom sailed back to Canada and took up his trade as photographer, he visited England from time to time. Crossing the Atlantic he must have thought back to the ten anxious days he spent at sea with the first contingent of the Expeditionary Force as they sailed to Devonport in 1914.

Years passed and Tom became well known as a photographer and film maker. As the Second World War drew to a close he filmed a parade in Vancouver. Canadian and American troops strode by. There were bands, airmen with bomb trolleys, tanks and jeeps. The onlookers waved and cheered as ambulances and artillery pieces drove by. Trailers carried huge portraits of Churchill and Roosevelt, the American president. Girls in uniform threw out their chests and stepped out confidently, the crowd cheered them on. Then at the end a chariot appeared, painted with a large swastika and pulled along by lads in German uniform, it was a joke. The crowd cheered, confident that the Second World War would end soon, with victory for the Allies.

Tom Whitefoot survived both wars, he lived to a good age, ninety-five years. Many men of his generation felt grateful that they had survived but guilty that so many good friends had not enjoyed their full share of life.

The Whitefoots carried on their trade in wines and spirits in the High Street (Tanner's today). Tom sailed back to Canada and took up his trade as photographer, he visited England from time to time. Crossing the Atlantic he must have thought back to the ten anxious days he spent at sea with the first contingent of the Expeditionary Force as they sailed to Devonport in 1914.

Years passed and Tom became well known as a photographer and film maker. As the Second World War drew to a close he filmed a parade in Vancouver. Canadian and American troops strode by. There were bands, airmen with bomb trolleys, tanks and jeeps. The onlookers waved and cheered as ambulances and artillery pieces drove by. Trailers carried huge portraits of Churchill and Roosevelt, the American president. Girls in uniform threw out their chests and stepped out confidently, the crowd cheered them on. Then at the end a chariot appeared, painted with a large swastika and pulled along by lads in German uniform, it was a joke. The crowd cheered, confident that the Second World War would end soon, with victory for the Allies.

Tom Whitefoot survived both wars, he lived to a good age, ninety-five years. Many men of his generation felt grateful that they had survived but guilty that so many good friends had not enjoyed their full share of life.

A chariot appeared, painted with a large swastika and pulled along by lads in German uniform, it was a joke. The crowd cheered, confident that the Second World War would end soon, with victory for the Allies.

Tom Whitefoot survived both wars, he lived to a good age, ninety-five years. Many men of his generation felt grateful that they had survived but guilty that so many good friends had not enjoyed their full share of life.

Chapter 4

Taking on the Turks

From the very beginning the Great War was a worldwide war. British and French troops invaded the German Colony of Togoland in West Africa five days after the declaration of war on the 4th of August. At the end of the month New Zealand forces occupied German Samoa in the Pacific. Indian troops were dispatched to German East Africa to take on the garrison at Dar-es-Salaam and the South Africans invaded German South-West Africa.

Yet the heart of the conflict was in Europe and help came from every corner of The Empire. The first elements of the Indian Expeditionary Force landed at Marseille on 26th of September. Three weeks later Canadians arrived at Plymouth. New Zealanders set sail from distant Wellington, and twenty thousand Australians were on their way to the Western Front. Many never arrived because they were caught up in the fight with the Turks who had thrown in their lot with the Germans.

The conflict began when Turkish warships bombarded Odessa and Sevastopol, Russian ports on the Black Sea. The Allies retaliated by shelling forts at the entrance to the Dardanelles, the narrow straits leading from the Aegean Sea to Constantinople (Istanbul today). The Ottoman Empire had once extended along the coast of North Africa as far as Morocco but they had been losing territory steadily for nearly a century. Britain had control of Egypt and intended to keep it that way, they had to retain control of the Suez Canal at all costs. Also vital to the war effort were the oil fields of the Middle East.

The war on the Western Front had reached stalemate by the end of 1914. To help the Russians in their campaign against the Turks and open up a second front an attempt was made to force a passage through the Dardanelles. A combined force of British, French and Anzac

(Australia and New Zealand Army Corps) troops was assembled and made preparations to land on the Gallipoli Peninsula.

Old 'Bridgnorthians' were going to be involved. William Ormesher was a well-respected young master and Pecy Nevett had been a star pupil. Bob Hutton kept his head down and survived skirmishes on the beaches. Bill Evans arrived too late to take part in the main event, but went on to distinguish himself in France.

The Gallipoli campaign ended with victory for the Turks. The decision was made to evacuate all Allied troops in January 1916. In one of the final exchanges a combined squadron of German and Turkish airmen shot down two aircraft of the Royal Naval Air Service.

Earlier, Petty Officer James Wightman, serving with the RNAS, had sounded optimistic in a letter to the school.

> *Everything seems to be going along quite alright here. I must say the Turks seem to have brave fighters, but they are no match for the Australian and New Zealand troops... Shall be more than delighted to receive the School Magazine if possible.*

He was certainly right about the fighting spirit of the Turks and the Anzac forces. A century has passed and the sacrifices made at Gallipoli are still remembered every year on Anzac Day, 25th of April.

SERGEANT (857) WILLIAM PERCY NEVETT – 12TH BATTALION AUSTRALIAN INFANTRY

Percy Nevett was miles from home when war broke out, in fact he was miles away from anywhere. He was at Day Dawn in the outback of Australia.

The surrounding landscape was flat and scorched and treeless, very different from the world he had known as a boy. A woodland drive led to the front door of the family home, Cotsbrook Hall. Green fields were all around, and nearby a reliable stream kept the mill-wheel turning.

At school Percy had excelled in the classroom and on the sports field. He went on to study engineering at Birmingham University and began his career with the Metropolitan Wagon Works in Walsall – a rough area. This was ideal training for his next job as engineer, maintaining the

© BES Library

water supply to the mining company at Day Dawn in Western Australia.

This dusty little settlement had boomed since gold was discovered there in 1890.

When war was declared the gold-miners downed tools and made for Black Boy Hill, a training camp outside Perth. Percy Nevett went with them. He had been a member of the Officer Training Corps at university and his experience at Day Dawn made him just the man to turn wild men into disciplined soldiers. He was promoted to sergeant on the day he joined.

The men of the 11th and 12th battalion of the Australian Imperial Force were some of the fittest men ever to set foot on a battlefield. They sailed from Freemantle and set up camp in Egypt in the shadow of The Pyramids.

Training continued in preparation for service in France, the desert was not the ideal training ground, there was too much sand and not enough mud.

Sergeant Nevett was singled out for promotion, he was better

qualified than most of the officers and Colonel Clarke recognised this.

"I'm sending you back to Australia for commissioning."

"I'd rather stay in the ranks, sir, with the men I know." The Colonel respected his decision.

There was change of plan. The Anzacs were not going to Europe, they were to be committed to the Gallipoli campaign. Percy Nevett made a will on the 5th of February.

The Royal Navy ferried the invaders from Alexandria to the Greek Island of Limnos. On the evening of 24th April 1915 battleships, minesweepers, troop transports and lighters sailed out of harbour and made for the coast of Turkey. The main force of French and British troops arrived in total darkness at the tip of the Gallipoli Peninsula. Further north Australians and New Zealanders were ferried ashore at 'Z' Beach.

In the poor light of the early dawn there was confusion. Believing they were too close to the promontory of Gaba Tepe one of the naval officers decided to steer north crossing the path of other units. Battalions were mixed and the chain of command broken.

Sergeant Nevett led his company ashore. The troops had expected to land on a gently shelving shore with cultivated land and orchards ahead of them. The planners had not done their homework. Laden with all their equipment they struggled through the waves. When they did manage to scramble ashore they found themselves on a narrow beach with near vertical cliffs above them. The Turks were in a commanding position. Machine gunners and snipers cut down the invaders before they could find cover.

Percy Nevett was hit above the knee in both legs, a comrade gathered him up and carried him out of harm's way. He died almost immediately. The day he died would go down in history. The 25th of April is Anzac Day when Australians and New Zealanders remember their lost sons.

Newspaper reports of the fighting at Gallipoli were alarming: *Battle Now in Progress – Australians Face Death – They Rose to the Occasion.*

At Cotsbrook Hall the Nevetts were desperate for news of their son. Percy's brother Tom, on leave in England at the time, did manage to make contact with the Sergeant Major of the Percy's battalion. He wrote back,

> *He was on the left flank on the Sunday we effected a landing here, and at this point the fighting was particularly heavy. Your brother was hit and carried to a place of more safety by Private Michie, another of our good men since killed. The wound was so serious that before the stretcher-bearers could get him to the beach, he died. He was one of our most popular NCOs, and my best friend.*

The bad news spread throughout the district. It may have been some comfort to the parents to read the tribute paid by the Reverend Dawes, Percy's old headmaster.

> *He was never beaten and temporary checks only served to increase his determination to win through. Yet with all this, he had such a charming personality, such an engaging manner, he was popular wherever he went.*

The British High Command underestimated the fighting capability of the Turks. Their army was ill-equipped, German advisers controlled what few planes there were to form an air force and the Turkish navy was

© Apley Estate Archives

described as ' a weird collection of scrap iron'.

The campaigns in the Middle East should have been a 'push over'. However, the military strategists did not take into account the grit and determination of 'Memet', the Turks answer to our 'Tommy'.

The invaders were trapped on the beaches and despite many heroic attempts to break out the Turkish defenders held their ground.

On the day William Percy Nevett died a young Grammar School master was also preparing to face the Turks at Gallipoli.

Lieutenant William Ormsesher – 16th Kings Liverpool Regiment, att. Royal Fusiliers

The Royal Fusiliers were held in reserve, William Ormesher did not join the fray until the 4th of July. The campaign was not going well and apart from the obvious danger of sniper fire and shelling by the Turkish artillery many troops fell ill. The scorching heat and the insanitary conditions in the trenches added to their misery. William was evacuated to Cyprus suffering from dysentery. At the time his excellent work supervising the repair of one of the trenches under heavy fire was rewarded with promotion to lieutenant.

© BES Library

On release from hospital he spent a few days at Mustapha Pasha, a rest camp at Alexandria. He wrote home.

> *I sit on a camp bed my feet on a floor of sand, alas very prolific in flies, fleas, lice and yellow and green lizards. I awake from a sleep induced by the loud bellow of bull-frogs in a nearby pond. I walk through the sand to the green sea, dive into waves – and sea-weed – and return to a strange breakfast, cooked by dark complexioned folk...*

Back at the regimental depot on Lemnos he met Lord Kitchener (a national hero and Secretary of State for War) who was on a tour of inspection. He knew the family would be impressed and wrote home to describe the meeting. This was his last letter. He was back in the trenches in November and this time it wasn't heat that caused a problem it was rain. An exceptional downpour created floods that swept down the hillside destroying the barricades and drowning a number of men in the trenches. It affected both sides and brought about an effective truce.

It did not last, hostilities resumed the following morning. The situation was recorded in the regimental diary.

The truce ended as strangely as it had begun and anyone showing above the trenches was liable to meet the familiar fate. Captain Shaw was shot dead. Lieutenant Ormesher was mortally wounded and with such an object lesson the bitter discomforts of the trenches were made to seem preferable.

William was taken to a hospital near the beachhead and then transferred to Limnos. His condition was stabilised and he was taken on board the hospital ship *Dunluce Castle* bound for Malta. He died on the 3rd of December and was buried at sea.

Both Lieutenant Ormesher and Sergeant Nevett are remembered on the Helles Memorial, overlooking the Mediterranean Sea.

Holding the High Ground

© CWG Commission

The Turks were not going to have it all their own way. Old Boys carried on the fight.

The most serious threat posed by Turkish forces was on the Suez Canal; this vital supply line had to be defended at all costs. Owen Williams played a part.

2ND LIEUTENANT OWEN EDGAR WILLIAMS – IMPERIAL CAMEL CORPS

Owen began his 'soldiering' as a Private with the Worcestershire Yeomanry, they arrived in Egypt in 1915. The beaches of Gallipoli were still held by forces of the British Empire but they could not break through and the cavalry were no help. The troopers were dismounted and fought as infantry, they landed at Sulva Bay in August. Owen and his comrades held on for four months until all troops were evacuated.

Worcestershire Yeomen and other mounted troops attached to the Camel Corps were now tasked with defending The Canal, which they did most successfully. The Turks retreated to Gaza.

Owen Williams was promoted, commissioned in the Welsh Regiment, and was killed in action on the last day of the Second Battle of Gaza. Nathan Mindel passed on, through Gaza to Jerusalem.

2ND LIEUTENANT NATHAN MINDEL – RAMC ATT. IMPERIAL CAMEL CORPS & ARMY SERVICE CORPS

Not everyone was comfortable in the saddle, especially on a camel. Private Mindel suffered a serious knee injury, he may have fallen off his camel. He was out of action for six months and during that time was commissioned as an officer in the Army Service Corps, a more comfortable position.

The Turks withstood assaults by British Forces, at Gaza in March and April 1917, but were finally driven out in November. General Allenby and his men pursued them, and rode into Jerusalem on the 9th of December. This was a triumph and particularly significant for Lieutenant Mindel, a Russian-born Jew. Also riding triumphantly into the Holy City were men of the New Zealand Light Horse.

ALAN HENRY HARRISON – NEW ZEALAND LIGHT HORSE

Samoa is literally on the other side of the world. Alan Harrison stepped ashore on this Pacific island in 1912 to take up a position as plantation manager at Puipa'a. This was certainly a big step, Samoa was then a German possession. Alan (he preferred to be called Jack) could not have known that within eighteen months troops from New Zealand would be landing to 'liberate' the islands.

The British government recognised that Samoa could have been used as a base for German warships operating in the Pacific and asked Australian and New Zealand forces to invade, they did so without a shot being fired. 'Jack' Harrison became part of the British administration until duty called and he joined the New Zealand forces.

A farm boy, from Chelmarsh, he was at home in the saddle and rode with the New Zealand Light Horse. It was a dusty ride back to England, first he had to face the Turks in Palestine.

In October 1917, on the road to Beersheba, the New Zealand cavalry charged the Turkish defences. They attacked with just a bayonet in one hand, their rifles slung across their backs. The captured four machine guns and over a hundred prisoners. The Australians went on to take Beersheba. This action was probably the last great cavalry charge in history.

Jack's brief war was over, he had been wounded low down in the back and was shipped to England to recover. The greenery of the Severn Valley must have seemed strange after the dust of the desert in the Middle East, and the bright blue of sea and sky seen from the shores of a Pacific island.

Perhaps to disguise it, maybe to draw attention to it, Jack had a tattoo placed over the scar on his back.

The Turks proved to be tough opponents. In April 1916, at Kut-al-Amara on the banks of the Tigris, 11,000 British and Indian troops surrendered to the Turks after a four-month siege. Those taken prisoner were force-marched along river to Baghdad and many died on the way. This was a humiliation that can be largely blamed on the Government of India- the supply of food and equipment was haphazard and disorganised – medical facilities were almost non-existent. Responsibility for the conduct of the war against the Turks was transferred to the British War Office. General Sir Stanley Maude, a meticulous planner, became army commander.

Captain Alfred Parsons had died in an earlier attempt to relieve the garrison. With Stanley Maude in command the tables were turned, Kut-al-Amara was retaken. Walter Barlow and the 30th Punjabis gave a hand, Lieutenant 'Joe' Jones of the Worcestershire Regiment lost his life. The Turks were in retreat, Tom Wilkes rode with the 14th Hussars and pursued them for a hundred miles to Bagdad and Phillip Hutton went beyond to finish the job in the Caucasus.

War weary and demoralised the Turks finally surrendered. There was no shame, they had driven the best of the British, French and Anzac forces off the beaches of Gallipoli and subjected the garrison at Kut to the most humiliating defeat in British military history. They had failed to take the Suez Canal or cut off oil supplies from Iraq or the Caucasus. They had even threatened the port of Aden.

Vast coal stocks were held there to fuel ships of the merchant fleet and the Royal Navy. Aden was given extra protection in 1917 when troops were sent from India.

SERGEANT (241217) STANLEY RUPERT NORTON – 1/6TH EAST SURREY REGIMENT

Stanley Norton wasn't exactly an orphan, he had grandparents, Edwin and Mary Norton. As an eight year-old he lived with them at 4 Church Hill, Madeley, and shared the house with his cousin Wilfred, a designer at the Tile Works.

His studies at the Grammar School gave him just enough knowledge to be an Elementary Pupil Teacher. The Norton household was reduced to two, Cousin Wilfred had gone and Grandfather Edwin was dead. Stanley Norton moved on, south to Surrey.

He was among the first to join the 1/6th East Surrey Regiment, raised at Kingston in August 1914. After barely two months training the battalion was ready to sail. They embarked at Southampton on the 29th of October to begin their passage to India.

They were over a month at sea, which meant they probably went round The Cape rather than the shorter route through The Canal. From the wharf at Bombay they 'entrained' for the trip to Lucknow, over eight hundred miles. Grubby villages and fields without hedgerows passed by. It was a strange land, *Why am I here?* Stan may have asked himself. At least when they arrived it was to a place most of them had heard of.

During the Indian Mutiny of 1857 several hundred civilians and a contingent of British and Indian troops were held under siege for six months. The siege was lifted at the second attempt. This incident had gone down in military history – every schoolboy had heard of the Relief of Lucknow. After six months there Stan Norton and his mates were probably ready for a change, and it came as a relief when they were moved to Rawalpindi.

Near to the Afghan border there was always trouble with the 'tribesmen', but nothing serious at the time. Disease accounted for most of the casualties in the ranks of the East Surreys. February 1917 and they were on the move, train to the coast, ship to Aden and action – not a lot of action. Turkish guerrilla bands were making a nuisance of themselves, harassing the Aden garrison, made up largely of Indian troops (7th Rajputs).

The East Surrey Regiment responded by sending out small reconnaissance parties. There was little contact with the enemy, one of the Turks fortified posts at Jabir and another at Hatum was destroyed.

The most serious incident occurred at Hatum in January 1918. To improve the defences the East Surrey Regiment dug in about a mile beyond the fort. The Turks replied with artillery and rifle fire, the defenders withdrew, fighting a rear-guard action, and 4 were killed and twenty-three wounded. The same month they returned to India to barracks at Meerut. In total the 1/6th Battalion lost 71 men during the war, the vast majority died of disease either in India or in the Gulf.

Sergeant Norton's contribution to the downfall of the Ottoman Empire was small. A schoolteacher, not a professional soldier, he was probably glad that he had not been called upon to make a bigger contribution.

Chapter 5

Duty Calls

There was no shortage of volunteers from the town, the majority joined the county regiment. The Territorials sailed for the Far East and did not see action in France until 1917, and then were thrown into the thick of it. Old Boys who had gone out into the world and returned to join the fray paid a heavy price, Smith and Burton came from Canada to die in 1915. Percy Nevett came from the gold fields of Australia to die at Gallipoli. William Ormesher, the classics master, fought there, died of wounds and was buried at sea, Guy Haseler has no grave.

Lance Sergeant Guy Broadfield Haseler – 5th Oxford and Buckinghamshire Light Infantry

The names of well over fifty thousand men are carved on the panels of the Menin Gate. Behind every name there is a story. Brief details are given in the War Graves register: address of next of kin, parents, widow and children are often mentioned. In the case of Guy Haseler his mother and late father are named and something unusual was added, 'Came from USA to enlist.'

Guy came from a well-known Handsworth family. He completed his education at Bridgnorth Grammar School and joined the family business. His father, John Haseler, was a manufacturing goldsmith with connections worldwide. In July 1913 Guy sailed from Liverpool on board '*La Negra*' bound for Argentina. The following year he was in New York. At the outbreak of war he booked his passage home and sailed back to Liverpool on Cunard's ill-fated '*Lusitania*'. He arrived safely at the Prince's Landing Stage. Back home in Birmingham he enlisted in the Oxford and Buckinghamshire Light Infantry.

The 5th Service Battalion was formed at Oxford and began training for war immediately. Leaders had to be found from among the new recruits and Guy Haseler was promoted to Corporal. Regular soldiers of the 2nd Battalion had landed in France ten days after the outbreak of war. Wounded men returning to the depot told of their experiences, there was nothing glorious about life in the trenches.

Born Leader

© BES Library

Lance Sergeant Haseler and 'C' Company were ready for action by the Spring of 1915. He came home, to Handsworth on leave, before embarking for France. It was not a joyful occasion. He attended the funeral of his father who died in March 1915. Guy's brother, John, a Private in the Warwickshire Regiment, was also on his way to France.

Annie Haseler lost the men in her life. She had for company, in the house in Devonshire Road, her unmarried daughter Ruth and Edith Martin, the 'cook domestic'.

The *Lusitania* that had carried Guy safely back to England set off on her final Atlantic crossing on the 1st of May. She was intercepted by

83

the German U-boat U20 on the 7th of May. Torpedoed off the coast of Ireland she sank within eighteen minutes, a thousand lives were lost. Guy must have 'thanked his lucky stars' that he was not on board. Now he was preparing for another boat trip across the Channel.

On the 20th of May Sergeant Haseler landed in Boulogne. The Ox and Bucks were moved swiftly to Ypres, a year earlier an attractive market town, now reduced to a shattered shell.

Today battlefield tours often start here and take the N8 out of town in the direction of Menin. Very soon the tourists arrive at a confusing roundabout with roads leading in seven directions. This was Hell Fire Corner and well named by military map makers, the target of artillery fire from the beginning of the war. From here it was but a short march to Railway Wood where the Ox and Bucks took over the front line trenches. In 1915 this place was a wood in name only. Leaves appeared on shredded branches in the Spring, only to be blown off by more shell fire.

Across no man's-land from 'C' trench the Germans had built a redoubt, a network of trenches and gun emplacements. On the 22nd of June two platoons of the 5th Battalion the Ox and Bucks were set the hopeless task of attacking the German positions. The assault failed, exhausted by their efforts the men returned, fell back into their own trenches. Guy Haseler did not return, his body was never recovered, his name is now among the fifty thousand on the Menin Gate. He served on the battlefield for less than a month, his brother 'soldiered on'.

2nd Lieutenant John Valentine Haseler DCM –
1st/6th Royal Warwickshire Regiment

At the war's end Annie Haseler welcomed home the son who survived. He began his service as an eighteen year old Private in the Warwickshire Regiment. He served with distinction and rose through the ranks.

In November 1916 he was awarded the Distinguished Conduct Medal for 'conspicuous gallantry in action'. When his platoon officer and sergeant had both been killed Corporal Haseler kept the men together and assisted the wounded.

Later when all but two of a Lewis gun team became casualties he kept the gun in action thereby facilitating the capture of a trench and taking several prisoners. His bravery and coolness were most marked.

Corporal Haseler was commissioned as 2nd Lieutenant in August 1917. He went on to serve with the North West Frontier Force on the border with Afghanistan. Clearly a travelling man, he met Miss Wilkes in Spain, they were married at the British Consulate in Barcelona in the 1930s, and as time went by they had four children together. Lieutenant John Haseler was in uniform again during the Second World War, serving as a paymaster. He died in Banbury in 1981. His was a full life, all a matter of luck.

Richard Hinkesman was very unlucky.

CORPORAL (497) RICHARD BOYCOTT HINCKESMAN – HOUSEHOLD CAVALRY – 1ST KING EDWARD'S HORSE

Richard Hinckesman was an exhibitioner, he benefited from the generosity of Edward Careswell. The Careswell Trust, which dated from 1690, gave him the opportunity to study at Christ Church College Oxford. This did not mean the Hinckesmans were a needy family, they were extremely enterprising, farming and trading in Shropshire since the time of the Civil War and always prepared to go further afield.

© BES Library

Richard's father, Thomas Boycott Hinckesman, went off to South Africa to do some prospecting. He changed his trade from corn merchant to gold miner. He ran into trouble at Tati near Bulawayo during an uprising that historians later called the Second Matabele War. He was killed in 1896. Richard was nine years old at the time.

Georgina Hinckesman was now the 'head of the household'. She moved with her three boys from Astley Abbots to 12 Victoria Road. She had 'private means', Tom Hinckesman left her £3250 in his will.

Richard left Bridgnorth Grammar School to take up his scholarship at Christ Church College. When he graduated he began teaching at Northampton Grammar School, and lodged with a seventy-two year old widow for five years.

The Hinkesman family dispersed. Mother moved back to Wales, her native land, to Trinity Road, Aberystwyth. In 1913 Richard said goodbye to Mrs Anne Hodson, his landlady in Lutherworth Road, Northampton. At Liverpool he boarded the *Virginian* and sailed to Quebec, en route to Toronto to take up a teaching appointment at Upper Canada College.

Richard's stay in Canada was short, he sailed home, on the *Tunisian* in June 1914, at the beginning of the school holidays. He arrived in Liverpool and made his way to Aberystwyth. The clouds of war were gathering, Richard did not return to Toronto, he waited for the storm to break. Ten days after war was declared Richard Boycott Hinckesman walked into Alexandra Palace to enlist, 'for the duration'. He joined 1st King Edward's Horse, an elite regiment, part of the Household Cavalry.

'For Empire and Liberty' Was the Moto

Most of the officers and men had seen service in the dominions and colonies of the British Empire, they were an exceptional group. Even though Richard was a graduate of Oxford University he was still only given the rank of Lance Corporal.

As a change from drill the regiment devised a competition, 'wrestling on horseback'. Pathe News filmed one of these events. A group of about twenty men, riding bareback, grabbed, tugged and punched each other in an effort to unseat a rival. The last man standing, or in this case sitting, was the winner.

By the Spring of 1915 they were ready for action. 'C' Squadron arrived in France on the 22nd of April 1915 to join the London Division at La Bassee. An important battle had been fought here in October 1914. When Lance Corporal Hinkesman arrived most of the fighting was concentrated further south. His regiment was having a quiet time, just the occasional shell to contend with.

Richard worked well and was well qualified, he was hoping for promotion. He was recommended for a commission. This would have meant retuning to England for officer training. He did not return.

Richard was supervising the loading of a wagon in a chalk pit, close to the front line, when a shell exploded nearby and he was trapped under a pile of earth. Frantic friends dug him out, but he died in a field ambulance on the 20th of October 1915, age 28.

A guard of honour of King Edward's Horse attended his burial in the nearby military cemetery at Louvencourt. (Plot 1 Row C Grave 12).

Guardian Angel

© BES Library

He was well remembered by all who met him, teachers and pupils in Northampton, footballers in Aberystwyth, Old Boys in Bridgnorth. His name was carefully written in ink on the Roll of Honour of Christ Church College, Oxford and cast in bronze on the Bridgnorth War Memorial. On the library stairs of his old school, under the stained glass window of St Michael, he is remembered alongside other boys 'called to higher service'.

A talented man, Richard Hinckesman, had sailed from Canada to join the fight and would have gone far had he lived.

A survivor who came from afar was Bill Evans.

Lieutenant William Henry Evans – Field Artillery Brigade, Australian Imperial Force

The stationary business of Robert Evans provided a comfortable living for his wife, Alice, and their three children. It was fortunate that Alice understood the printing business because she had to carry on alone, Robert died prematurely. The children were given a good education and expected to make their own way in the world. William went to the other side of the world, to Australia, to Moonee Ponds on the outskirts of Melbourne.

Return Ticket to the Old Country

© National Archives of Australia

William married and made a living as a grazier. When he wasn't herding stock he rode with the 19th Light Horse. Many of his companions went to enlist in the Imperial Force at the outbreak of war. A year passed before Bill Evans decided to join in. He was a married man, the decision to leave Marjory and a comfortable life at Moonee Ponds was not easy. His mind was made up in Albert Park in Melbourne in September 1915 when the 4th Field Artillery Brigade was raised.

From the point of view of the army he was exactly the kind of adventurer they were keen to recruit, a man with military experience, used to the outdoor life. In August 1915 he was drafted into the infantry. Within a month of joining he was promoted to Sergeant.

New recruits were well aware of the dangers they faced. The Gallipoli campaign had cost the Australian Imperial Force dear, twenty-six thousand casualties, eight thousand dead. Those that survived were withdrawn to Egypt and then shipped to the Western Front. Sergeant Evans went to join them there. Ten days before the Christmas of 1915 he disembarked *HMAS Wiltshire* at Suez.

Three months later he sailed from Alexandria to Marseille. The Brigade were then given the opportunity to see something of the country they had come to defend as they travelled 800 kilometres by train to Le Havre. Here they collected transport vehicles and the 'eighteen-pounders' they were going to use to pound the enemy. Then they were on their way to Armentieres. The fighting here was not as intense as other places along the Western Front and the allies used the location as a 'nursey sector' where new units could be 'blooded'. The 4th Brigade fired on the German positions for the first time at Armentieres on the 8th of April 1916.

Bill Evans and 12 Battery moved south to Sausage Valley near Pozieres. The Battle of the Somme was raging, and they were in constant action against the enemy, for six weeks. There was some relief in September when they were moved to Ypres but returned in November. As the harsh winter set in they experienced the first gas attack.

Sergeant Evans had shown himself to be a very capable leader of men. In November he was promoted to Lieutenant, 'in the field'. This was a particular honour, often awarded after demonstrating leadership under fire. During the winter months both sides held their ground, hostilities resumed in earnest in the Spring of 1917.

© Imperial War Museum

ALL QUIET ON THE WESTERN FRONT

The Germans had made a tactical withdrawal to establish a more secure front line, the Hindenburg Line. A central feature of their defences was the village of Bullecourt. On the 10th of April an attempt was made by six battalions of Australian Infantry to take Bullecourt. The assault failed, they lay in snow in no man's land overnight until ordered to retire. Fresh troops attacked again the following day and failed to break through. They did not lack courage, they lacked leadership. General Hubert Gough's mismanagement cost the Australians over two thousand casualties.

Lieutenant Evans was out of action, nothing serious, 'mild tonsillitis'. He was back with his battery within a week, and preparing to support the infantry in yet another assault on the enemy lines. The battered 4th Division was replaced by the 2nd Australian Division.

In the early hours of the 3rd of May they advanced across no man's land. Artillery batteries worked tirelessly, pounding the enemy positions. Despite the efforts of Bill Evans and the gunners of the 4th Field Artillery Brigade few gaps were made in the wire protecting the German trenches. Sent in to support the weary Aussies were Welsh Fusiliers and a battalion of the Honourable Artillery Company.

Although they did not know it at the time, two Old Boys were now fighting side by side at Bullecourt. Eric Owen serving with the Honourable Artillery Company was captured by the Germans within hours of joining the battle, Bill Evans carried on the fight for nearly a fortnight.

The fifteenth of May was the day Billy Evans' 'soldiering' came to an end. Wounded in action he was 'patched up' at the front before transfer to No. 14 General Hospital at Wimereux the next day. The gunshot wounds to his right hand and left leg were serious. It was clear he would not return to duty for months. Within twenty-four hours he was in England, ferried from Boulogne across the Channel on board *HMHS St. Andrew*.

Lieutenant Evans spent four months at No. 3 General Hospital London before he was discharged to Weymouth. Granted sick leave, he would have been able to visit the family in Bridgnorth. Alice Evans had moved from the High Street to 'Garth' on the Wenlock Road. In October she said goodbye to her son. He embarked for Australia, together with other casualties of war.

Waiting at Moonee Ponds, Marjory must have known Bill was on his way. How or where they were reunited we may never know. He had a limp and he had lost a finger, but his wounds were certainly not serious enough to prevent him tackling the many tasks around the house that his young wife had lined up for him.

As the war drew to a close the Australian Government arranged passages for 'native born Britons' to visit the Old Country'. The *Wyreema* cast off from the dock in Sydney harbour on the 14th of October 1918, by the time she arrived in England the war was over.

Chapter 6

Town and Country

The Stewards were the chemists, everyone for miles around knew that. They had a cure for everything, coughs and sneezes, cuts and bruises and quite a few unmentionable complaints. There must have been few who had not been through the door of the Medical Hall at the end of the High Street.

Minding the Shop

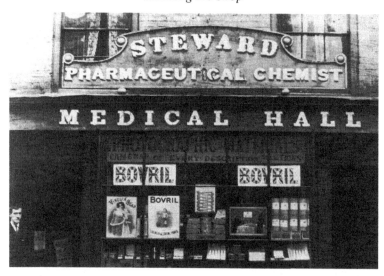

© the Steward Family

George helped his father keep the business going while his brothers went to war. They served with distinction.

Out of town, farmers, like the Pages and the Robins, were often more concerned with the health and welfare of their stock than of their families. Horse liniment was just as effective on a wagoner's knee as on one of his team, and a sip of dark liquid that would cure coughing in a flock of sheep would do a man no harm, or so they believed.

There were differences between the townsfolk and those who came in once a week to market but when war came they were united. Fred Head was a typical townie.

Private (28655) Frederick Head – 1st North Staffordshire Regiment

Fred was a quiet boy, not an athlete, not the sort the army could turn easily into a warrior. Farmhands, bricklayers, gamekeepers, working outdoors in all weathers they could be made into soldiers in no time. Fred was a 'pen-pusher' working as a clerk for Gertrude Jones and surrounded by shop girls selling drapery at Waterloo House. He dressed smartly and filled in the ledgers in a 'neat hand' but he did have one quality the Army could use, he was an excellent shot.

Fred shared lodgings with a dozen young folk, mostly drapers' assistants. Fred was a hardware clerk. Maude was a draper, Ethel a dressmaker, Alice a domestic and Edith was in 'fancy goods'. To escape these cackling women, Fred put on his battledress once a week and marched down to the Drill Hall.

Fred seated on the left

94

He was a member of 'F' Company (Bridgnorth) 4th Battalion KSLI (TF). Their commanding officer Captain Westcott rewarded Fred's skill with the Lee Enfield rifle with promotion to Corporal. It didn't give him the bearing of a soldier but that didn't matter, he could still hit the target.

The 4th Battalion were enjoying their annual camp in Wales when war was declared, they were mobilised immediately. As territorials they were not required to serve overseas but the majority agreed to do so. In a matter of weeks they were sailing to the Far East to relieve the full-time professionals at the Singapore garrison.

Private Head wore the Imperial Service Bar on his tunic to show that he was prepared to serve overseas, however he stayed at home, his mother was widowed, he was her only son. For a year he carried on with his clerical duties at Waterloo House and helped with the training of young territorials at the Drill Hall. In November 1915 he 'attested' and became a member of the regular army. In July the following year he transferred from the KSLI to the North Staffordshire Regiment and as a member of the Training Corps sailed for France.

Twenty thousand British Troops died on the first day of July 1916. The Battle of the Somme raged on and men died every day. Troops freshly arrived from England were thrown straight into the fray. The battle for control of Delville Wood began on 15th of July. For six weeks one infantry division after another went out to face enemy fire. At the end of August it was the turn of the Queen's Regiment, the East Surreys, West Kents, and North Staffs to do their damnedest – 'to do or die'.

It was five months since Fred Head had left his home town, he had been in France for four weeks and, during three days of fighting at Delville Wood, his regiment had suffered over three hundred casulties. Fred was killed in action on 31st of August. Mary Head received the news at her home in Rose Lane.

Boys in blazers and caps passed by on the way to school just as her boy had done, only they were on their way to the new school, not the Old Grammar School in St Leonard's Close. When Mary went out to shop in the High Street everywhere there were reminders of happier times when Fred was a boy at school.

"If only we could put the clock back, and boy soldiers would be schoolboys again."

© BES Library

Now there were boys in kakhi all over the town, making the best of their leave before they went back to the front. There were some like Bill Steward who would not return.

Sergeant (1138) William John Steward – 22nd Royal Regiment of Fusiliers

Bill Steward joined the Royal Fusiliers in 1914 at the White City when the 22nd Battalion was formed by the Mayor of Kensington. Bill was working as a pharmacist in London at the time. A year later the Battalion landed at Boulogne to fight on the Western Front until the end of the war.

So many died in battle in July 1916 that the task of 'tidying up' their affairs sometimes took months. Families, anxious for news, waited, hoping for the best, fearing the worst. Men, at first believed to be missing, were confirmed dead, lucky ones appeared on the Red Cross lists of prisoners.

In some cases letters written by the company commanders appeared impersonal, they simply did not know the man. Sergeant Bill Steward was well known, letters of condolence from Colonel Barker and Captain MacDougal of the 22nd Royal Regiment of Fusiliers were unusually detailed. On the 14th of July Colonel Barker wrote:

I am very sorry to have to inform you that your son Sergt. W. J. Steward was killed last night about 11pm. He was out repairing the parapet, when the Germans turned a Machine Gun on the party. He was killed instantaneously and had three bullets through his head. I saw him buried today by the Chaplain at 2.30 p.m. He is buried in the Lovane Valley with many other of his Comrades. The Lovane Valley is at the foot of Vimy Ridge, quite close to the Bethune, Arras Road and about 18 miles from Bethune.

No words can tell you the very high opinion we all had of your son. He was a most gallant fellow, always eager to volunteer for any dangerous enterprise. I looked upon him as my best Sergt. and had hoped to have him for an officer later on. I knew him very well personally and had the greatest admiration for him, as he always endured any hardship so cheerfully, and was an example to everyone.

You have my deepest sympathies.
Yours truly, R. Barnett Barker

Only hours before his death Bill Steward had been chatting with Captain MacDougal, who recalled the conversation in the letter of sympathy penned to Bill's father.

Dear Sir
I very much regret to tell you that your son was killed last night while on duty in the front line. He had just replaced another Sergeant, who had been badly wounded, and was hit by a Machine Gun, death being instantaneous.

I think your son was the most popular NCO in my Company and his death has cast a gloom over us all. It was his unfailing cheerfulness and his smile, ever brightest in adversity that endeared him to his comrades. He has been in my Company from the day we joined the Battalion and I cannot call to mind a single occasion when he was cast down or out of humour, and I had absolute confidence in him whether things were going well or ill.

He went on

I am afraid this will be a sad blow not only to you all but to his fiancée. I do not know her name, but I should like you to convey to her the sympathy of the Company in her sorrow, and I should like you to realise in the intensity of your grief that there are others, many comrades and officers, whose grief is only less poignant than your own, and that they may like to share some part of your burden. Your son had numberless friends and assuredly no enemies, his sweet and gracious character made enmities impossible.

A Place of Rest

It was only an hour before his death that he was talking to me of his two brothers who are further south and of his anxiety for their safety. I sincerely hope that they may return to you when this great storm has subsided.

We have just buried your boy. Our chaplain who he liked and admired immensely read the service over him and the Colonel and I and several other Officers were present.

He lies buried in a small valley within earshot of shell and rifle fire and our own Pioneers are making a cross to put over his grave.

We have lost many men here, and your boy lies surrounded by gallant comrades.

Yours very sincerely, A. MacDougal Capt.

In his last conversation with Captain MacDougal Bill had expressed his concern for the safety of his brothers. They did not end the war unscathed but both did survive.

Major Alan Steward MC – Royal Garrison Artillery

Alan, the Steward's youngest son, went straight from school to the Military Academy at Woolwich and was commissioned in the Royal Garrison Artillery.

The 27th Siege Battery proceeded to France in September 1915. Their task was to disrupt supply lines carrying enemy troops, rations and ammunition to the front line. They were equipped with heavy howitzers capable of flinging huge shells for miles across the battlefields. Alan rose through the ranks, he was a Captain in 1918 and, as the war came to an end, he was awarded the Military Cross.

Near Inchy-en-Artois on the morning of the 27th of September 1918 the Battery was being shelled. The section officer was killed. No 1 Gun was put out of action and practically the whole detachment became casualties, besides some men on other guns. He went out under heavy fire to superintend the removal of the wounded and rallied the remaining men. By his cool courage and example the guns were kept in action at a critical time.

Alan must have been proud to wear the medal that set him apart from other men. What may have pleased him more was his performance on the cricket field. In 1920 he strode out to bat for the town against Highley and scored a 'rapid 26' to finish them off. This made him a local hero.

LIEUTENANT CYRIL STEWARD – ROYAL ENGINEERS AND ROYAL GARRISON ARTILLERY

Brothers Alan and Cyril Steward had chosen not to train as chemists. Cyril studied civil engineering at Birmingham University. When Alice Steward's fair-haired, blue-eyed boy completed his studies he joined the Royal Warwickshire Regiment a month after the outbreak of war. He was quickly transferred to No 2 Special Battalion, Royal Engineers at Chatham. This was the 'chemical section', responsible for gas warfare.

In August 1915 he began his service in France. Clearly he knew the effects of gas, it was a fearful weapon, against which there was little defence. Corporal Steward must have decided that, with his training, he was better suited to more conventional warfare. On Boxing Day 1916 he submitted his application for transfer to the Royal Garrison Artillery.

He came home in the New Year and trained at Mansfield Park until May. Corporal Steward was now 2nd Lieutenant Steward of the RGA. He returned to France for 'on the job' training at No 4 Artillery School, then he took up his duties as a gunnery officer.

The opposition had equally skilful gunners who could return fire. Gun emplacements were the obvious targets. On the 4th of November Cyril was wounded, he remained stubbornly on duty. If he had retired for treatment he might not have been wounded a second time twelve days later. The Battery was on the receiving end of a gas shell.

From the Casualty Clearing Station Cyril was transferred to No 3 General Hospital and shipped home from Le Havre to Southampton on board H S *Exquibo*. He recovered from his wounds, and sat out the war in England.

It was ironic that a man who had been part of a unit specialising in gas warfare should himself have been 'on the receiving end'.

A lad who had been brought up on fresh country air was Tom Robins.

*

School transport for some of the farming families meant saddling a pony, riding to town and stabling at The Swan, an easy ride for Tommy Robins, across Morville Heath, from The Croft. He might have made a jockey, he had the right build.

What Tom lacked in stature he made up for in personality. His headmaster remembered how he managed to stand out in a crowd.

Private (2288) Thomas Hoblyn Robins – 6th Battalion KSLI – formerly of the Shropshire Yeomanry

A Little Terror

© BES Library

He was one of our most sporting Old Boys, full of life and vigour, full of fight. Looking back over the past one thinks of him first as a very tiny boy running between the legs of the big boys, the Captain of School, a strapping six-footer, was a sight worth seeing. As he grew up he distinguished himself by being foremost in every rough and tumble enterprise that required daring and skill.

The countryside around the family farm, the fields and valleys, streams and wooded hills were not unlike the landscape he would look out over in the Valley of the Somme.

The war was not unexpected, Tom and troopers of the Shropshire Yeomanry had been preparing for it. When the order came to mobilise they set off for Shrewsbury in high spirits, raring to go. From every corner of the county they rode in to Brogynlyn Park near Oswestry. The regiment was brought up to strength, equipped for battle; the troopers manoeuvred on horseback and drilled on foot. After a month they believed they were ready for action. They crossed the country by train to East Anglia and there they 'kicked their heels' while the strategists at the War Office 'scratched their heads'.

'How could the cavalry be used to good effect?'

They were at their best on open ground where the going was firm. Over in Flanders's fields it wasn't only the mud that would trouble them, it was the trenches, shell holes and endless coils of barbed wire.

Some lucky troopers sailed with their steeds to Egypt. Those left behind were dismounted. Tom Robins transferred to the 6th Battalion KSLI – still no action, they stayed put, camped in England.

Tom fretted at the length of his training in England and was all eagerness to get into the firing line, but although his wish was granted to him he was not destined to have a very long time on the battlefield.

Private Robins had been in uniform for well over a year. At last, surrounded by familiar faces, he sailed for France. Battalions of the county regiment, already fighting in France, had gained plenty of battlefield experience. Sometimes they fought side by side, more familiar faces. The 6th Battalion went into action straight away.

Successful raids were made on the German trenches and fists-full of medals were awarded for individual acts of bravery. On the 14th of July the Shropshires were moved into trenches at Flerbaix alongside the Australian 5th Division. They went into action together on the 19th, the following morning they went out to collect the dead and wounded. With less than a week's rest they were sent back into the trenches opposite Serre and 'found them waist deep in our dead'.

The 6th KSLI had been so seriously reduced in numbers that it was sent back into reserve. Training began again for another attack on Guillemont, twenty more were killed before the battle began. Perhaps, by now, even Tommy Robins was losing his appetite for battle.

After Guillemont the battalion marched to Morval to play a part in the Battle of Transloy Ridges. Simply taking over from the Royal Warwickshire Regiment cost the 6th Battalion seventeen casualties.

There was constant shelling, danger everywhere, not just in the front line. Men died repairing dugouts, carrying messages, shaving, writing home, sharing a mug of tea, playing cards – some were lucky, some were not. Not everyone could bear the uncertainty. 'Does this shell have my name on it?'

On the 6th of October two men were taken to the Regimental Aid Post with self-inflicted wounds. This was noted in the war diary:

6 pm, relief of the battalion by 6th Ox and Bucks commenced and the Btn moved into reserve. – Large parties found for digging assembly trenches and carrying to the front line. –19 wounded, 2 self- inflicted. No unusual activity – One killed.

The dead man wasn't named, he was just another 'Tommy', and in this case it was Tommy Robins. Such was the chaos at the time that Tom's body was never recovered. His passing was later recorded on the Thiepval Memorial, on a brass plaque in Morville Church and in the library of his old school.

Chapter 7

All Pals Together

The Lord Mayor of Birmingham and his Committee set about forming the 1st Birmingham Pals in September 1914. They was no shortage of recruits. At Sutton Park Alderman William Bowater looked out across a sea of cloth caps, there were a few bare-headed lads and the odd trilby hat. Somewhere in the crowd were four Old Boys of the Grammar School.

Dain, Stokes and the Findon brothers began their conversion from bank clerk, shop assistant and schoolmaster to professional soldiers at Sutton Coldfield. After weeks of drill, days spent on the rifle range, hours polishing boots and not a minute's rest they were ready for the passing-out parade. The time had come to pose for the Company photograph.

Cheer Up Lads

© Royal Warwickshire Regimental Museum

Private Dain was in 'D' Company, Corporal Richard Findon and his brother Frank were in 'B' Company. Anyone of a superstitious nature, looking for ill omens, might have been disturbed when they scanned the names of others gazing into the crystal ball of the camera lens. The Quartermaster Sergeant of 'B' Company was Dark (F. Dark) and the Sergeant Major of 'D' Company was Black (W. Black). There were more cheery characters in the ranks, Privates Gosling and Yapp, Lusty and Bliss. No matter, they were trained soldiers now, nothing could harm them, they would all sail to France and come home as heroes.

From Sutton Coldfield they were moved to a huge tented camp in the grounds of Bolton Hall in Wensleydale, and then down to Salisbury Plain, nearer to the Channel coast.

On the 21st of November 1915 the 'Pals' landed at Boulogne. There was a period of training given by men with first-hand experience of life in the trenches, and visits to the front line were arranged to 'familiarise' the new draft with conditions there. In the New Year they spent three days digging trenches within a hundred yards of the German line. They came out with a 'clean sheet', not a single casualty.

They retired to Vaux to clean up and receive more training. Some members of the 14th Battalion were singled out for special treatment. They were given accommodation in a nearby chateau, kept in isolation while they recovered from German measles. This was something the enemy could not be blamed for, German physicians had made early studies of the disease and hence the name. The whole battalion was out of the line for two months and spent some of the time digging 'sump holes' to drain away the vast quantities of mud from the roads.

Spring came, the countryside dried out, raids and skirmishes were organised and there were casualties. The Generals, meanwhile, were planning a really 'Big Push'.

The Battle of the Somme began on the 1st of July and came to a bloody end in mid-November. The suffering was beyond belief. At 7.30 am on the first day a hundred and twenty thousand men rose up along a twenty-eight mile front and made their way deliberately across no man's-land. The waiting Germans emerged from their shell-proof shelters and set up their machineguns. The slaughter began. Wave after wave came on, to be cut down in turn. Fifty thousand men fell, twenty thousand were dead.

The second half of the year 1916, from July to December, was the bloodiest of the war for the nation, the town and the school. Old Boys were wounded, missing, made prisoner and the unfortunate ones 'called to higher service'.

Private (305149) Charles Norman Wightman – 1/8th Royal Warwickshire Regiment

Bridgnorth Cricket Club celebrated a famous victory in the summer of 1912. In a needle match with Shrewsbury Town they won by an innings and forty-eight runs. They were helped to victory by a number of old boys, Dyer, Dain, Piper and Charlie Wightman (standing third from the left).

Batting for the Town – Batting for England

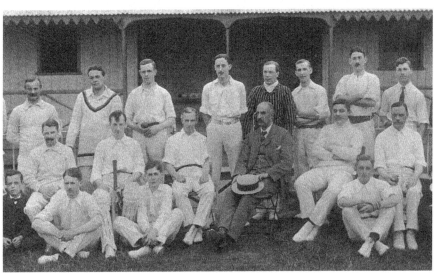

Two years later most of the team changed from cricket 'whites' to army khaki and went out to bat for England against the Germans. Some were 'caught', others 'bowled out', and the rest carried their bat and returned to the pavilion at the end of the game.

Charlie Wightman strode out to open the innings on the first of July. There was just a hint of mist on the meadows at daybreak in the Valley of the Somme. The sun rose up into a cloudless sky, a glorious day,

106

© BES Library

the best of the summer so far. The troops were in good heart, the artillery had pounded the German lines for a week, it would be 'a walk over'.

What followed was carefully noted in the war diary of the Royal Warwickshire Regiment:

2.0 am Battalion reported present in forming up trenches.

4.30 am Reported that everyone had a good breakfast. Artillery bombardment was intense.

7.0 am Very intense artillery on both sides.

7.23 am Enemy machine guns opened up all along the line. Three minutes later our troops are lying on the parapet ready to advance.

7.30 am Advance begins. Enemy first line reached and passed very quickly as also was the second. Having heavy casualties from machine gun fire in enemy third and fourth line. We reached our objective 35 – 40 minutes from Zero Hour and began consolidating and cleaning rifles.

By this time the next Battalion was arriving but had had so many casualties that they could not go through us so helped consolidating. This happened with all Battalions following us.

We had to retire to the third line. No supply of bombs were coming from the rear so could not hold on and retired again. Enemy machine guns and snipers were doing a great amount of damage all the while.

7.30 pm Held on to this position until relieved by a battalion from the rear. Throughout the action no troops were seen to our right or left.

11.00 pm Arrived at Mailley- Maillet and were put into billets.

It was a similar story all along the line. The Germans had anticipated the attack and withdrawn from their front line trenches to more secure positions. The artillery hardly damaged the concrete pill boxes from which they emerged to pour machine-gun fire into the ranks of the advancing infantry.

The following day what remained of the Battalion lined up for Roll Call.

Colonel Innes was dead. Major Caddick was dead and six other officers. The Battalion had paid a heavy price, 251 were missing, 255 were wounded and fifty-seven were dead.

Charlie Wightman was missing. Harry Jones, Ted Lay and John Dain were wounded. Harry Jones was shipped off to England, Ted Lay was fighting fit in no time. George and Isabella Wightman waited for months for news of their 'missing' son. Finally they were informed officially that he had been 'killed in action' on the 1st of July.

The enormity of the military disaster on the first day of battle did not deter General Douglas Haig.

"The enemy has been severely shaken. Our correct course is to press him hard with the least possible delay".

In the first week of July encouraging reports appeared in the newspapers, the true picture was very different. Tens of thousands of letters and telegrams sent from France told a different story.

The Dain family received some news from the War Office. A boy ran up from the Post Office to 20 Victoria Road with a telegram for Mr Frederick Dain. It informed him that his son, *Private J. L. Dain (882), 14th Warwicks, is dangerously wounded and lying at 12 Stationary Hospital.*

Private John Leslie Dain – 14th Royal Warwickshire Regiment

The Dain family were well known in the town. Frederick Dain managed a wine business in the High Street. John Dain dressed smartly, it was expected of all the clerks employed by Lloyd's Bank. John worked at the

© BES Library

Ironbridge branch, his old classmate Harold Gibbs was behind a till in Birmingham. When war was declared they both set aside their pens and ledgers. Harold was commissioned in Royal Field Artillery, John served as a Private soldier and went into battle with a rifle instead of a field gun.

Wounded during the opening exchanges of the Battle of the Somme, John Dain died of his wounds, on the 4th of July. Carried from the battlefield to the Stationary Hospital at Rouen the medical staff must have believed he had a chance of survival, moving him to Le Havre where he might have been be shipped home. He was buried in the St. Marie Cemetery, near No 2 General Hospital at Le Havre.

July 1916 was the blackest month of the War for the 'Old Boys'. Charlie Wightman and John Dain died in the first week, next to fall was Bert Johnson.

Sergeant (266341) Albert Johnson – 2/7th Royal Warwickshire Regiment

The Hen and Chickens in St Mary's Street had been serving ale for centuries. Within its walls young men had boasted of their actions on far flung battlefields, in the Crimea, the Sudan, India and South Africa. The landlord, Joe Johnson, listened patiently as lads in uniform compared their experiences with veterans of the Boer War.

©BES Library

"You should have been at Spion Kop my lad, then you'd know what fighting was all about."

There was no comparison, the South African wars were minor events compared with the battles raging across the Channel. Joe Johnson knew this, his sons Albert and Charlie were both out there.

In the autumn term of 1916 the youthful editors of the School Magazine brought their readers up to date with 'Old Boy Notes'.

Westrop brothers had both been awarded the Military Cross... Captain Lloyd was home on leave and 'looking as hard as nails'... Lieutenant Barlow was in Mesopotamia after an exciting voyage up the Tigris...and... "We regret to report that Sgt. A. J. Johnson and Signaller A. Stokes are still among the missing. We sympathise most deeply with their parents who are suffering such terrible and protracted anxiety."

They were missing for months. Neighbours no longer enquired

about the boys, if there had been any good news it would have spread through the town in a day. If Albert Johnson's name had turned up on list of prisoners there would have been free drinks at the Hen and Chickens. Joe Johnson's regular customers had asked for news of his son in July, but after three months there was little to say.

Albert was an after-thought, born ten years after his brother and sisters, spoilt no doubt by Hilda and Emily. He did well at school and was working as an articled clerk for an auctioneer in Rugby at the outbreak of war. Already in uniform, he was a Territorial, he went through the formality of 'attestation' in January 1915, and joined the 2/7th Battalion of the Royal Warwickshire Regiment. This was a reserve battalion and not expected to serve overseas, although the majority of recruits had agreed to do so if called upon. They trained at Northampton before moving to Salisbury Plain. Albert rose steadily through the ranks and was promoted to Sergeant in May 1916, just before the battalion sailed from Southampton to Le Havre.

Travelling across France by train to Beisnelles, like the thousands who had gone before them, there would have been excitement and apprehension but very little fear; they were surrounded by friends, nothing could harm them. After some training at Bethane the Battalion took over trenches near Quesncy in June, it was relatively quiet.

All hell broke loose on the 1st of July when waves of infantrymen swarmed out of their trenches on the first day of the Battle of the Somme. This proved to be the worst day in British military history, sixty percent of the officers who fought on that day were killed, and 20,000 men died. Instead of reviewing the battle plan General Haig ordered more slaughter at Albert and Bazentin Ridge. Nothing was gained, more good men were lost. Then he planned a 'diversion' at Fromelles.

Warwickshire Pals moved to Laventre on the 15th of July, and for four days surveyed 'no man's land' that separated them from the enemy. They were part of the 61st (South Midland) Division preparing to fight alongside the Australians, hardy and fearless but without battlefield experience. They were all being asked to do the impossible, take the high ground of Aubers Ridge, in broad daylight under heavy fire. When the whistles blew on the 19th of July wave after wave of Aussies were cut down.

Sergeant Johnson led his Company onto the battlefield, and all went well at the outset, two lines of trenches were captured, then the Germans rallied and the Warwicks withdrew leaving casualties. Albert Johnson was missing.

The battalion regrouped behind the lines and tried to make sense of what had happened. Albert's company commander wrote to a few lines to Joe Johnson.

> *Owing to the attack failing on the flank a number of our men were cut off. We have hopes that a number of these are prisoners. This, I hope, was the case with your son, who was a splendid NCO, highly efficient in every way.*

There was still hope that he had survived the battle, but shortly afterwards Albert's death was confirmed – 'killed in action', 19th of July 1916.

The action at Fromelles had been a disaster. Two thousand Australians had died on the day, and the South Midland Division had lost heavily. Two years on, when peace was declared, an Australian war correspondent wandered over the battlefield of Fromelles.

> *We found the old 'no man's land' full of our dead, the skulls and bones and torn uniforms were lying everywhere.*

In time a cemetery was made on Aubers Ridge and the remains of the fallen brought in from the surrounding countryside. Two large plots were created – Plot I holds 120 Australians, largely unidentified – Plot II an equal number of men of the South Midland Division. They had all finally taken the high ground of Aubers Ridge.

Albert Johnson had served in France for just fifty-nine days. His personal effects were sent to his family in St Mary's Street. When the brown paper parcel was opened out on the kitchen table Albert's sisters, his mother and father must have looked down in disbelief. Was this all that remained of their loved-one? Agnes Johnson died within a year – of a broken heart? Medals, a scroll and a memorial plaque were sent to Joe Johnson after the war, this was no consolation.

Tragedy for the Findons was two-fold.

© BES Library

SERGEANT (223) RICHARD FINDON – 14TH ROYAL WARWICKSHIRE REGIMENT

Before he left for France Sergeant Richard Findon was granted leave. From Salisbury Plain he travelled to Hansworth to visit the family and to marry his childhood sweetheart. He posed outside the family home in 'full battle order'.

The Findons had moved from Bridgnorth but Richard's old headmaster well remembered the antics of Dick Findon, "The light-hearted 'sport' with an infinite capacity for getting into scrapes, irrepressible, not to be depressed by untoward circumstances."

His character had not changed in the years since he left school to make his way in the world.

The Battle of the Somme was really a series of battles. There were attacks on High Wood and battles at Guillemont, Fler-Courcelette, Morval and Transloy.

In July Dick Findon ran into trouble, he was wounded – it was only a scratch, no need to report it. Three days later the Warwicks took over from the Royal West Kents in the front line trenches and prepared for another assault on the German positions at High Wood. Patrols were

113

sent out to gather information. The Germans knew what was coming. Shells rained down on the Warwicks, there were casualties before the battle had even begun.

Throughout the day, 22nd of July, troops 'eager to get on with it' checked and rechecked their equipment. The timing was precise, at 9.50 two Companies emerged from their trenches and advanced under a protective artillery barrage. At 9.55 the troops spread out, a manoeuvre they had practised before. The Germans anticipated this and cut them down with machine-gun fire. Reinforcements moved in, they were mown down in turn. The artillery barrage should have moved on, the guns brought to bear on the enemy trenches, they failed to do so. At nightfall the Warwicks withdrew. It had been a disastrous day.

At least twenty officers were killed, wounded or missing, thirty-six 'other ranks' were dead, 195 were missing and over two hundred were wounded. The following morning patrols went out to recover the dead and wounded. Sergeant Richard Findon's body was never found.

A letter arrived at 30 Comer Road, Moseley. Dick Findon's young widow read and reread Captain Richmond's words. "I trust you will accept my deepest sympathy... I shall miss him tremendously... He died gallantly, leading his platoon in an attack... He had been wounded three days previously." It was small comfort.

At least his brother Frank was still safe.

It was months before the fate of many was known, families must have feared the worst but still clung, on hoping that their boy was in German hands. This was the hope of Elizabeth Stokes of Hopstone House.

Signaller (1689) Alfred William Stokes – 14th Royal Warwickshire Regiment

Putting on a uniform seemed to change the character of some young men. Shop assistants and errand boys were turned into fearless warriors by the photographer. This was not the case with Alfie Stokes he still looked like a choir boy and sensitive young schoolmaster. Looks could be deceiving, his mother, Elizabeth Stokes, was made of stern stuff. This young widow brought up four children and ran a farm, Hopstone House, near Claverley.

She was blessed with bright and capable children. Her eldest boy,

© BES Library

Cecil, worked alongside her on the farm, George was a schoolmaster and Alfred was planning to follow his example. He was admitted to Bridgnorth Grammar School in September 1907, a 'county scholar'. Alfred did well, after training he began his teaching career in Handsworth.

He joined the Warwicks with the Findon brothers and John Dain. They had shared memories, of childish behaviour at school, and more childish behaviour on Salisbury Plain during infantry training.

Signaller Stokes' first view of the battlefront was from the trenches below Vimy Ridge. The Germans held the high ground. A hundred thousand French troops were either killed or wounded attempting to dislodge them. It was not until 1917 that the Canadians finally overwhelmed the German defenders.

The Royal Warwicks and the Royal West Kents went into battle side by side and suffered badly on the 23rd of July. Private Alfie Stokes was still unharmed. His battalion hung on for a week but were then driven back, the battalion was reduced to about three hundred men. They were taken out of the line to recover, drafts of fresh troops arrived and the Battalion prepared for battle again.

At High Wood Alfred was slightly wounded, patched up and sent back into the line. The 14th Battalion faced the enemy again at Guillemont.

The battle began at 9 o'clock on the 3rd of September 1916. They watched the King's Own Scottish Borderers lead the attack on Falfemont Farm, a strong point in the German defences. It didn't look much like a farm, not like the farms Alf could remember, not like Hopstone House.

Hopstone – a Fine Prospect

© Graham Jones

He could recall every detail of the farm kitchen, the smell of his mother's cooking, and his last meal with the family, a year earlier, before he returned to camp and waited to cross the Channel for France.

The Scottish Borderers advanced, 'very gallantly and in splendid order'. They disappeared over a ridge and contact was lost. Nothing was heard of them for hours, no messages were sent back. At mid-day 'C' Company of the Warwicks attacked a gun-pit, an hour of fierce fighting followed before they overran the German position. Then they learned that the Scottish Borderers had failed in their attack. This meant that as the Warwicks advanced their right flank was exposed to heavy machine-gun fire from Falfemont Farm.

The entry in the battalion war diary did not disguise the difficulties the 14th Battalion had faced.

Under these conditions the impossible was being asked. Both Companies advanced very gallantly and in splendid spirit, but at once came under very heavy M/G fire and losing heavily they began to wither away. 'A' Coy on the right bore the full brunt and soon dwindled away to a few remnants, which however still continued to advance in the most undaunted manner. 'B' Coy on the left suffered almost as severely but struggled on, managed to occupy and hold the front trench of the position, just south of 'Wedge Wood'. In conclusion I would say that the behaviour of the Battalion was throughout magnificent, and it was by no fault of theirs that the attack failed.

At the roll call following the battle some of Alfred Stokes' comrades reported that he was last seen lying wounded, he was listed as 'missing'. The family waited for more than a month for news. When the official casualty lists were published he was still 'missing', there was

Made a Mess of the High Street

117

still hope. Perhaps he was a prisoner. In early December the youthful editors of Bridgnorth Grammar School Magazine noted that three 'old boys' were missing, Albert Johnson, Charlie Wightman and Signaller A Stokes.

> *'We sympathise most deeply with their parents who are suffering such terrible and protracted anxiety.'*

The Red Cross must have confirmed that Alfred was not a prisoner of war. Just before Christmas the family accepted that he had died in front of Falfemont Farm on the 3rd of September. Guillemont had been an attractive village, it was reduced to ruins, the surrounding woodland shredded by shells.

The loss of her son must have been hard to bear. Quietly kneeling in the parish church of All Saints, Claverley, or standing to sing familiar hymns Elizabeth Stokes could remember the days when Alfred was a chorister and Sunday-school teacher. How proud she must have been of her boy, who had shown so much promise. All Saints had not only lost a chorister, the church had lost its bell ringers. Ernie Drew, the tower master, Bill Owen and the Boucher brothers. Sarah Findon was still grieving for the loss of a son, Richard.

Frank Findon was still on the battlefield.

PRIVATE (68) FRANK LEONARD FINDON –
16TH ROYAL WARWICKSHIRE REGIMENT

Frank must have been special. He was the baby of the family, the youngest of Sarah Findon's twelve children. Feeding such a large family could not have been easy. What helped was the family business, the Findon's grocery at 38 Whitburn Street.

By the outbreak of war all the children were capable of looking after themselves. Frank was working as a clerk for an estate agent in Handsworth. He was one of the first recruits (Private 68) to join the 16th Battalion of the Royal Warwickshire Regiment. He celebrated the first Christmas of the war with the family and the next with his Warwickshire Pals in France.

The 16th Battalion and the 14th, his brother Dick's 'mob', often served side by side, relieving each other in the front-line trenches. We do not know how Frank learned of his brother's death, perhaps through the regiment, but more likely in a letter from home. No doubt he wrote back to assure the family that he was safe, not in any danger. This was not true.

In July and August 1916 thousands had been lost in a succession of battles on the Somme. On the 18th of September the 16th Royal Warwicks moved from Mericourt to Waterlot Farm and occupied trenches and shell holes nearby. It was a wet and miserable place. On the bright side, according to the war diary there was 'nothing to report' and 'casualties nil'. It was the same story when Frank and his chums moved back into Chimpanzee Trench. This may have cheered them up.

"They've made monkeys of us all, right enough."

When the order was given to move up to the Quadrilateral they knew that this was no laughing matter. They had been there before. The Germans had built an elaborate redoubt above a deep wooded ravine; a network of trenches protected by masses of barbed wire allowed the defenders to move from dugouts to machine-gun posts with a clear field of fire before them.

During the days before the planned attack on the 25th, when patrols were probing the German defences, men went 'missing', were wounded and died. The Warwicks were given a hopeless task. On the day they put up a brave fight but were forced to withdraw. Private Frank Findon and those who survived trudged back to Oxford Copse, a place of relative safety. German and British gunners carried on the fight, shelling each other's positions.

Brief notes were entered in the war diary for the 26th of September – 'weather fine' – 13 wounded – 6 killed, they were not named. Sarah Findon had lost another dear son, she would never know where he lay.

The Thiepval Memorial to the Missing of the Somme was unveiled in 1932. It bears the names of seventy-two thousand men who have no known grave.

The Royal Warwicks are easily found. The names of one thousand eight hundred men of the Royal Warwickshire regiment are carved on panels immediately to the right, beside the steps leading to the central arch. Frank Findon is among them.

© CWG Commission

One Old Boy who shared the same dangers as the Findon brothers, Bert Johnson, Alfie Stokes, Charlie Wightman and John Dain was Bill Pratt.

Captain William Richard Pratt – Royal Warwickshire Regiment

Bill Pratt was among the first to join the 'Birmingham Pals'. He was near the head of the queue when they lined up to 'sign on' – they gave him a regimental number – 44. He was over thirty, the managing clerk of an electroplating company. Mature and responsible he was promoted to Sergeant almost immediately.

The men of the Service Battalions, who agreed to serve for the duration of the war, were keen but untrained. Within a year they were ready for battle. Sergeant (44) William Pratt was selected for further promotion. He landed at Boulogne on the 21st of November 1915, the same day as the Findon brothers. The following day his commission as a Second Lieutenant was confirmed.

Bill survived the battles in which other 'Old Bridgnorthians' were

lost. He fought in Italy in 1917, and returned to France the following year. Promoted to Captain by the end of the war, Bill Pratt was a very lucky man.

Chapter 8

In the Air and in the Bag

The Somme was a dangerous place for everyone, the PBI (Poor Bloody Infantry) bore the brunt of it. Gunners shelling German positions were in turn targeted by the enemy artillery. Dodging the shells above, airmen flew back and forth, bombing, spotting for the artillery, gathering intelligence and scrapping with their rivals in the air. Perhaps the luckiest were those cut off at the front and taken prisoner, greeted by their captors with a few welcoming words.

"Für Sie Tommy ist der Krieg vorbei"…"For you Tommy the War is over".

On the 2nd of June 1916 Clem Deighton, serving with the Canadian Mounted Rifles, was taken prisoner, and in May the following year Ernie Owen serving with the 2nd Battalion, the Honourable Artillery Company was also in the bag. Meanwhile Clem's cousin, Milner Deighton, had a bird's eye view of events as a forward observation officer with 7 Squadron. He was one of a handful of Old Boys who tried their hand at aerial combat.

SQUADRON LEADER PHILLIP DAVIES – ARGYLL AND SUTHERLAND HIGHLANDERS – ROYAL FLYING CORPS AND RAF

Alexander Davies, the headmaster of Norton School, was provided with a house close by. Compared with most of the homes in Village Road it was a substantial modern dwelling, with three bedrooms. They were rather small and as the Davies's five children grew the bedrooms felt even smaller. The youngest boy, Phillip, was born in 1897 at School House.

Clearly his father knew the value of a good education and sent his son to the Grammar School in Bridgnorth. The boy did well and took the Oxford examination in 1914, but instead of becoming a student

© Graham Jones

at university he became a soldier. He claimed to have been born in Edinburgh and joined the Argyll and Sutherland Highlanders.

On the 2nd of May 1915 Phillip arrived in France. The Argylls always seemed to be in the thick of it, and Private (2489) Davies appeared to relish the action.

> *We moved to a different part of the line and our position on taking it was fine and quiet, both sides agreeing to as little fuss as possible.*
>
> *Only a rifle shot or two fired every hour, a wee few more at night of course, and at dawn and dusk.*

On the third morning, however, in the small hours, they got a tremendous shock, or rather, three shocks, 60 yards of their trench was demolished, thrown into the air, turned right over.

...even now a fortnight after the event, it looks like the top of a volcanic crater and is of course irreparable.

As a result they shelled us every day after that, only stopping at night time. At about 3 o'clock in the morning of the last day in the trenches they bombarded us for half-an-hour, giving us in that time between six and seven hundred explosive shells with a few shrapnel thrown in. The shrapnel is not so bad when there is good shelter for everyone, as we had there, but the high explosives are not so nice. We can hear them coming, but can never see them, and one landing on the parapet is sufficient to blow it right in, although it may be five or six feet in thickness. Results for the Germans' expensive shells: nine wounded – hardly worth it was it?

Being a signaller now – my latest role – I was attached to a company telephone office in the firing line and we had a rather busy time mending broken wires, etc., and getting reports back to headquarters.

For more action Phillip transferred to the Royal Flying Corps. He flew missions over the front line and against all the odds survived the war. Returning home Phillip renewed his friendship with the Harrison boys. They all shared an interest in cricket but more importantly they introduced Phillip to their cousin, Isabella. They married in 1927.

Phillip was still flying in the years leading up to the outbreak of the Second World War. He was a civilian instructor and an officer with the RAF volunteer reserve. A man who had experienced war in the air at first hand was someone the next generation of airmen could look up to. Squadron Leader Davies still found time to pursue his passion for cricket.

Although protected by pads and gloves batsmen still expected to receive a few 'knocks'. One fateful September afternoon Phillip was hit on the leg, there was a nasty bruise. Phillip died, a blood clot to the brain the most likely cause. He was buried in Bridgnorth Cemetery in 1941, leaving a young widow and his dear daughter Jane. This was a man who had made light of shells and shrapnel in the trenches and flown flimsy aircraft over battlefields, only to die playing the game he loved most.

© Graham Jones

Roy Kelly was another young man who experienced war on the ground before he took to the air.

2ND LT. ROY HAMILTON KELLY – PRINCESS PATRICIA'S CANADIAN LIGHT INFANTRY AND THE ROYAL AIR FORCE

The Kelly family, William and Annie and children Mildred and Roy, came from Somerset and moved into a modest home on Albion Terrace. Roy completed his education at the Grammar School and was apprenticed to a High Street chemist. For companionship and a bit of excitement he joined the Shropshire Yeomanry, he was a 'weekend' soldier.

Eric Burton and Tom Whitefoot both left secure family businesses in the High Street and went adventuring, over the sea to Canada, Roy Kelly went too. A chemist no more, he found work as a bank clerk with the Imperial Bank of Canada in Saskatoon, he also found a wife. Arrangements were made for the wedding in 1914.

A month after war was declared Mabel May Gower and Roy Hamilton Kelly were married. Meanwhile young men were flocking to the recruiting centres eager to join in the fight in Europe. Newly-wed Roy

Hamilton held back for a year, then he agreed to serve 'for the duration of the war' with a University Company.

In November 1915 The Bridgnorth Journal reported that ten 'varsity students left Saskatoon and would remain in Montreal for a short period prior to their departure for the war zone'. Roy Kelly sailed for France.

In 1916 he transferred to Princes Patricia's Canadian Light Infantry. Princess Pat's already had a reputation as determined fighters. At the Battle of Frezenberg they defended a ridge at great cost, they lost 500 men in three days. Eric Burton, his old school friend, had been one of them, killed in action in 1915. Roy Kelly had written to his mother to offer words of comfort at the loss of her son.

Mrs Burton kept in touch with another boy from the town, Tom Whitefoot. He was also serving with the Canadians and she asked him to try to contact Roy. A meeting was arranged as the Canadian Division prepared for battle. "Tom is looking awfully fit, and is soon coming over to Bridgnorth on leave. Am trying to get in touch with him again".

Private Roy Kelley's first experience of trench warfare came in July 1916. When he came out of the line he wrote home to his parents.

June 7th, 1916, I was very glad to get a letter from you and M (his wife), when we came out. It helped me a great deal. Many thanks also for sending the papers; they came just before we went in, so I took them with me, and read them the first day we were in.

I wish I could give you an idea of the whole business, but that is impossible. It is safe to say that our company was practically blown to bits, and almost surrounded, it retired to the first supports (support trenches) and could not be moved.

Fritz was getting in by a communication trench, and they wanted help to block it up with sandbags so three of us did that. We fixed bayonets, and beat them with our fire. I hope I got a few. The bombardment was awful – just a rain of high explosives, with some shrapnel. We were buried, and soaked, and buffeted. It was only by God's mercy that I was spared, but I did my best and meant to go like a soldier.

Later on, in our new line, I found Charles Garvice's 'A Girl of Spirit' in a ruined dugout and read that to steady my nerves. It helped a good bit.

Garvice was a popular author of the time, he could churn out a novel a month, to a formula. The stories often involved a virtuous woman overcoming obstacles and achieving a happy ending. Roy was a troubled man and anything to take his mind off the horrors of his surroundings would have helped. He had survived the opening days of a battle that would last for over four months.

What became known as the Battle of the Somme was in reality a series of battles, fought in appalling conditions between July and November 1916. By September Roy's battalion had been strengthened with fresh drafts of Canadian lads.

On the opening day of the Battle of Fler-Courcelette, 15th of September, the Canadian Division overwhelmed the Germans and, with the help of tanks, captured Courcelette. There was no breakthrough however, and the battle ground to a halt after a week. By then Private Roy Hamilton had already left the battlefield. Wounded on the first day, he was on his way to England.

With wounds to his right leg and thigh he was 'progressing favourably' in the Military Hospital near Nottingham. He wrote home to assure the family that he *never enjoyed himself so much in all his life as he did while the fun was on*. Roy recovered from his wounds and remained with Princess Pat's until May 1918, when he transferred to the newly formed Royal Air Force as an officer cadet. In June he was declared 'fit as a pilot' but there was an unusual comment entered in his record, 'smokes too much'. At the time everyone smoked but chain-smoking may have been a symptom of a more serious problem, a nervous disorder perhaps.

He completed officer training and flying training as the war came to an end and was commissioned in the Royal Air Force. The repatriation of servicemen took some time and it was September 1919 before 2nd Lieutenant Kelly returned to Canada as a civilian. Roy and Mabel moved into the Park View Apartments in Saskatoon and planned for the future. Roy had changed his trade again, he wasn't a chemist or a bank clerk, nor a soldier or an airman. Now he claimed to be a farmer.

In that part of the world one thing was certain, the temperature would fall as winter tightened her grip, by January it might be down to minus twenty, and there was little that could be done by way of farming. Christmas came and there was some 'good cheer' for a day or two, the New Year arrived, the future was uncertain.

On the 4th of January Roy Kelly died, from a 'war related injury/ condition'. He took his own life. He was buried in Lawnwood Cemetery in Saskatoon, mourned by his young wife who had prayed that he would survive the war, only to lose him in peacetime.

Now we understand more of the mental scars of conflict, it is called post-traumatic stress disorder. In his letters home he had made light of life in the trenches – "never enjoyed myself so much in my life as when the fun was on". In another letter to his parents he described an incident that revealed his inner thoughts.

The worst trip I had was one night. We wanted water, so I beat it down the trenches to get it. The parapets and parados were down in places, so had to take a running chance and crawl along, in other places – over dead bodies and bits of bodies. Luckily it was getting dusk, and their faces were dirty, do I couldn't recognise any pals. High explosives are hellish. During it all I was so glad there was a Hereafter, where I might have M. and you all again.

Fading images, the faces of loved ones, his wife, mother, father, sister, lost comrades, and peaceful scenes of home, childhood, and schooldays may have passed before him as he drifted into oblivion.

There was a happier outcome for the Owens.

Private Ernest Ronald Owen – Honourable Artillery Company and Royal Sussex Regiment & Private Arthur Thomas Owen – Civil Service Rifles

The Owens lived modestly in Mill Street. Ellen Owen had no domestic servant to 'help in the house'. Arthur worked as a clerk for a law firm in the town. They had three sons and wanted the best for all of them, sacrifices had to be made. Annual fees for the Grammar School amounted to 24 guineas, this was more than six months' pay for a farm labourer at the time, as a clerk Arthur must have been paid more. The investment paid off.

Ernest and Arthur, the two oldest boys, made their way to London, they had family in the capital, Ellen Owen was born in Bermondsey. In 1915 Arthur was working in the head office of Macdonald, Gibbs and Company. They were specialists in heavy engineering and so vital to the war effort that Lord Kitchener, Secretary of State for War, commented:

I should like all engaged by your company to know that it is fully recognised that they, in carrying out the supply of munitions of war, are doing their duty for their King and Country equally with those who have joined the Army for Active Service in the field.

Nevertheless, young men, not in uniform, did feel uncomfortable walking the streets of London. Arthur joined the Civil Service Rifles, a territorial reserve regiment. Battalions were formed from this regiment that did fight in France, but there is no record of Arthur Owen in their ranks.

At the same time his brother, Ernest, was working as a clerk with Cox's Bank in Charing Cross. He joined the Honourable Artillery Company in January 1917, and after only two month's training he was sent to France and straight to the battlefront. He arrived on the 3rd of April.

The Germans had made a tactical withdrawal to establish a more secure and defendable front line, the Hindenburg Line. The Honourable Artillery Company were positioned to back up the Australians preparing to attack the fortifications at Bullecourt. The first assault on the 10th of April was aborted and a fresh attempt the following day failed.

Bullecourt was a place name a generation of Australians would always remember. Here some of their finest men suffered the worst losses on the Western Front. Here they lost faith in the British High Command, and General Hubert Gough in particular.

A second attack was planned for the 3rd of May – the result could have been predicted. Once again the Australians were to take the lead. They made an early start, 3.45 am. The full horror was revealed as dawn broke and the advancing troops moved forward treading over the bodies of their fallen countrymen that had lain on the battlefield for over a fortnight. This day would later be described as 'memorably bloody and ill-rewarded'.

After twelve hours of bitter fighting the 'Aussies' were exhausted. As darkness fell fresh troops from the 22nd Brigade stepped in – the 1st Royal Welsh Fusiliers and the Honourable Artillery Company. There was confusion, there were more casualties, Privates Charrington, Creswell and Springate were dead, Private (9934) Owen was missing.

There was no more fighting for Ernie Owen, after only a month on the battlefield he was made a Prisoner of War. The captured troops, largely Australians, were marched away to Lille and held in a huge dugout they called Fort MacDonald or the Black Hole. Their captors called them 'Vergeltungsgefangene', Prisoners of Respite. There was no 'respite', they were treated harshly and this was deliberate. The Germans had made a request to the Allies that their prisoners should not be held in camps closer than thirty kilometres from the front line – the request was ignored.

Prisoners from Fort MacDonald were forced to work repairing the German defences under shell fire from their own side. They survived on a diet of bread made with a mixture of flour and sawdust, and turnip soup. Many did not survive. Prisoners of Respite were encouraged to write to family or anyone of influence describing the conditions, so that the conditions that German prisoners were held under might be improved.

For all concerned, captors and captives, civilians and soldiers, conditions worsened as the war wore on. Ernie Owen survived nearly eighteen months of captivity. When lads like him came home anxious mothers tried to 'feed them up'. This was a mistake, they 'couldn't stomach' a roast Sunday dinner, it took months for them to adapt to a normal diet.

Ernie Owen did adapt, he was buried in the town cemetery in 1972.

The Great War produced, in every community, a local legend, and everyone certainly knew of the exploits of Milner Deighton.

Captain Denis Milner Deighton AFC – London Regiment, Army Service Corp, and RAF

Without vaccines to treat the disease, polio or infantile paralysis could have life-changing consequences. Headache, sore throat, stiff neck could be symptoms of the common cold, if there was loss of sensation in arms or legs this meant something more serious. Milner Deighton was not at the family home in St Mary's Street in 1911. At the time of the national census, he was at the Queen Victoria Nursing Institute on Bath Road in Wolverhampton suffering from poliomyelitis. The treatment was expensive, for just four patients there were six nurses and four domestic servants working under the direction of a matron. Milner Deighton pulled through and regained his youthful vigour.

The Deightons had various business interest in the town and when Milner left school he could have chosen an office job. Perhaps to 'build him up' he was taken on by Bill Bishop as a farm pupil at Posenhall. The war interrupted his outdoor education but he would be getting plenty of fresh air over the next four years.

Already in uniform, a territorial with the Shropshire Yeomanry, he enlisted on the 29th of September 1914. His commission as a 2nd Lieutenant in the London Scottish was confirmed on the 18th May 1915. He

With My Compliments

was dispatched to France in November and joined the 43rd Divisional Train of the Army Service Corps.

Divisional Trains were the supply lines, carrying everything from bandages and blankets to bully beef and machine-gun bullets to the battlefront. Each company was made up of about four hundred men and almost as many horses, with carts and wagons and at least two dozen bicycles. Exposed, easily spotted from the air, and targeted by enemy artillery, this was dangerous work. Supplies had to get through whatever the weather. The winter months on the Western Front were particularly miserable and lowered the morale of some, not Milner Deighton. He had a way out of the slush and mud. He joined 7 Squadron in March 1916 and took to the skies as a Flying Officer Observer.

The squadron was equipped with Bristol BE2s, two-seater biplanes, light bombers used on reconnaissance missions over enemy lines. The pilot took the front seat and the observer the rear, he was the one who did the bombing. Milner had plenty of practice over the valley of the Somme as the great battle raged below.

In November the Battle of the Somme ground to a halt. Lieutenant Deighton had been 'chauffeured' round the battlefront, for four months, by his pilot and somehow they managed to avoid trouble, but Milner wanted to take control.

He had natural ability and passed the pilots' course with flying colours.

He has shown himself to possess ability very much above the average. His landings, flying approaches have always been extremely good.

He served as an assistant instructor with the 1st Reserve Squadron until August 1917 when he was transferred to the School of Special Flying.

To keep up to date with latest developments Milner attended a course at the No 2 School of Aerial Gunnery at Turnberry on the Ayrshire coast. This was something he must have enjoyed, swooping over the golf course in a Sopwith Camel and firing at ground targets, silhouettes of enemy aircraft made from sheet metal. There was a very satisfying clatter when the target was hit with machine-gun fire.

The Sopwith Camel F1 shot down more enemy aircraft than any other Allied plane. Unfortunately it had a reputation for vicious stalls and spins and claimed the lives of many inexperienced pilots. Part of the training included mock battles over the golf course, the efforts of the young pilots were recorded on the gun cameras. The Vicker's machine guns were only firing blanks but it was still exhilarating stuff. In the evening they could relax in the luxury Turnbery Hotel and the trainees could listen to the 'old sweats' tales of aerial combat over Flanders fields.

At the Mayfair Hotel in London the same stories could be told again. Off duty, this was the place to stay because the management offered free board and lodgings to young pilots. A certain amount of glamour surrounded them, they appeared to face danger with casual 'devil may care' attitude. However Milner did have some anxiety, he did not want to be 'shot up the bottom'. The problem was solved by his flight mechanic who cut a plate of steel to fit under a cushion in his seat.

Flying was dangerous, with an enemy taking pot-shots from below. That was to be expected but no one expected a fellow airman to crash

I Am Speechless

With permission from David Deighton

133

into your aircraft on the ground, but this is exactly what happened to Lieutenant Deighton. A fellow aviator, taking off in an Avro flew into the back of Milner's Sopwith Camel.

The instructors apparently had special privileges, in August 1917 Milner flew home to take his father on a tour of Severn Valley. Few people had ever seen the dome of St Mary's church from above. As the pair glided over the Northgate they looked down on the upturned faces of the townsfolk in the High Street before they disappeared, flying over fields to bank and turn at Astley Abbotts. Following the river and railway line back towards the town Milner 'pulled on the stick' as the track disappeared into the tunnel under the town, it reappeared just short of the station. A porter with hands on hips looked up.

Then Milner Deighton did something that made him a legend in the town. He swept over the river, turned and flew back low over the footbridge that passengers used to cross from the station to New Road. He considered, briefly, his next manoeuvre.

"Yes it is possible".

Little Room for Manoeuvre

Lieutenant Deighton repeated the whole operation, only this time he flew under the footbridge.

Milner was posted to the Central Flying School before the end of the war. In some ways instructing nervous young pilots was almost as dangerous as flying over German guns in the valley of the Somme. He had done both and for this he was rewarded. His courage was recognised with the award of the Air Force Cross.

A fine collection

When the war was over, Milner spent almost a year ferrying every type of aircraft to bases all over England. He was released from duty in July 1919 and put on the reserve list of RAF officers.

There was a special bond between men who had served together through dangerous times, friendship that often lasted a lifetime. 'Ossie' Manning and 'Curly' Deighton never lost touch. At least once a year they would remember the day they stood side by side in All Soul's Church Marylebone, on the occasion of the wedding of Winfred Hope Wyndham to Denis Milner Deighton. Ossie Manning was the best man.

The Wyndhams lived in Cavendish Square, within a stone's throw of the Mayfair Hotel where young airmen came to relax and socialise. Young wives often try to reform their husbands, but if Winifred did try she failed.

The thrill of flying was something Milner could not give up. To celebrate the end of the war he had put on a display, in January 1919, that certainly impressed a reporter for Autocar magazine,

> *I have never beheld so dazzling a display as that of Captain Deighton, for he passed from one feat to another with such rapidity that the eye could scarcely follow him. The machine, a Sopwith Camel, similarly darted about at high speed, at all angles, just like a dragonfly, and even improved on natural flight by the careering along upside down.*

Any spare time he had was spent with a 'flying circus' raising money for the RAF Benevolent Fund. No one was better qualified. He became a close friend of Bertram Mills. His circus, with clowns, trapeze artists and a lion-tamer was based at Olympia, Milner's children were given ring-side seats.

Curly on the left

As a pilot on reserve Milner had to demonstrate his ability at the De Havilland Civilian Flying School in 1924, and annually for the next two years.

Has shown himself to possess ability well above the average. His landings, flying approaches have always been extremely good.

If this was ever in doubt the examiners could have watched a film of one of his displays over the seafront at Margate.

When Milner Deighton died in 1966, three hundred people attended his funeral at St Leonard's Church. A lasting memorial to him is fixed to the wall of the council chamber in the old Town Hall. His son, David Deighton donated the wooden propeller from the aircraft that he flew under the footbridge in 1917 – a feat that will never be repeated.

Milner's uncle 'Clem' had a similarly adventurous spirit.

Clement George Deighton 1st Battalion Canadian Mounted Rifles

Clement Deighton was sixty-seven when he died in Toronto in 1947. In Prospect Cemetery, a simple tablet, 'in loving memory' marked his grave – Pte. Clement G Deighton 1st CMR CEF.

At the time everyone knew what these initial meant, he had served with the Canadian Mounted Rifles and been part of the Canadian Expeditionary Force. Many of his generation had shared the same experience, half a dozen letters could not convey the full story. His life was not without incident.

Clem's earliest memories were of the 'Hollies' in St Mary's Street, a large comfortable house with a garden and shrubbery in which to hide from his sisters Mabel and Lucy. Sarah Deighton managed the household and Thomas made a good living as a chemist.

The Deighton family firm of estate agents and auctioneers had been in business for over fifty years, and so it seemed the natural thing to do to be a part of it. At the turn of the century Clement George Deighton was indeed practising as an auctioneer with the prospect of a secure and comfortable life ahead. Clem had other ideas, he took the train to Liverpool and took ship, the *Teutonic*, to New York on his way to Winnipeg and a different life in Canada.

He met an Irish girl in Winnipeg, and in 1907 he married Irene McKinney.

Manitoba was a prairie province booming with immigrants and outside investors. The couple moved south to Boisevain, close to the border with North Dakota. This was where the best land was to be found. The Deightons began farming.

When war was declared in Europe, the Canadians were quick to respond, 18,000 Manitobans enlisted in the first year. Many of them were British born adventurers, exactly the sort of men the army was looking for. In April 1915 Clem attested, signed the document that made him a soldier. When he volunteered for service he was nearly 37 years old, almost too old to serve. He gave his occupation as 'farmer'. He was over six feet tall, a fit, sturdy individual, he was readily accepted. His wife did not enjoy the same good health.

All in the same boat

Before the 1st Battalion sailed for Britain 'A' Squadron of the Canadian Mounted Rifles posed for a photograph outside the Dominion Government Building in Yorkton, Saskatchewan. Somewhere in the ranks stood Private Deighton. Standing in the back row was Private John

Gunn who would be wounded and taken prisoner at Hooge on 2nd of June 1916. Unfortunately he would not be the only one.

The Canadian cavalry were raring to go, keen to see action, and for many there was the excitement of returning to 'the old country' and an opportunity to see family and friends. They sailed from Toronto in June and, after ten days at sea, landed in England.

They were welcomed by the folks of Shorncliffe. The sight of men in uniform was nothing new, there had been a garrison there for over a century. The Canadian cavalry set up their headquarters and began training for war. Riding lessons were not needed, in their spare time men of the Mounted Rifles entertained local children with displays of expert horsemanship. The infantry meanwhile dug trenches and marched for miles. The camp was overflowing, the lucky ones were moved from their draughty tents to be billeted with local families.

Clem had been in Kent for just over a fortnight when he received devastating news, his wife Irene had died on the 5th of July 1915. She was only twenty-eight. There was little time to grieve, the battalion was mobilised for war. He did not care, he had lost his dear wife there was little left to lose.

The Mounted Rifles rode in style to the docks at Folkestone, their own brass band on the quayside and pipers to pipe them on board. They landed in France on the 22nd of September.

It soon became clear that the battlefields of Flanders were not the same as the Canadian prairies or even the rolling downs of Kent. Even the finest war horses could not charge through barbed wire or over bomb craters filled with mud. The Canadian Mounted Rifles were dismounted and retrained as infantry.

Private Clement Deighton and his companions got their first taste of real battle in the spring of 1916. Rain and constant shelling had turned the battlefield of St Eloi into a quagmire, mines detonated by the British had created huge craters. Despite the conditions the Third British Division fought their way across this filthy landscape, pushed back the Germans and set up a new line of defence. The Canadian Division arrived the following day to take over their positions but there was no time to 'dig in'. The Germans counter-attacked, the Canadians were pinned down by a storm of shells. For a week they strove to hold the line but so many men were lost that in the end they had to accept defeat. The only reliable intelligence came from aerial photographs which showed clearly that this was an impossible position, the generals issued the order to withdraw.

William Walker who had transferred from the Mounted Rifles to the Flying Corps, was one who flew over this wasteland. Buffeted by wind and rain he looked down, 'I see where my regiment CMRs have almost been wiped out. I always knew they would fight like tigers'.

Over a thousand men had been lost, what these young men had been through was unimaginable. A bank clerk from Calgary described the scene,

When day broke, the sights that met our gaze were so horrible and ghastly that they beggar description. Heads, arms and legs were protruding from the mud and dear God knows how many bodies the earth had swallowed.

The battle was lost but nevertheless the Canadians had shown courage and doggedness, and won the respect of all, including the enemy.

Two months later in June 1916 the Third Canadian Division was preparing for battle once again. The Battle of Mount Sorrel threatened to be a repetition of the action at St Eloi. On the morning of the 2nd of June the trenches held by Mounted Rifles were almost completely destroyed by shellfire, so when the German infantry advanced in the afternoon they met with little opposition, a few knots of dazed survivors surrendered or died fighting. The Germans were unable to press their advantage to the full, Canadian reinforcements arrived to hold up the advance and planned a counter attack. It failed, the village of Hooge was lost.

Among the casualties were General Mercer, killed by a burst of shrapnel, General Williams, wounded and captured, and Privates Gunn and Deighton were missing, but not for long.

Uberleuntnant Hebestreil had beautiful handwriting. He carefully wrote out a list of twenty-one men, neatly in alphabetical order, over half of them were men of the Canadian Mounted Rifles. Private Clement Deighton was the eighth on the list. He had arrived at Gefangenen – Lager Stendal and this was where he would stay until the end of the war.

Conditions for Prisoners of War at Stendal were not as awful as one might imagine. They were sheltered from the elements, fed daily with black bread and thin soup, and they received letters and parcels from home, and were far removed from gunfire and flying shrapnel.

The Red Cross provided prisoners with a new uniform. Photographs were taken of smart and cheerful lads and printed as postcards to send home. This was propaganda to show the world how well the men were treated. French prisoners formed an orchestra and put on regular concerts. At Christmas there was a pantomime. Throughout the year 'international' sporting events were arranged.

We have a Captive Audience

It wasn't all play, prisoners were expected to work. The lucky ones were billeted with farming families, the unlucky ones sent to slave in salt mines.

As the war ground to an end food became scarce, and the prisoners relied more and more on the Red Cross and parcels from home. Many food parcels went astray, the Germans were starving too. After the Armistice came into effect in November 1918 Canadian officers arrived to arrange transport back to the regiments and then home. Lee and Lane, Sanders and Smith, captured at Ypres with Clem Deighton, must all have made plans for the future during the winter months of 1919. They had something to go back to. In March they sailed across the Atlantic, were demobilised and dispersed.

Clem returned to the farmstead at Boisevain, Irene was buried nearby. They had been together for only six years.

He moved on, near to Winnipeg, and made a fresh start. Two years later he married Sarah Herbinson sixteen years his senior. They were together for twenty years.

He may have had regrets, life might have been easier in a quiet market town in Shropshire. He never returned. He saw men leave Canada again to fight in Europe in 1939 and wished them luck. With the rest of the nation he rejoiced when victory was achieved and those, like him, who survived, could begin again.

Chapter 9

Bellringers and Butchers

George and Ann Walker had four sons, two went to war. Ben and Fanny Boucher had four sons, they all volunteered to serve. The Bouchers and the Walkers both lost a son – on the same day.

The Walkers were High Street butchers, Ben Boucher was a wheelwright on Rudge Heath, Claverley. Both families earned a good living and gave their boys a good education. In 1913 Denis Boucher was awarded a School Certificate by the University of Oxford. He had satisfied the examiners in seven subjects including German – a knowledge of French might have been more useful.

Denis, second from the left

Claverley Church lost nearly all its hand-bell ringers in September 1914. Ernie Drew, Bill Owen and the Boucher brothers, Cyril and Denis, all lined up at the Drill Hall in Bridgnorth to join the county regiment. Denis (Private 13134) and Cyril (Private 13135), and (Private 13136), Ernie Drew, were very close, and time spent together on the battlefield would make the bond even stronger.

Private Denis Boucher & Private Cyril Boucher – Kings Shropshire Light Infantry

Ernest, Ben Boucher's eldest son had taken up his father's trade as wheel-wright. Cyril was a gardener, and Denis a pupil teacher, neither of them was qualified to 'carry arms', but nor were scores of other lads who arrived at the Depot in Shrewsbury, in September 1914.

There to greet them were four officers and thirty professional soldiers from the battalion in Tipperary who would turn them into fighting men over the winter months. As Companies were formed they were dispatched to Blackdown Camp near Aldershot. Uniform and rifles were issued, the rifles were almost immediately withdrawn and sent to France. Losses of men and equipment in the Retreat from Mons had to be made good. To practise arms drill, rifles were fashioned from planks of wood, no matter,

Cold beer anyone?

the recruits were still full of enthusiasm and optimism. The loss of their rifles was disappointing, but disappointment was something they had to get used to.

Training began in earnest, round the clock, every day of the week, except for a fortnight in the summer during a heatwave. Even farm boys and gardeners, like Cyril Boucher, used to working in all weathers, were glad to move into the shade.

Training continued, through the autumn and into the New Year. On the 23rd of January the 5th Battalion paraded, with thousands of other troops, in front of Lord Kitchener, the Secretary of State for War. It was bitterly cold, greatcoats were not allowed. Standing, shivering, snow gently falling, it was hard to believe that training had been held up by burning sunshine.

In March, King George and Queen Mary attended a cross-country competition and awarded first prize to Private Stewart, the Shropshires cheered. In May there was an outbreak of measles, the Battalion was moved into quarantine, out of barracks and put under canvas on Watts Common. It snowed. This was excellent training for life in the trenches.

On the 20th of May, men of the 5th Battalion began the journey to France – train to Folkestone, ferry to Boulogne. Denis and Cyril Boucher were left behind. Their comrades first came under fire at Zillebeke near Hill 60. Sergeant Alfie Diss was the first man to die, a professional soldier, he had survived the South African War to die after a week on a battlefield in France. Over the next two months more men died and the wounded were sent home.

Fresh troops were called for, now it was the Boucher boys' turn, they joined the fight on the 26th of July. These were troubling times for Ben and Fanny Boucher on Rudge Heath. Not only were Denis and Cyril on the battlefield, their eldest son, Alec, also sailed for France the same month.

LIEUTENANT ALEC EDWARD BOUCHER MC –
11TH ROYAL WARWICKSHIRE REGIMENT

When Alec completed his studies at the Grammar School, he became at pupil teacher at Worfield School under the watchful eye of Mr Lloyd, the headmaster. To become a fully qualified teacher he went on to Saltley Training College and then was appointed as an assistant master at a Council School in Halesowen. Ann Chesterfield, a widow, took in lodgers at 16 Laurel Lane; all were schoolteachers and that included Alec and his sister Lilian.

Alec moved to Cambridge to teach at Barnwell Boys' School and to study at the university. Then came the War. Keen to join, he was given the rank of Lance Corporal in the 9th (Service Battalion) Gloucestershire Regiment. To begin their training they were billeted at Codford St Mary in the Wiltshire countryside. Alec was very quickly singled out for promotion and was commissioned as a Second Lieutenant in the Royal Warwickshire Regiment in February 1915.

This is a Serious Business

© BES Library

The training on Salisbury Plain over, he landed in France on the 30th of July 1915, Flanders Field was a far more dangerous place. Attack and counter attack over the coming months made little difference to the position of the either side. Winter was on its way, 11th Battalion Royal Warwickshire Regiment mounted an attack, perhaps the last before the weather turned against them. It was the last of the year for Alec Boucher,

146

...recovered a wounded comrade from no man's land and returned to the trenches, receiving wounds himself.

A telegram, dated 18th of December arrived at Rudge Heath to inform the family that Alec had been admitted to No 2 Red Cross Hospital at Rouen and that more information would follow. It was too late, the family already knew that he had been carried from the battlefield to 19 Casualty Clearing Station.

Sister-in-charge (E D Small) had written to Alec's mother.

Dear Mrs Boucher
I am sending a few lines for your son A E Boucher who came into station wounded 2 days ago. He has several wounds in chest and abdomen. The chest wound is superficial but the abdominal wounds are more serious. Yesterday Colonel Alex Thomson came in consultation with the other medical men and it was decided that an operation was necessary. Your son stood the operation well and has had a wonderfully good night. I told him I would write to you – he sends his love and whenever he is able he will write himself. The doctors are doing everything for him that can be done but for 2 or 3 days one cannot tell how things will go with him. I shall write you a daily note telling you how he is. We shall do everything we can possibly do for him and give him every comfort in our power. He is such a good patient – with much sympathy in your anxiety, I remain
Yours sincerely E D Small

By Christmas Alec was 'on the mend'. In the New Year he was promoted, and for his bravery he was rewarded with a Military Cross. After convalescence and home leave he was back on the battlefield. At a time when wounding and death were daily events in every community, stories of survival were considered good news.

Ernie Drew, one the Claverley bell ringers, was wounded. On hand to help him to the dressing station was his boyhood friend Cyril Boucher. Within days Cyril was wounded too, a gunshot wound to the head, they both survived and returned to the front to carry on the fight. Ernest,

I Want My Mum

Uncle Dennis in Full Bloom

the Boucher's eldest son, was unharmed by war, the tragedy in his life occurred before war began.

STAFF SERGEANT (TS 7537) ERNEST WILLIAM BOUCHER – ARMY SERVICE CORPS

Benjamin Boucher was a wheelwright by trade and Ernest was the only one of his sons to take up the trade. His knowledge of horse-drawn vehicles meant almost instant promotion to Staff Sergeant in the Army Service Corps. Food, equipment, ammunition, most of this was carried on the final stage of the journey to the front line on carts drawn by horses, donkeys and mules.

Sergeant Boucher's regimental number (TS 7537) revealed that his company had responsibility for this type of work and 'S' meant 'Special'. Ernest did not join in 1914, he had family commitments, to his father's business and his own little boy's upbringing.

Beatrice Whitney and Ernest Boucher were married in 1912 and started a family immediately – Cyril William Boucher was born. He was only a year old when his mother died In June 1914, two months before the outbreak of war.

The Boucher and Whitney families took on responsibility for the care of the little boy. Fanny Boucher had brought up four sons and two daughters, she had plenty of experience. Harriet Whitney, was single, seven years younger than her deceased sister, living nearby at Quatt and willing and able to take care of the boy. She cared for his father also, in 1917 Harriet Whitney married Ernest Boucher, her brother-in-law.

The war ended and Ernest returned to the family home, wife and son, and his trade as wheelwright. He was in many ways more fortunate than his brothers.

PRIVATE (13135) CYRIL BENJAMIN BOUCHER – 3RD AND 7TH BATTALION KSLI

Cyril Boucher crossed the Channel half a dozen times, always with mixed feelings. July 1915, surrounded by boyhood friends full of bravado, going out to 'give the Hun a bloody nose'. After six months in the trench they realised it was not that easy. Home for Christmas and back to the Depot, 'this is the life', leave it to others to carry on the fight. Spring 1916, May blossom in the hedgerows, off to France, not for long, gunshot wound to the head, 'only a scratch'. Well away from the Somme, home leave, looking forward to another Christmas at home.

It was not to be, he was back with the 7th Battalion in cold, cheerless huts at Bus on Christmas Eve. Some of the huts were without floorboards, the whole area a sea of mud and crackling ice. Stirring tunes blasted out by the Divisional Band and an extra ration of rum did bring some cheer and helped the boys celebrate Christ's birthday.

They moved on to better quarters at Franqueville in January. Fresh troops arrived to bring the battalion up to strength. Training continued in preparation for the forthcoming battle at Arras. Here the Shropshires took over from the Suffolks and carried on with the task of building fortifications and enlarging caves and the tunnelling system. They were very happy to do so, a whole battalion could be accommodated in the caves, and some of the tunnels extended for three miles to the front line trenches. No more scampering over open ground.

Nevertheless men were still killed and wounded. During the month of March, six were killed, six were wounded. Cyril Boucher's right arm was broken by a shell fragment and ended his war on the 18th of March 1917. It was not a simple break, he was back on home soil within a week, and his shattered arm was saved.

Cyril spent almost a year on 'light duties', with the 3rd Battalion at Pembroke Dock, before he was discharged in November 1917 – home for Christmas this time. The medical board at Oswestry had acknowledged that he was no longer physically fit for war…that 'the extent of capacity for earning a full livelihood in the present labour market is lessoned to 80%'. Cyril was given a cash allowance for twenty weeks and a Silver War Badge.

He did find work as a gardener, at Newton Hall, Pattingham, and to celebrate the end of the war he married Miss Margaret Crump.

The war did not end happily for all, the Bouchers were still mourning the loss of their son, Alec.

LIEUTENANT ALEC EDWARD BOUCHER MC –
11TH ROYAL WARWICKSHIRE REGIMENT

Newly promoted and rewarded with a Military Cross, Alec was back on the battlefield in 1916 and ready to play a part in the great Battle of the Somme. It began on the 1st of July, Alec Boucher, who led a Sniper Section, survived several skirmishes with the enemy. There was no breakthrough, by November both sides were weary, and ready to call halt to hostilities as winter approached.

Alec was out of the firing line, conferring with officers of the Royal Artillery when a 'whiz bang' came over and fell among them – shards of shrapnel flew everywhere.

From notes, made by a junior officer, the battalion war diary for the day was later typed up.

STATION ROAD

18th... 'D, Co. supplied ration carrying parties for the three Companies in the front line. During this operation 'C' Company suffered 40 casualties from hostile shell fire.

18th... Lieutenant A E BOUCHER MC was killed. Two sections of the 112th MGC were attached to the Batt.

19th... The Batt. remained in reserve in STATON Rd.

Locally, news of Alec's death was reported in the Bridgnorth Journal, the Grammar School Magazine and the Diocese Magazine. Letters of condolence came from fellow officers in France. Notes were received from the War Office – a list of 'personal items' to be returned to the family – location of place of burial – a record of the final payment into the account of Lt. Boucher.

None of this revealed the true nature of the man, until Fred Cope put pen to paper. Out of the blue, in July 1917, a year after the Battle of the Somme began, a letter arrived at Rudge Heath from the Military Hospital, Southall. Fred Cope was still being treated for the wound he received on the day Alec Boucher died. He wrote:

Dear Sir
You will probably be surprised to hear from me, but I've often thought how I would like to write and just tell you now things have settled down a little of what a fine Officer

Mr A E Boucher was... I know what good work he used to do on patrol and know that his Military Cross was a well-earned one... After he was wounded and came back to us he took great interest in a Sniper Section... I was picked for his section which was very nice and he taught me a lot...any man who I know was never afraid to go out with him. I was his orderly and when we were going to another regiment with a message two artillery officers came up and asked Mr Boucher just to let them have a look at his map and as soon as we stopped a shell came over and killed Mr Boucher, wounded the two officers, a sergeant and myself in the foot, which caused me to be in hospital until now and I cannot walk yet. I am very sorry that Mr Boucher didn't get wounded only for he was one of the best men who ever put feet on French soil.
Yours Truly
L/C F H COPE

Mrs Boucher replied to Fred's letter almost immediately and in return received more details.

Dear Madam
I was very pleased to receive your very nice letter and to know that you did not mind hearing from me... Now you say you would really like to know more about his injuries... I believe I have told you before that we were going round to the 6th Bedfords in front of us, and two Artillery Officers seeing I suppose with maps in hand Mr Boucher was our intelligence officer, asked him to let them have a look at a certain map, so he did. No soon had they said this when there was a shell came and six of us who were standing half a second before were laid down. The shell being a wizz bang which are as quick as lightening and come very low had a terrible force. My own experience was this. It blew me senseless for about a minute and I felt as if my stomach had been forced into my chest, then Iooked round first thing I saw was Mr Boucher right opposite absolutely white and on is back. This was

before I saw my foot, I was half silly for a minute or so, and
I could not find a mark on Mr boucher anywhere, this also
makes me think he was not wounded. When he stood and
when he fell he was still facing where the shell bursted so
I really think that the awful force which came was the cause.

Fred described his own wound. He foot had been operated on twice, the treatment was not complete after a year. He sounded optimistic, but in reality he would be crippled for life. His own life and that of the Boucher family would never be the same again, Fred expressed his feelings very clearly.

I'm sure he was always prepared to die and always went
about so fearless. It takes me all my time to write because
I am always thinking and always have done. What would
I give if I could have the days and his presence back again?

The bond between this man and his officer was so strong, it was more than just friendship.

November 18th was a date Fred Cope from Walsall, and the Bouchers of Rudge Heath, and the Walkers of Bridgnorth would never forget.

The Walkers and the some of the Boucher boys were taught by the same schoolmasters in the same classrooms. Ernie Boucher, Ben's eldest son, did not take up the chisel and the plane, the tools of their father's trade. Unlike Bob Walker, who with knife, saw, and meat cleaver could dismember lamb, pig or bullock.

These were anxious times for any mother with sons of conscription age. Caleb Walker was over thirty and Frank was only thirteen. Denis and William were farming and might be exempt.

Private (S/22520) William Ewart Walker – Argyll and Sutherland Highlanders

It is not clear why anyone from a Shropshire market town should choose to join a Scottish regiment but Colin McMichael looked fine a kilt. Doctor 'Llew' Rhodes was attached to the Argyll and Sutherland Highlanders, and both Phillip Davies and William Walker served with the same regiment.

Three years before the war William Walker was a pupil at Kingsley Farm, Tasley, and he returned to the land when the war was over.

Bob, his elder brother, was working as a butcher alongside their father. Bob had blood on his hands even before the outbreak of war. He did not appear to be a bloodthirsty man, quite the opposite.

PRIVATE (27830) ROBERT HARRY WALKER – 11TH BATTALION, BORDER REGIMENT

Someone Else Can Do the Killing

© BES Library

Private Bob Walker's military career was brief. When he signed on he was given a number (4566) and assigned to the Herefordshire Regiment. During training, encamped on Prees Heath, he met a Welsh girl, Mary Lloyd, she was a telegraphist, and she was special. In the summer of 1916, before he left for France, they were married at Oswestry. They were happy, and must have made plans for the future – a secure home, children and a garden for them to play in, family gatherings in Bridgnorth and Harlech – all this when the War was over.

Bob was granted leave in August. Old Boys, school friends, who had served in France, told him it was grim but assured him that, with any luck, it would soon be over.

All the infantry regiments had suffered greatly in the opening battles on the Somme. To keep them up to strength as fighting units men were frequently transferred between them. In September, Private Walker of the Herefordshire Regiment became Private (20566) Walker of the King's Shropshire Light Infantry. He landed with them in France on the 3rd of October, and a week later he was transferred to 11th Battalion Border Regiment. He hardly had time to change his cap badge.

Shropshires, Herefords, Argylls, infantry from every corner of the land, prepared for battle in the valley of the Ancre on the 18th of November. Sleet and rain fell on their backs as they advanced across the mire of no man's land. A score of men from the Border Regiment were wounded or taken prisoner on the day, and others died. Private Robert Walker was 'killed in action'. His body was recovered and hastily buried nearby.

Next of kin, Mary Walker, his wife of less than six months, was informed. She went home to Wales to be consoled. Editors of the School Magazine added their condolences to the family in Bridgnorth and noted that Bob Walker was the fifth Old Boy to die in battle during the autumn term.

The Walkers and the Bouchers had both lost a son. For both families, and forever, the darkest day on the calendar would always be the 18th of November.

Three years later, just before Christmas, Ben Boucher was informed that a new war grave cemetery had been created and it was 'found necessary to exhume the bodies buried in the area and re-inter them'. This must have been distressing although Major Stopford did assure him that 'reburial has been carefully and reverently carried out'.

Private Robert Walker (VII D 46) and Lieutenant Alec Boucher MC (VII C 40) now lie together in the Ancre British Cemetery, Beaumont-Hamel.

Chapter 10

In the Cradle of Civilisation

As schoolboys, Wilkes, Barlow and Parsons were taught that Mesopotamia was the 'cradle of civilisation' – the fertile lands in the valleys of the Tigris and Euphrates where the wheel was invented, cereal crops were first planted and mathematics and astronomy were popular pastimes. Arriving in troopships at Basra they did not recognise this land, 'the cradle of civilisation', from the description given to them by their old masters. It was a hot, dusty, fly-blown place.

Politicians and generals in 1914 did recognise the importance of 'Mesop', not because of the wheel or the corn harvest but because of the oil installations of the Persian Gulf. The Turks controlled the region. They joined the Central Powers and declared war on the Allies in October 1914. The British response was swift. The Indian Army was mobilised and a joint force, with Royal Navy support, captured the port of Basra on 23rd of October 1914. The Turks counter-attacked but were easily pushed back. Emboldened by this, the High Command ordered General Townsend to explore the possibility of pursuing the Turks up the Tigris to Baghdad.

The expedition set off in April 1915, capturing Amara in June, Nasiriya in July and Kut-al-Amara in September. They should have held this important town but instead pressed on to Ctesiphon. With lines of supply extended, and outnumbered by the Turks, they were forced to retreat to Kut, and were besieged. Two attempts were made to relieve the starving garrison, both failed, and in April 1916 more than ten thousand troops surrendered. Tom Wilkes avoided capture.

Private Tom Wilkes – 14th Hussars

The early years were not easy for Tom Wilkes, he had no memory of his mother. She died the year after he was born in Morville, in 1893. At least he was given a good education and guidance from his grandfather. At the outbreak of war he was working alongside him at Common Farm, Shirlett.

Farm boys like Tom Robins and the Wadlows could ride, they joined the Yeomanry but were soon dismounted. Tom Wilkes joined the Hussars and stayed in the saddle. The 14th Hussars were attached to the Indian Army. They were ready for battle at the outbreak of war but were not mobilised for over a year. On the 8th of November 1915 the regiment embarked at Karachi. The 490 horses outnumbered the men.

After a week at sea the troopers and their steeds must have been relieved to step ashore at Basra, even if they were entering a war zone. No sooner had they disembarked than the men were transferred to four river steamers, and their horses were tethered in lighters roped to the side. The horses, ninety in each lighter, were unhappy with this arrangement and kicked the wooden partitions to pieces. Filling the nose-bags and water-buckets was a dangerous business.

Sketch by Private Baggott

They arrived at Kut, disembarked and pressed on, upstream to Azizyeh, to support General Townsend, retreating from Ctesiphon. The Hussars and the Bengal Lancers were very welcome. Highly mobile, they were able to protect the flanks of the retreating column, harried by a combined force of Turks and Arabs. In one notable encounter their approach to the enemy was covered by a sandstorm. Taken by surprise, the cavalry swept through their ranks as if on a training exercise. 14th Hussars were not only fine horsemen, who could wield a sabre at close quarters, they were also a regiment of marksmen capable of picking off the enemy half a mile away.

Townsend's weary troops arrived back at Kut and strengthened the defences, anticipating the siege. There was some talk of keeping the cavalry so that horsemeat could be used to feed the garrison. A handful of men, sick and wounded, did stay, the bulk of the regiment fell back to Ali-al-Gharbi. Private Tom Wilkes and the 14th Hussars spent four miserable months there, under canvas awaiting supplies. Men and horses suffered from disease, heat and poor diet.

When reinforcements and fresh supplies arrived, an attempt was made to relieve the starving garrison at Kut in January 1916. Captain Walter Barlow and Captain Alfred Parsons arrived to take up the fight.

Captain Alfred Parsons – Gurkha Rifles

Fifteen years separated Alfred Parsons and Cecil Barlow but they still had much in common. They had both spent their childhood in East

Dressed for the Occasion

Castle Street and their fathers were both ministers of the church.

Alfred Parsons graduated from Keeble College Oxford in 1903 and was commissioned in the Royal Irish Rifles. He chose to serve with the Indian Army and transferred to the Gurkha Rifles. Cecil Barlow was still a schoolboy at the time.

In 1912 there was joy in the town, the bells of Saint Mary's rang out to celebrate the wedding of Lieutenant Parsons and Miss Gladys Maddison.

Three years later Alfred was fighting in France. At Festubert he was among the Irish again, the Gurkhas moved into the front line to relieve the Royal Innishkilling Fusiliers. Out of a force of a thousand men they had suffered 700 casualties. There was more fighting to be done at Givenchy, then a change of scenery for Captain Parsons and his men. They were shipped to Basra to take on the Turks.

The situation in Mesopotamia was desperate. In January 1916 General Aylmer led an expedition to relieve the siege at Kut without success. Captain Parsons was wounded. These were anxious times for his family, particularly his wife and two small children. Alfred recovered and joined another expedition in March.

Conditions for men and horses were no better here than in the trenches of Europe, icy rain producing knee-deep mud, food for men and horses in short supply.

The Turks held a heavily fortified redoubt at Dujaila. Heavy rain delayed preparation for the battle to take Dajaila for two days, which gave the defenders some warning. The attack failed, petered out 700 metres short of the fortifications. There were well over three thousand casualties. Without reinforcements they could do no more. There was no alternative, the garrison (around 13,000 men) surrendered on the 29th of April.

Captain Alfred Parsons was not there to see it, he had died on the 8th of March 1916, his body was never recovered.

The bells rang out once again from Saint Mary's Church. A muffled peal was rung to honour the memory of Alfred Parsons. Among the bell ringers were young men he had played with as a boy and were now players in a deadly game. Henry and Alice Parsons lost their only son, Gladys lost her husband of just four years, and his two children lost the father they hardly knew.

His name is cast on one of the panels on the town memorial and carved on a panel of the Basra memorial, one of the forty thousand who died in Iraq during the Great War. The memorial was originally sited on the quayside at Basra but was moved thirty kilometres inland on the road to Nasiriya in 1997. A major battle was fought here during the First Gulf War.

In later life, Alfred Parsons and Cecil Barlow, with shared memories of childhood, and dusty battlefields along the banks of the Tigris, might have had plenty to talk about but Alfred's life had been cut short. Cecil Barlow won the Military Cross, travelled widely, and married twice, his was a full life.

Captain Walter Northey Cecil Barlow MC – 30th/ att. 28th Punjabis and 32nd Sikh Pioneers

Editors of the School Magazine could not possibly include all the reports of the war sent to them by Old Boys. In the autumn edition of 1916 they noted that C Barlow was in trenches in Mesopotamia having had 'an interesting and exciting voyage up the Tigris'. His parents at 23 East Castle Street no doubt knew the full story.

Walter's father, a clergyman, would have been a man of peace. He had married Constance Northey, her family had many military connections including Colonel Frank Northey. He had died a bloody death during the Zulu War in 1879. The blood from a severed artery spilled on the battlefield was no different from any other soldier, although the Northey family could claim to have inherited royal blood from the Plantagenet kings. By the time it reached Walter's veins it must have been much diluted. However, with so many military men in the background, a chance to serve in the army at a time of war was not to be missed.

Walter Barlow completed his training at the Quetta Military Academy and was commissioned in the 30th Punjabis. He arrived in Mesopotamia after the failed attempts to relieve the garrison at Kut.

General Townsend and his men were in captivity and the Turks took over the town. Now it was the Turks' turn to be besieged. They constructed formidable defences, trenches, dugouts, machine-gun posts, artillery batteries. Infantry men from the Midlands were sent in to test the Turks' resolve. Lieutenant Maurice Jones was about to arrive to give a hand.

2ND LIEUTENANT JOSEPH MAURICE JONES – 6TH/ATT. 9TH BATTALION WORCESTERSHIRE REGIMENT

Born in Oswestry, schooled in Bridgnorth, Maurice Jones was commissioned in September 1915 in the Worcestershire Regiment.

A year later he found himself under the command of General Townsend who had been given the task of recapturing Kut. Gloucesters, Staffords and Worcesters chipped away at the Turkish defences, they gave a good account of themselves in the opening skirmishes. The Worcesters however were in a precarious position, and it was decided that half the battalion would withdraw and build a more secure line of defence. 'C' and 'D' Companies set about the task with a will and constructed a series of large dugouts that became known as Worcester City. It was completed before Christmas, and on Boxing Day the whole battalion was reunited.

There was more good cheer on the 28th of December when a new draft arrived to strengthen the 9th Battalion. Everyone expected a 'rough time' in the New Year and a hundred extra men would certainly help. The draft included three young lieutenants, C H West, P W Harrington and Maurice Jones from the 6th Battalion.

In preparation for the attack, a system of trenches was dug, moving yard by yard towards the enemy. This was dangerous work. Digging in the open, even at night, men were lost. Lieutenant Harrington had arrived with Maurice Jones in December, within a fortnight Harrington was dead.

Gradually, throughout January, the Turks were pushed back by British and Indian infantry, supported by the Artillery to the rear and the Royal Flying Corps overhead. A strongpoint in the Turkish defences was the Liquorice Factory, many Turks died in its defence. Over eight thousand of General Maude's men were made casualties before The Factory was in their hands. Between the 14th and 15th of February two thousand Turks surrendered, and the Battle of Kut was over.

Maurice Jones did not take part in the celebrations, he died, killed in action on the last day of the battle. He was buried, far from home, in the Amara Military Cemetery (XXI L11), in present-day Iraq. Most of the Commonwealth Cemeteries are in peaceful places but, even after a hundred years, Amara is still a dangerous place.

The fight to push back the Turks to their own land, and to secure the oil fields so vital to the war effort, went on. Alfred Parsons and Maurice Jones had given their all.

Old Boys, Barlow and Wilkes, went on to complete the mission. The Turks retreated from Kut in February 1916, a month later they were driven out of Baghdad. The 14th Hussars were ordered north to defend the city, and they did not have long to wait before they found some opposition at Delhi Abbas. The Turks suffered badly, this proved to be an important encounter. It allowed General Maude to consolidate his position during the summer months.

Tom Wilkes rode on to Baghdad. General Maude was a poor administrator, but he was a tactician and made good use of cavalry. The Hussars were given the opportunity to engage the enemy, on horseback and dismounted, and casualties were light compared with the actions in France.

Take It Easy, Boys

© Imperial War Museum

Although there are no details given, Tom's record shows that his first action, back in 1915, was on the Hedjaz Railway. The Turks had constructed a narrow-gauge track to link Damascus to the holy sites of Islam on the Arabian Peninsula. This became an important supply line for Turkish forces operating in Palestine, and threatening the Suez Canal. It was here that T E Lawrence, 'Lawrence of Arabia', made a name for himself.

In Iraq, Tom Wilkes took part in minor battles fought around Ramadi and Tikrit, towns familiar to men who fought more recently in the Gulf Wars. There were casualties, the 14th Hussars lost their commanding officer, shot in the back. Colonel Hewitt died in an ill-equipped hospital in Faluja. The most senior casualty was General Maude himself, he died of cholera. Trooper Wilkes was unharmed.

Lieutenant Barlow's 'exciting voyage up the Tigris' must have become even more dramatic. In August 1917 his name appeared in the London Gazette on a list of young officers who had all been awarded the Military Cross.

This was the year of the Russian Revolution, and this complicated the position in the Middle East. The oilfields on the shores of the Caspian Sea were no longer defended by the Russians. The Turks could now take control of this vital resource – something had to be done

An armoured column, under Colonel E J Bridges, and including Tom Wilkes, was dispatched to pave the way for General Dunsterville and Corporal Phillip Hutton

CORPORAL (152377) PHILIP HUTTON – ROYAL ENGINEERS

Dunsterforce was charged with securing the oilfields at Baku and the pipeline to the port of Batum on the Black Sea. Even the commander, General Lionel Dunsterville, described the task as a 'mad enterprise'. One of the men selected to take part was Phillip Hutton, a dispatch rider with the Royal Engineers.

He was very fortunate, he was not a foot soldier, trudging along with a heavy pack; he was not a trooper with a horse to feed, and as long as there was fuel in the tank of his motor bike he 'tootled along' quite happily from Baghdad to Caucasus.

Following the Bolshevik Revolution, the Russians signed a peace treaty with the Central Powers and no longer protected the oilfields in the region. The Turks threatened to cut off supplies. It wasn't all 'plain sailing' for Dunsterforce, there were setbacks along the way, confusion, and men were lost, but the oil fields were secured before the end of the war.

Phillip Hutton came home and made plans of his own.

A hundred years have passed and troubles in the region are still not resolved: oil, tribal squabbles, religious fanatics and Russian politics, continue to destroy the lives of many around the Black Sea, in Syria, Iraq, and Afghanistan. Richard Smith could not have imagined that this was how it would be.

2ND LIEUTENANT RICHARD H SMITH – 2ND QUEEN VICTORIA'S OWN SAPPERS AND MINERS

Of course Dick and Marion Smith missed their boys when they went off to the 'ends of the Earth', but they were not short of company. They were busy keeping their customers happy at the Cross Keys, in the High Street.

When war began Leslie made his way home, he crossed Canada with the British Columbia Regiment and sailed back to the 'old country'. Granted leave during training on Salisbury Plain, Les was reunited, briefly, with the family, before he sailed for France.

Meanwhile, brother Richard, two years his senior, was sweating it out in Madras on the west coast of India. Even here the residents had already had a taste of World War. Far from the battlefields of Europe, it came as a shock when the oil terminal was shelled by the German light cruiser *Emden* a month after war was declared. It was clear that oil was going to play an important part in the war. Madras was the only Indian city to be attacked. The Belgian town of Ypres was attacked repeatedly.

In April 1915, 7th Battalion British Columbia Regiment advanced towards the German trenches in support of a Highland regiment. Caught in the open, artillery shells burst among them, there were many casualties. Private Leslie Smith was the first Old Boy of Bridgnorth Grammar School to be Killed in Action. Bad news travels fast, and far, as far as Madras.

Over the centuries a very fine city had developed, with fine buildings and the sort of recreation that the well-to-do could enjoy, on the golf course, at the riding stables and hockey field. On hearing of his brother's death Richard Smith was in no mood for sport and recreation. He made repeated requests to his employer, the Madras Government, to release him from his duties. It was over a year before they decided to do so. He wrote to his old school and they published an extract from his letter.

I am writing to tell you that the Madras Government have at last allowed me to go on Military duty and that I was gazetted Sept. 28th as a 2nd Lieut, Infantry Branch. At present I have no orders as to what station or regiment I shall be posted to but I expect to have marching orders before the end of this week. I hope to go to Bangalore and be attached to the 2nd QVO Sappers and Miners.

He did indeed join his chosen regiment. 2nd QVO Sappers and Miners served in Mesopotamia from Oct 1916 until January 1918. Their battle honours included Kut-al-Amara.

A force of fifty-thousand men, mainly from British India prepared to retake Kut in December 1916. On the outskirts of the city Sappers and Miners cut trenches in forward positions, yard by yard towards the enemy defences. Kut was recaptured, not all the Turkish garrison were trapped inside, many retreated in good order. They were pursued up the valley of the Tigris for over fifty miles, as far as Aziziyeh. General Maude's men regrouped and marched on to Baghdad. This was good news for the nation and good news for Smiths in Bridgnorth. It was 'drinks all round' at the Cross Keys, Lieutenant Richard Smith was still fighting fit. He returned to India in January 1918.

Richard did not return to a desk job with the Madras Government, there was still soldiering to be done. There was trouble on the North West Frontier. The Afghans had stayed neutral during the war although some of their politicians had been tempted to join on the side of the Turks. Fortunately relations with the British were good at the time, and Britain had taken responsibility for the Afghans' foreign affairs. When peace came the situation changed, the Afghans wanted a bigger say in the running of their country and hostilities broke out. The Afghan Army was helped by tribesmen on the border with India who were always looking for a fight.

The Third Anglo-Afghan War lasted for only three months, from May to August 1919. A peace treaty was signed, the Afghans had control of their foreign affairs. They established a special relationship with the new Soviet Government, this would end badly. It seems we learn nothing from history. Parsons and Jones died in Iraq, Hutton and Wilkes fought to protect oil supplies, Richard Smith returned from Afghanistan to a government office in Madras.

Returning to Europe, to visit family in his home town, Richard would hear at first hand the tragic story of his brother Leslie, lost in France.

He would recall that one Old Boy, Cecil Barlow, had had a similar wartime experience to his own. They had both been trained at the Quetta Military Academy, in present-day Pakistan, and both travelled along the banks of the Tigris, from Basra to Baghdad. They had seen the havoc that arms, oil, and religion could create in the region, and does to this day.

Service in this campaign did help Cecil Barlow in peacetime, he became a petroleum salesman.

Chapter 11

1917 – New Year – Nothing New

January 1917, and still no sign of an end to the War. The American president, Woodrow Wilson attempted to bring the war to an end by diplomacy. He asked the warring nations to outline their terms for peace. While 'notes' passed between diplomats, men died. There was no agreement.

Unwisely, the German government attempted to negotiate an alliance with Mexico and Japan against the United States. In February diplomatic relations between the US and Germany were severed.

The conduct of war was changing. Germany announced unrestricted submarine warfare and threatened to sink hospital ships. U-32 sank *HMS Cornwallis* off the coast of Malta and a torpedo flotilla sank *HMS Simoon* in the North Sea.

There was better news from the Middle East. Kut, the scene of the humiliating surrender of British and Indian troops, was retaken by General Maude. His shrewd tactics won the day.

Following the success of Maude's men at Kut the Turks were in retreat on two fronts, beyond Bagdad and along the coast of Gaza. They began the war by threatening to take the Suez Canal and thereby cutting supply lines between Europe and the Far East. Cavalrymen sent to defend the Canal had practised their manoeuvres in grassy fields, not sandy deserts. Men used to saddling and riding a pony had to accept that the camel was a different animal. Owen Williams had to adapt.

2ND LT. OWEN EDGAR WILLIAMS – WORCESTERSHIRE YEOMANRY,
IMPERIAL CAMEL CORPS, & 1ST/4TH WELSH REGIMENT

James Williams was a practical man, the manager of a factory in Halesowen producing fire bricks. He believed in a good education and sent his son Owen to Bridgnorth Grammar School and King Edward VI Grammar School. Owen was subsequently apprenticed as an electrical engineer, he completed his apprenticeship before the outbreak of war.

Owen Williams and the Earl of Dudley were well prepared. Owen was a Private in the Worcestershire Yeomanry and the Earl was in command. Skilled in musketry and confident cavalrymen the Worcesters were ordered to Egypt in 1915.

They were 'dismounted' and for four months prepared to fight as infantry, and in August they landed at Suvla Bay, Gallipoli, to support the Anzac forces attempting to break through the Turkish defences on the hills overlooking the beach.

The Gallipoli campaign failed and all troops were evacuated in January 1916. The Worcestershire Yeomen were reunited with their horses at Chatley Camp near Alexandria, they had been spared the months of misery on the beach at Suvla Bay. Next they were dispatched to Suez to strengthen the defences on the canal. The Regiment was given responsibility for the stretch around Qatia.

Owen Williams and other Hussars were attached to the Imperial Camel Corps. The camel was better suited than the horse to operations in this terrain. They faced a determined enemy. In defence of the garrison at Oghratine over a hundred men were killed and many more wounded. The Turks established a base at Romani, defended by over forty-thousand troops. They were planning to use this as a base to seize The Canal. British and Anzac forces struck the first blow and drove out the Turks, who retreated along the coast and made a stand at Gaza.

Meanwhile Private Owen had been singled out for promotion. He was commissioned as a 2nd Lieutenant in the Welsh Regiment in March 1917, and missed the action of the First Battle of Gaza on the 25th.

The cavalry did well and captured the high ground, the infantry were less successful. Concerned that they could not secure a water supply, General Dobell dithered and ordered withdrawal at dusk. Realising that this was a mistake, he attempted to resume the battle the next morning. The infantry were exhausted, the Turks had reinforcements and the attack failed.

Over the following three weeks the Turks improved and extended their defences. On the 17th of April General Dobell launched a second assault. He decided on a frontal attack, with the infantry supported by six tanks and the artillery using gas shells. Transfer from the Camel

Corps to the Welsh Regiment meant that Lt. Owen Williams was at the front and fighting on foot. The tanks and the gas shells proved to be dismal failures. The improved Turkish defences held out and after three days the Second Battle of Gaza was called off.

This had been a costly failure. It cost Owen Williams his life. He was killed in action on the 19th of April, the last day of the battle, and buried nearby with other men of the Welsh Regiment. His final resting place is in the Gaza War Cemetery (XIII B 5).

Earlier in April, one of his old classmate, Bernard Cookson, died in France, and was buried where he fell on Wancourt Ridge.

2ND LIEUTENANT BERNARD COOKSON – ROYAL FUSILIERS & 1ST EAST YORKSHIRE REGIMENT

Taking Life Seriously

© BES Library

Bernard Cookson parted from his fellow boarders, at School House in St Leonard's Close, in the spring of 1912 and began his training as a chartered accountant. Two years later he joined the 19th Battalion

Royal Fusiliers as a Private soldier (6425). The Battalion, (2nd Public Schools), was formed at Woodcote Park near Epsom and made up of young professionals. It was expected that most of the volunteers, who joined as Private soldiers, would become officers.

From Woodcote Park the battalion moved to Clipstone Camp in the heart of Sherwood Forest. Five thousand men, all four of the Public Schools Battalions, were the first to arrive. Building work was still on-going and conditions were basic. Eventually there would be flush toilets and electricity, but not before Bernard's training was complete.

Office boys, who had exchanged city suits for army tunics, had to get their hands dirty now, digging trenches to train for war. They set about the task with enthusiasm. Some of the trenches they dug then have been 'restored' and are visited by school children a hundred years on. In August the 19th Battalion moved to Tidworth to complete their training, and landed in France in November 1915.

During the winter months there was little action, just mud and misery and the opportunity for the public school boys to get a taste of life in the trenches. Most of the men in the ranks were encouraged to apply for a commission. Many were selected and the 19th Battalion was disbanded in April 1916. Commissioned in August, Private Cookson became 2nd Lieutenant Cookson of the 1st East Yorkshire Regiment. Promotion to 2nd Lieutenant in an infantry regiment meant taking the lead in any attack, they were the targets for the enemy, life expectancy was short.

Home on leave Bernard could enjoy home comforts. The Cooksons had gone up in the world, Henry Cookson was promoted from clerk to colliery manager, and on retirement the family moved from Dawley Brook to 'Rusholme' in Western Road, Hagley.

Bernard joined his new regiment on the Western Front. They had already survived battles at Fler- Courcelette, Morval and Le Transloy. Bernard spent another winter in France, there seemed no end to the war.

The French planned a major offensive. To divert German troops away from the French sector they asked the British to mount an attack near Arras. Field Marshall Haig would have directed his armies further north to Ypres but he was 'persuaded' to co-operate with the French, by Lloyd George, the British Prime Minister.

The East Yorkshires, part of the Northumbrian Division, were given the task of taking Wancourt Ridge. The Battle of Arras began on the 9th of April. German gunners and the Royal Artillery exchanged fire. Bernard's battalion was fortunate, there were no casualties as they 'formed up' for the attack. They crossed no man's-land, the German wire was intact, they were held up and men died before they could break through. George Holmes, Bill Green, Vic Jalland and Ron Morrison, a nineteen year old, all Second Lieutenants in the 1st East Yorkshire Regiment, all died leading their men into battle. The following day another young officer was killed in action.

Over 400 men were buried nearby. In time more were brought in from other areas and a final resting place created at Wancourt. Bernard Cookson and his fellow officers were reunited, five of them, laid side by side in Row A of Plot VIII.

Accountants are very particular, they like to 'keep the books straight'. In due course their professional body, Incorporated Accountants, created a register of all their members who had given their lives in the Great War. Carter & Co, of Birmingham, had lost a promising employee.

The Second Battle of Arras, begun on the 9th of April, ended officially on the 16th of May and cost close to 150,000 casualties, among them Harold Dove.

Rifleman (S/27123) Harold Francis Dove – Bachelor of Arts & 13th King's Royal Rifles

There can be few more peaceful names than Dove, unless of course it happens to be Peaceful.

Private Tommy Peaceful was buried in Flanders in June 1915, while Harold Dove was helping to discipline boys in the Grammar School cadet force. It wasn't difficult, he was their English master and he had been a member of London University College Officer Training Corps for three years while studying at Reading.

During 1915 a number of Old Boys, whom Harold had taught, had already been sacrificed on the battlefield, and his friend and colleague Bill Ormesher had been buried at sea. There was nothing glorious about the war.

At the end of the year there was one happy event, at All Saint's Church Forest Gate, Harold and Alice Dove were married; they looked forward to a happy life together. Any plans they had for the future would have to wait.

Every able-bodied man was required to enlist unless he was in a reserved occupation. Lieutenant Cooksey, responsible for recruitment in Bridgnorth, wrote to the Education Department in Shrewsbury and asked for guidance in the case of Wightman and Dove. It was decided that James Wightman, an assistant master at St. Leonard's School, 'can be spared to join His Majesty's Army', and the governors of the Grammar School decided that Harold Dove could also be spared.

Harold's physical development was described as 'good' by the medical officer in Shrewsbury, he weighed about fifty kilogrammes. Wearing glasses he looked studious. Without glasses he could read only the top line of the optician's chart with his right eye. A Rifleman would be expected to have sharper vision.

Nevertheless, Harold was declared fit for service, and in June 1916 he was kitted out with the uniform of a Rifleman in the King's Royal Rifle Corps. A man with his background and education should have been an officer. He allowed himself to be carried along by events. He was twenty-seven, he was newly married, he was intelligent, and he probably wanted no part in it.

After three months training Rifleman Dove sailed for France. The ferry made its way down Southampton Water and into the Solent, they sailed past Stokes Bay, Harold's birthplace and where he first saw the sea – happy days. From the docks at Le Havre new recruits went straight to the Rifle Brigade Depot to listen to stories of life and death on the front line. In November Harold finally went 'up the line' with the 13th Battalion KRRC (The Prince Consort's Own). Neither the Prince Consort nor any of his descendants were anywhere to be seen.

Harold spent a miserable winter going 'in and out of the line'. This was no place to spend his first wedding anniversary.

Any spare time he had was spent writing home to Alice at Forest Gate. All letters were censored, he could not say where he was nor could he express himself freely knowing that every word would be read by a stranger before the letter reached his young wife.

While the PBI were doing what they could to keep warm and stay cheerful in the trenches at the front, the generals and staff officers were warming themselves in a comfortable chateau at the rear. They were not idle, they were planning another 'big push' around Arras in the spring.

The Battle of Arras began on the 9th of April 1917. On the 10th,

172

Rifleman Dove's battalion was given the task of taking a German position which lay eight hundred yards ahead across no man's-land. In preparation for the battle Harold must have made sure that his precious glasses were secure, without them he was lost, although, no one could see very much when they set off in the gloom at 3.45 am. They had expected some help from the artillery but none came. Harold Dove and his companions stumbled on through heavy fire. Four tanks appeared to deal with some troublesome machine-gun nests. After five hours of fighting they had reached their objective. The cavalry arrived.

Whose idea was this?

© Imperial War Museum

They were fresh and eager to help the struggling infantry. Dismounted they deepened shell holes, set up machineguns and attended the wounded. A defensive line was established, there was no question of a breakthrough. All along the battlefront there were casualties, hundreds of cavalrymen were lost and just as many of their 'war horses'. The men could take cover when they were shelled, the horses were tethered in the open and slaughtered. The KRRC were relieved by another battalion and withdrew. In less than a fortnight they were back in action.

At Gavrelle they were given three more objectives and they were successful. The highlight of this action was the capture of a white charger belonging to a German officer, defending the trenches opposite. This fine animal went on to win a prize at the next regimental horse show.

Behind the lines the King's Rifles counted the cost of their recent 'scrap'. The adjutant couldn't say much about the casualties. He knew another three fellow officers were dead and several wounded, scores of Riflemen were dead or wounded and many could not be accounted for.

Alice Dove was told that her husband was 'missing', he was never found. It was later confirmed that he was KIA (killed in action) on the 23rd April 1917.

The War Office and the Rifle Brigade Office tied up the loose ends. The widow's address was confirmed – Forest Gate E 7. She was to receive a widow's pension, thirteen shilling a week. Alice put in a request for his 'personal effects'. A lot of paperwork was involved for just two Field Cards and one photograph – she appeared so happy. Those who did not have her husband's gift for words sent field cards to their loved ones. By deleting five or six statements a message could be composed – *I am quite well – I have received your parcel – letter follows at first opportunity.*

Alice examined the field cards, they were blank, there was no last word from her husband. Harold Doves talent with pen and paper was never fully expressed. His name will remain forever carved in stone on the Arras Memorial.

Alice returned to the academic world of Reading University, where she and Harold had first met. Alice applied for her husband's medals, they arrived at St Andrew's Hall, a calm and comforting place. 'The Great War for Civilisation' was the inscription on one of Harold's medals.

A Place of Solitude and Learning

Alice examined the engraving on the edge – *2679 Rfman H F Dove KRRC* – nothing more.

She looked out over the flower bed and the carefully trimmed lawn. A lone student strolled by, it wasn't Harold.

Harold Dove must have read of the exploits of famous military leaders such as the Duke of Wellington

Arthur and Alice Wilson must also have read of Wellington's famous battles.

Private Arthur Wellesley Wilson – 9th Royal Fusiliers

The heroics of Arthur Wellesley were well know, as Duke of Wellington he had defeated Napoleon at the battle of Waterloo. He had been less successful as Prime Minister but still held in high regard by the public.

His achievements were commemorated worldwide, from Wellington, capital of New Zealand, to an impressive memorial at the end of Park Lane in London. Everyone had heard of the Wellington boot and tens of thousands of mugs and plates had been produced to gather dust in humble homes everywhere. There may well have been a piece of Wellington potery on a shelf in Alice Wilson's kitchen.

When Alice and Arthur Henry Wilson were trying to decide on a name for their second-born son, Arthur was their first choice, and why not add Wellesley to give the boy something to live up to, even if they did not expect him to be a great soldier? They were not alone in coming to this decision, Arthur Wellesleys appeared in parish registers all over England.

Early life for Arthur, his brother Alfred and his sister Mary appeared precarious, the family home clinging to the face of Castle Cliff. At the boundary of the tiny garden there was a thirty-foot drop through brambles to the entrances of caves carved out of the crumbling red sandstone.

During the Civil war the castle was held by Royalists; the Roundheads laid siege to the town. When Colonel Lavington and his men began to tunnel into the Castle Cliff to undermine the Royalists holding out above they soon surrendered. The tunnels were later enlarged and made into extra rooms for the simple dwellings built at the foot of the cliff.

More substantial houses were built above, 23 and 24 St Mary's Steps were particularly grand; solid, three-storey, brick built family homes. The children, looking out on the world from any one of the windows

© Graham Jones

overlooking the Severn, were treated to an ever-changing scene. Carts, carriages and even the occasional motor car went back and forth across the river bridge. On weekdays barges loaded and unloaded goods on the quayside opposite Harbour House. At weekends pleasure boats carried their passengers from the landing stages in the grimy shadow of Southwell's Carpet Factory to the clear waters and sunny meadows under High Rock. Grazing cattle looked up, and courting couples waved as they passed.

On Sundays the bells of St Mary's rang out above the Wilsons' chimney pots, drowning out the bells of St Leonard's in the distance. Close by, across St Mary's Steps, the 'Russellites' (Jehovah's witnesses) in sober black trooped into the Kingdom Hall.

In 1900 Arthur Henry Wilson was working as a cashier for a land agent and Arthur Wellesley Wilson was a scholar at Bridgnorth Grammar School. Ten years later father was calling himself an accountant and his son was a bank clerk in the town. The family drifted apart, Alice Wilson died, Mary Wilson moved to Berkshire. Father and Alfred, a carpet designer, stayed in the family home. Arthur Wellesley Wilson was working in Birmingham at the outbreak of war.

He joined the Royal Berkshire Regiment as a Private (20160). Later he was transferred to the London Regiment, 9th Royal Fusiliers. The battalion landed in France in May 1915 and spent the rest of the war in and out of the front line, playing its part in minor skirmishes and major battles. The Battle of Loos, which lasted a fortnight, cost the lives of 20,000 good men. The Fusiliers were sent over the top again in 1916 to do battle at Albert, and Pozieres and Le Transloy.

The River Scarpe, just north of Arras, may have reminded Arthur Wilson of his childhood, fishing for 'tiddlers' in Well Meadow or practising his first strokes in the calmer (and cleaner) waters of the Severn, upstream from the town. There was nothing calm or tranquil about The Scarpe, a series of bloody battles were fought on its banks.

Casualties from the First Battle were high and yet General Haig did claim some success after five days of fighting. The Second Battle of the Scarpe only lasted a day, 23rd -24th April. Conditions were appalling, freezing fog, the battlefield littered with the fallen. There was stalemate. In the first week of May the 9th Battalion Royal Fusiliers prepared for battle once again, German trenches were captured but there was no breakthrough. Arthur Wilson and his mates came out of the front line. Washed and shaved, and with a hot meal inside them, they began to feel human again.

They were not out of danger, still within the range of German artillery. To 'consolidate their position' another assault on the enemy was ordered. Private Wilson did not take part, he was killed by a shell as preparations were being made for the attack. He died on the 8th of May 1917, two days later one of his officers wrote to his father to offer *'sincere sympathy at the loss of a fine fellow, cheerful on all occasions.'*

He was buried nearby in St Catherine Cemetery. The village just north of Arras was taken from the Germans in 1916 and held until the end of the war. Only when the guns fell silent in 1918 could those buried there 'rest in peace'.

Father died 14th January 1919 leaving all his property to his daughter. Mary never returned to the family home. Castle Cliff was sold to Alfred Lloyd, a bootmaker and draper, in March the same year for £500. It seems that Mary had to accept life as a spinster, as did thousands of young women of her generation; so many eligible young men had died during four years of war.

All soldiers were advised to make a will, 'just in case anything should happen'. Arthur left what he had to his unmarried sister. A clerk at the War Office worked out his back pay, £12. This was the sort of work Arthur could have done in his head. Later Mary received £837 from Arthur's estate. This was a considerable sum, her bank-clerk brother certainly knew how to handle money. Private Arthur Wellesley Wilson was twenty-six when he died.

Raised overlooking the river in the Severn Valley, he was laid to rest in the Valley of the Scarpe.

Chapter 12

Casualty Clearing

Of the thousands of battlefield casualties the majority were single young men. When they were hurt it was only natural for them to cry out, "Mother, help me!"

Mother was a long way away. A comrade might help, but if they were advancing towards enemy lines they would have been ordered to leave the casualties and 'press on'. It was the duty of stretcher bearers to gather up the wounded and bring them back to safety, these were brave men. The Regimental Aid Post would 'patch up' anyone lightly wounded, more serious cases were passed on to the Field Ambulance.

In Safe Hands

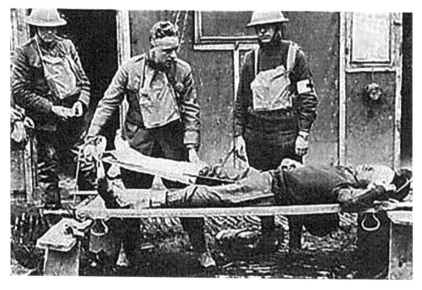

This was not a mobile unit, it was staffed by a team of medical officers and well trained men of the Royal Army Medical Corps. Some casualties were returned to their battalion after treatment. Serious cases were moved on by any means to the nearest Casualty Clearing Station – the horse-drawn cart was the least comfortable method of transport. Here they were at a relatively safe distance from the front line, where serious operations such as amputations might be carried out.

Those with life-changing injuries were moved on by road, rail or canal to a Base Hospital or direct to one of the ports to take ship to 'Dear Old Blighty'. The system devised for the treatment of casualties was something Ryder and Rhodes knew well.

Captain Edward Llewellyn Noott Rhodes – Royal Army Medical Corps

Ellen Rhodes gave birth to a baby boy in 1882, if there had been any complications help was at hand. Her husband, William, was not only a Justice of the Peace he was also a Surgeon, Physician and General Practitioner.

Little Edward Rhodes grew up surrounded by medical paraphernalia: shiny steel instruments, jars and bottles containing ointments and evil-tasting medicines, rolls of bandages and slings for broken arms. It was not surprising that he should go on to study medicine at Selwyn College, Cambridge.

The Grammar School had a poor reputation in the 1890s, it was not until 1897 when the Reverend Dawes replaced the Reverend Price that matters improved dramatically. Bromsgrove School on the other hand had an excellent reputation and this was where Edward Rhodes (he preferred to be called Llew) completed his schooling before he began his medical training.

Newly qualified, he returned to Bridgnorth to work alongside his father. Nothing could have prepared him for the tragic event at Northgate House in September 1908.

William Rhodes had been in poor health for some time, it may have helped if he had heeded words from the Bible – *Physician Heal Thyself*. Concerned with the welfare of his patients he neglected his own condition – 'the cobbler always wears the worst shoe'. Whatever his physical condition, a more serious problem was Doctor William Rhodes' mental health.

Just before midnight one Wednesday evening in September, Llew said goodnight to his father. It was not unusual for them to be working late and rising early. The following morning William was late. Concerned for his wellbeing, Llew burst into his dressing-room and found his father dead. The cause of death, poisoning, a bottle of carbolic acid was nearby.

We will never know why he chose to end his life in such pain, knowing the burning pain to mouth and windpipe the acid would cause, when there were benign drugs to hand, that would have ensured a peaceful end.

A private family funeral was arranged. Dr Rhodes had been practising in the town for well over twenty years. A man who had done much for the community: a Justice of the Peace, Churchwarden of St Leonard's, founder of the Rowing Club and former mayor to Bridgnorth. There were many who would have wanted to pay their respects – not only the town 'worthies' but ordinary folk, including residents of the Workhouse; he had cared for many of them. The report in the Journal made this clear.

The respect felt for the deceased gentleman, both rich and poor, was shown by the partial closing of business premises and drawn blinds at private residences and a large number of cottages in the town.

Dr Edward Llewellyn Rhodes moved away to further his medical career. In 1911 he was elected a Member of the British Medical Association and took up an appointment as house surgeon at Richmond Royal Hospital. Accommodation was provided for the staff, young doctors were outnumbered by unattached nurses. Many cheap romantic novels have been written about doctor and nurse relationships. There was nothing cheap about Laura Beatrice Bradford, she was the daughter of a home-counties architect. Before the war Edward and Laura must have 'come to an understanding'. Everyone's life was put on hold in 1914.

At time of war skills of every sort were called for – navvies and farm hands to dig trenches, clerks and storemen to supply the shovels, map makers and mining engineers, and on the front line, sailors, airmen, gunners and riflemen to do the damage. To pick up the pieces were the MOs and the medics.

As Medical Officer, Captain Rhodes was attached to the Argyll and Sutherland Highlanders, probably the 10th Battalion. The Argylls were noted for their tenacity and were often chosen to take the lead in battle. During the course of the war, in total, nearly seven thousand Argylls were killed and at least twenty thousand wounded; plenty of work for the medical staff. Llew Rhodes fitted in well, athletic and fearless, he had represented school and college on the rugby field.

Captain Rhodes arrived in France on the 6th of June 1915. Preparations were already underway for a joint attack by French and British forces. Tunnellers were at work under the front line. Supplies of ammunition and chlorine gas were being stockpiled. Untested young recruits were drilled in the art of war by lads in their early twenties.

The Battle of Loos went off with a bang when the mines laid by the tunnellers were detonated. The gas intended for the German defenders blew back in the faces of advancing infantry. The artillery were short of shells and failed to cut the barbed wired, that snared many and made them easy targets. Against all the odds the 'Jocks' fought on and took the high ground of Hill 70. Here Richard Hilton a Forward Observation Officer commented,

All that we needed was more artillery ammunition to blast those clearly located machine guns, plus some fresh infantry to take over from the weary and depleted Jocks. But alas neither ammunition nor reinforcements were available and the great opportunity was missed.

Later, Llew Rhodes gave his own account the first day of battle, to his mother, who wrote it down.

Saturday, September 22nd, 1915

On Friday 24th at 11pm Noeux-les-Mines, about six miles behind the firing line. From 4 to 6 a.m. the guns that had been concentrated during the night, near Loos began to fire like mad. This continued until 7 a.m. when the infantry attack was launched. At 6.20 a.m. gas and smoke were sent

off by the British, although there was very little wind to drive them.

At the start of the fighting the 45th Brigade was nearly three miles from the British front line trenches. As soon as the leading regiment of the Division began to charge, we began to move and occupied, in succession the British front-line trench, and then the German front-line trench. While occupying these trenches we saw a large number of prisoners being brought in... We were ordered to advance over the open ground to Loos and occupy Hill 70, which lies just beyond that town... On the top of the hill was a German redoubt.

About two in the morning, the Germans made a vigorous counter attack, which was heavily repulsed...and at 9 a.m. a charge was launched against the Germans who by this time had been strongly reinforced. The charge was stopped by machine-gun fire. About 3 p.m. we were ordered to retire from Hill 70, some did and some didn't...

So far in his account he had given his mother no personal details. Ellen Rhodes said, "Well now I should like to know where you were and what you were doing in the Battle".

I followed on foot and when we reached the German front line trenches I dressed the wounded of the other Brigades who had gone on. I then found that the Battalion of the Argylls had gone on to Loos but could not find them, so for a time looked after the wounded of the 9th Gordons, who could not find their doctor. Later I found the Argylls and formed a dressing station in a house at the foot of Hill 70. This was occupied by a French woman and four children. This house was not touched during the battle although shells were continually dropping all around. Most of Loos had been destroyed by our artillery fire before the attack. During the Battle some Scots soldiers and an officer took refuge in the house where there were some French women. They were being sniped at from some houses nearby. One of the French women snatched the officer's revolver, went through the back door, crept up to the German snipers and shot them both dead.

A French woman and a child came out of Loos and helped some of our wounded. While doing so a wounded German soldier wounded both of them, and the machine gun sergeant of the Argylls chopped the German soldier's head off with an axe."

Ellen Rhodes said, "I suppose motors came up and took away the wounded as you dressed them".

Llewellyn was working without his orderlies who were lost, he replied,

No, I sent two notes and three messages telling them to come. There was a tremendous scrap about that; so I filled a row of houses with the wounded.

Heavy casualties had been anticipated by the High Command, and arrangements made to cope with at least forty thousand. The Advanced Dressing Stations and Casualty Clearing Station were expected to accommodate ten thousand wounded at any one time. Buses and trucks and seventeen ambulance trains were on standby, even canal barges were to be used to evacuate the wounded.

Captain Rhodes could confirm that despite the detailed planning there was still chaos on the battlefield.

The battle lasted for over a fortnight. Battalions from nearly every Scottish regiment fought at the Battle of Loos and suffered a huge number of casualties, thousands were killed. Almost every town and village in Scotland was affected by the losses at Loos.

The Argylls were awarded a Battle Honour for their sacrifice at Loos, and Captain Rhodes was given a Mention in Dispatches. Over the winter months fresh troops arrived to fill the ranks and prepare for battle again on The Somme. Thousands of casualties were treated in this series of battles between July and November 1916. There was little rest for Llewellyn Rhodes and his team of medical orderlies, but at least there was some joy for him when the Battle of the Somme came to an end.

Home on leave in November, Captain Rhodes and Laura Bradford were married at Saint Mark's Church, Surbiton.

© the Rhodes Family

After the honeymoon he may have been lucky enough to spend Christmas visiting old friends in his home town, well away from the misery of the front line. This was an opportunity to catch up with local gossip and learn the fate of some the Old Boys. Not all of the stories had a happy ending.

Of particular interest would have been the activities of Surgeon Lieutenant Richard Thursfield serving with the Royal Navy off the coast of Africa – lucky man. Also on the High Street were the families of other Old Bridgnorthians, Cooksey and Price, Beaman and Walker.

At the opposite end of the High Street, close to the Thursfield's medical practice was the Ryder's drapers shop. Alf Ryder was not a medical man but he certainly knew what the inside of a Field Hospital looked like.

Alf Ryder was just one of the scores of eager lads who flocked to the regimental depot in Shrewsbury to join the KSLI. Only the best were selected to serve in the county regiment. Butchers, bakers, farm hands, miners, and posh boys attending Shrewsbury School were all willing, but they were not warriors. Alf Ryder was a draper's assistant with none of skills of an infantryman, he was expected to learn quickly.

Not Friends with the Germans

Within a matter of weeks drill sergeants of the Royal Marines had knocked them all into shape at Blackdown Camp. They moved on to Chidlingfold, and in January 1915 formed up at Witley to be inspected by Lord Kitchener, the Secretary of State for War himself. It was a memorable event, it was bitterly cold. The recruits stood without greatcoats as snow fell steadily on the flat tops of their forage caps. A visiting French general, well wrapped up, was heard to say, "C'est manifique!" His remark was lost on the rank and file.

In March they were in comfortable quarters at Aldershot and parading before the King and Queen. A cross-country competition was arranged between rival regiments, and Queen Mary presented first prize to Private Stewart of the 5th KSLI. The whole battalion felt special. Six weeks later they were all singled out for special treatment.

Measles broke out and they were put into isolation, under canvas on Watt's Common; no cosy hospital ward for them. It was unseasonably cold, there was more snow. Believing that things could not get any worse everyone was looking forward to a move to the battlefront. No matter how thorough the training may have been nothing could have prepared them for what lay ahead.

Horses and mules and a hundred men set off by train to Folkestone and crossed to Boulogne on the 19th of May 1915. The rest of the battalion followed on the next day. They were reunited at Erkelsbrugge in Belgium, they were now within artillery range of the front line. Preparations were made to move on to Dickebusch. On the 30th they arrived in the trenches and began to dig in. Here the Battalion came under fire for the first time. The Colonel and half his men worked at night to strengthen their position. It wasn't dark, the Germans fired flares to illuminate the scene, and took pot-shots at anything that moved. Sergeant Diss was killed and three of his lads were wounded.

This was a blow but as time went by incidents like this became commonplace and accepted. A dozen were killed and sixty wounded at Bellwarde in June, more casualties at Railway Wood and more still at Hooge in August.

Back at Railway Wood in September Alf Ryder and 'B' Company were at the 'apex of the salient', which meant 'at the sharp end'. They attacked on the 27th and reached the second line of German trenches. Surrounded on three sides they withdrew. When the roll call was taken the next day and the company clerks had 'totted up' the figures it was revealed that 440 were killed, wounded or missing.

King George visited Belgium in October and a detachment of men from the 5th KSLI who had distinguished themselves in battle attended a special parade. A better place to be was the brewery at Poperinghe where there were hot baths and hot food, ale and loose women.

Drafts of fresh troops arrived to fill the gaps in the ranks. The idea that war was glorious was quickly dispelled by 'old sweats' in their teens.

Winter set in – "there are few places in Europe more unpleasant than Belgium" one well-travelled officer remarked.

Christmas was celebrated but there was no longer any fraternising with the enemy. More misery was forecast for the New Year. Lieutenant Richard Butt was killed in January, he had been in Belgium less than a month. Morale was low, then in February there was some good cheer. The 6th Battalion arrived to take over from the 5th, this chance meeting with old friends was very welcome. The Germans spoilt the party, they mounted a bombing raid. The raiders were driven off but in this exchange ten were killed and seventeen wounded, including Alf Ryder.

Amos Ryder broke the news to Sarah that their son had received severe gunshot wounds to his left hand and was recovering in No 22 General Hospital, Wimereux. Nursing his sore hand he had time to think back over the events of 1915 and be grateful that he was 'still in one piece'. He was wounded but this was not a Blighty wound. Alf re-joined the Regiment in France after a spell of home leave. He would miss home cooking and he knew exactly what lay ahead, more action, more danger and quite possibly more pain.

King's Shropshire Light Infantry were on the move, the 5th Battalion was relieved by the 6th and retired to billets at Wormhout. They 'entrained' and travelled south away from what was 'generally considered to be the most unpleasant spot in Europe'. With the Ypres salient behind them they were on their way to Arras. The final step of the journey turned out to be one of the longest route marches of the war, with mud underfoot and snow storms along the way. Their reward was comfortable billets at Ronville, a suburb of Arras, less than a mile from the front line.

Fresh troops and young officers arrived to bring the battalion up to strength. Private Ryder, away on sick leave, may have missed the march but he was certainly on hand to prepare for the great Battle of the Somme. Officially the 5th Battalion was 'at rest', which meant parades, exercises and visits to the front line. There was rifle practice – Alf's left hand was damaged, but the trigger-finger of his right hand was still in working order.

Battle commenced on the 1st of July. The number of casualties passing back through the lines of regiments on standby at the rear was beyond belief. There was no rest for Royal Army Medical Corps, Captain Rhodes and his staff worked tirelessly. Alf Ryder examined the scars on his hand and waited. It was no secret that sooner or later the 5th Battalion would be involved.

At the end of the month they set off on foot to a 'livelier' sector of the front in the Valley of the Ancre. Weighed down by full packs they marched to the rail junction at Candas. Snow storms they had experienced earlier in the year would have been welcomed in the sweltering heat of August. Local villagers along the way cheered them on. On the 7th of August they arrived at journey's end, Buire-Sur-L'Ancre. Small-scale attacks were made on the enemy positions over the next two weeks.

With the King's Royal Rifles on the right and the Ox and Bucks on the left, the KSLI moved into the front line and kept their heads down for days while the artillery pounded the German positions in Delville Wood.

Thickets of hazel, mature oaks and birch trees with grassy rides between must once have been a sanctuary for fox, squirrel, badger and birdlife. Not now, the oaks were shredded stumps, barbed wire replaced the brambles, frightened men cowered in the fox holes. The German defenders held on. The South African Brigade attacked, the Germans counter-attacked. For six weeks the advantage continuously changing from one side to the other. The South African Brigade were exhausted, it was the turn of the Light Division to take on the enemy.

The attack began at 5.45 on the morning of the 24th of August and, as far as the 5th Battalion was concerned it was a success, the enemy was cleared from the edge of Delville Wood, over a hundred prisoners were taken. However the King's Royal Rifles were less successful, without their support the KSLI were forced to retreat. In this brief encounter two hundred of the Shropshires were killed and many gravely wounded.

Private Alf Ryder was in a mess, wounded in five places. He was handed on from Aid Post to Casualty Clearing Station to Base Hospital, and this time by Hospital Ship across the Channel and back onto home soil. Recovery was slow, by December he was 'progressing satisfactorily' at a Convalescent Home in Surrey. Alf's soldiering days were done, in February 1917 he was discharged and returned to civilian life and the family business.

Back on the steps of 'The Friendly House' on Waterloo Terrace, he greeted lads in uniform he had known all his life, pleased to see that they were still in good heart and unscathed.

On the lapel of his jacket he wore the Silver War Badge to show the world that he had been in the firing line. This was not necessary, the terrible wound to his skull was plain to see. Captain Edward Rhodes had seen many similar injuries and worse.

Doctor Rhodes returned to the town and set up home with Laura in East Castle Street. Walking back and forth to his surgery at Northgate he would be greeted by old patients and old friends. Daily life on the High Street appeared to have returned to normal, but it could never be the same, with so many missing and so many damaged by war.

The dreary decade of the 1920's passed, followed by the dangerous decade of the 1930's that ended in another World War. Youths in uniform appeared in the High Street almost overnight. Old soldiers were kitted out in khaki to join the Home Guard.

Alf Ryder had been declared 'unfit for service' but he was given a position that suited him perfectly. Private Ryder was promoted to 2nd Lieutenant and given responsibility for the Army Cadets. If there was one activity the boys enjoyed above all others it was target practice with the 22 rifle. The Territorials had a range at the Drill Hall in St. Mary's Street. For his cadets Alf Ryder set up a rifle range in the basement of his shop on Waterloo Terrace. The boys knew this was a dangerous game, a glance at the battle scars of their officer would remind them.

Peace returned and this time the decade that followed was more optimistic. The Health Service was established and money spent to improve education – and there was a boom in babies. Babies became toddlers and parents wanted the best for them, wanted them to be happy, particularly at Christmas time. Alf Ryder arranged visits to see Santa in his grotto.

Clutching a sixpence, boys and girls descended the spiral staircase, Mr Ryder sat at the bottom to greet them and collect the entrance fee. He was wearing a sombre suit not a red dressing gown; Santa was waiting at the far end of the crumpled cardboard grotto. He didn't have much to say, he seemed to be shaking his head, moving it from side to side and sometimes it got stuck. Disappointed children examined his damaged ear and the steel rods that ran down his neck and disappeared under the collar of his threadbare coat. Concerned parents explained that this was not the real Santa, this was an automaton, with a complicated clockwork mechanism hidden in his chest. The children moved away, passed the shelves filled with dolls, jigsaws, rubber daggers, chemistry sets, and boxes of Meccano. Mr Ryder gestured to a tub of sawdust close to his knee. In turn the young visitors rummaged around until they found a little parcel, then scurried on up the stairs.

The story, told in school playgrounds, was that there was something unique to be seen in Ryder's underground grotto, not a two foot high clockwork Santa puppet, but Mr Ryder's brain. Sure enough as they climbed the stairs and glanced back at the seated figure below, the terrible gash in his skull was exposed. To confirm what they had seen some questioned their fathers when they got home.

"Ah yes, Alf Ryder, 'e caught a packet at Devil Wood." It sounded better than 'hit by a piece of hot shrapnel'.

Doctor Rhodes returned to set up home in East Castle Street and practice medicine at Northgate. He could not dwell on the terrible sights he had seen during four years of war. Although, perhaps as he walked back along the High Street, after a day in his surgery, he was reminded from time to time of the fate of Surgeon Lieutenant Thursfield, killed in Northern Russian, and of the scars inflicted on Private Alf Ryder at Delville Wood.

Any man who had served on the front line and came away unscathed was a lucky man. When Leslie Hughes looked in the shaving mirror in the morning he would be reminded of a painful day in September1916, when good men died and he was scared for life.

Private Leslie Owen Hughes (2873) Shropshire Yeomanry, (26894) 6th KSLI, later Lieutenant, Reserve Infantry Regiment (Cheshire Regiment)

Serving with the county regiment in France Les Hughes must have lost close comrades, but this could not compare with an earlier tragedy – the loss of his own mother. Ellen Hughes died in 1910 when Leslie was twelve years old. His grandparents stepped in to 50 Mill street, Lucy Hughes to run the household and Sam to work alongside his son, Rowland, as a house painter.

Leslie may have expected to join the family firm, but the war intervened – a part-time soldier with the Shropshire Yeomanry, he transferred to the 6th Battalion KSLI and was serving with them in France in 1916, when they were preparing for the Battle of Passchendaele.

Nineteen-sixteen was a busy year for the 6th Battalion, in June they distinguished themselves at the Battle of Mount Sorrel, good men were lost, but they stood their ground. There were more casualties at Guillemont in September. The 6th Battalion held the trenches in front of Waterlot Farm. German raiding parties attacked their positions but were easily fought off. The enemy replied with heavy artillery and over the course of a week the Shropshires suffered casualties, a handful were missing, over thirty were killed and at least eighty were wounded. Those seriously injured were sent home for treatment.

Private Hughes wrote a cheery letter to the editors of the School Magazine. He was a lucky man, evacuated from the battlefield, he was recovering from a wound to the face at a military hospital in Cheshire. No doubt he also kept in touch with some of his old pals serving in France and at Christmas perhaps he received a card.

Season's Greetings

© Shropshire Archives

There was no glitter, no baby in a manger, no wise men, and no children opening presents or rosy-cheeked landlords handing out jugs of ale. This was the reality for the 6th Battalion, scrawny lads plodding across a dark landscape with picks and shovels, and a rifle over their shoulder

Les Hughes' duty on the front line was over.

With the benefit of a Grammar School education he began training as an officer at Kinmel Park, near Rhyll. Trenches were dug as a training exercise for recruits without battlefield experience – not necessary for 2nd Lieutenant Hughes or his commanding officer, John Holland, he had won a Victoria Cross in France. Leslie Hughes return to Cheshire to serve out the war with the Reserve Infantry Regiment.

Five years later medals were awarded, and a box addressed to Mr L O Hughes arrived at Catstree Farm. Leslie had not taken up house-painting, the trade of his father and grandfather, and he was not inclined to paint a new sign, changing Catstree Farm to Waterlot Farm. It was here that he was hit by shrapnel and he did not need any painful reminder. George Brown had a similar tale to tell.

PRIVATE (2402) (267869) GEORGE ARCHIBALD BROWN – 4TH KSLI & 6TH CHESHIRE REGIMENT

Allam Bridge, near Alveley, with its mill and waterfall, was a most attractive place to spend childhood, but George Brown had to grow up quickly, he had responsibilities, supporting his widowed mother. He was head of the household when he was sixteen. Two years later (October 1914) he was a soldier.

At the Recruiting Office in the High Street, George filled in the Attestation Form. Major William Westcott checked the details and witnessed his signature, he noted that George Brown gave his trade as 'Horse Keeper'. Many Old Boys of The Grammar School were professional men, accountants, solicitors or the sons of famers and shopkeepers. Life was not so easy for George, he had content himself with any work he could find – grooming pit ponies at Highley Colliery. Now he had a profession, solder, infantry man, with the 4th Battalion KSLI.

Fortunately, he was spared almost two years of battle and did not serve in France until September 1916. A year later, after a comparatively easy time the 4th Battalion was preparing for the Second Battle of Passchendaele.

On the 4th of October they set off from Hardifort and marched to Houtkerque, arriving on the 7th. Here they spent a fortnight preparing for battle and took over trenches on the canal bank at Ypres. There was water everywhere, running down the canal, falling out of the sky and filling up the trenches. Clothing and equipment was lost and morale was low. They moved on, to Irish Farm, and on again to Albatross Farm on the 29th of October.

The Germans were aware that troops were on the move all along the front, that an attack was planned, they began shelling the Allied positions. According to the Official History of the Regiment,

> *No casualties were suffered until the allotted positions were reached, but during the consolidation some 30 occurred, including Lieuts. Greene, Charlton and Lowe, who were hit by overhead shrapnel while waiting to deploy.*

George Brown was not mentioned but he was one of the thirty 'other ranks' to be wounded. Without delay, George was transported to the coast and carried on board HM Hospital Ship *Princess Elizabeth*. Next of kin, Elizabeth Brown, was notified. By the time the letter arrived at Netherton Cottage in Highley her son was safely tucked up in a hospital bed in Cheshire.

His injury was described as 'severe', a gunshot wound to the head that had fractured his skull and created a 'depression' certainly was 'severe' – but George survived. George's treatment lasted for ninety-one days that included a few weeks convalescence at the Princess Club in Bermondsey.

This hospital, opened by Princess Mary Louise in 1914, occupied 106 and 108 Jamaica Road. There was a Smoking Room, it was doubtful if anyone could see across the room – for those who wanted a view and fresh air, there was a roof garden. This sort of luxury was offered to men who had shown 'gallant conduct'.

George was transferred to the Cheshire Regiment and was discharged from the Depot in February 1918, 'no longer fit for military service'.

George Brown, Les Hughes and Alf Ryder all bore visible scars. Many others had deeper wounds, in the mind, that would never heal.

George's Reward For Services Rendered, a Silver War Badge

Chapter 13

Taking The High Ground

The month of July was the wettest that anyone could remember and for anyone doing battle in Flanders it was a month they would never forget. The conditions in the trenches were appalling – when it wasn't raining 'cats and dogs' there were still shells raining down. Above all, keeping dry was the main concern, for each and every 'Tommy'

Field Marshall Douglas Haig's main concern was how to break through the German lines, clear the Belgian ports of the U-boat bases and bring the war swiftly to an end. In April 1917 the front at Arras was pushed back six miles, and in June Messines Ridge was taken. Haig believed the tide was turning, Lloyd George, the Prime Minister, was not so sure, he did not want a repetition of the Battle of the Somme.

All sides were war weary. Mutinies among French troops were carefully concealed by the authorities. Strikes and anti-war demonstrations in Germany were weakening their resolve. Russian troops had joined the revolution against the oppressive regime of the Czar. The Russians were no longer prepared to support the Allied cause.

Lloyd George reasoned that with so much uncertainty the best course of action was to wait until the Americans arrived in force. He was overruled by the War Cabinet. So began a series of battles that would change the lives of many, including Harry Dyer, his brother Arthur and Jesse Marston.

Lance Corporal Jesse Marston – Shropshire Yeomanry and 6th Battalion KSLI

In July 1914 King George V was going to visit The Royal Agricultural Show at Shrewsbury. The Yeomanry were going to provide the escort.

They were given extra drill in April and May. In June they practised musketry. No one objected, they were keen to bring their soldierly skills up to the standard of the Regular Army. On the 3rd of July the King arrived and was very pleased with the way the Yeomanry conducted themselves.

Troopers and officers alike now looked forward to the next big event on the regimental calendar, the annual camp, planned for September. It did not take place. War was declared on the 4th of August and the Shropshire Yeomanry were mobilised within a week.

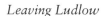

Leaving Ludlow

Lads from Wenlock and Bridgnorth, who formed 'D' Squadron, made their way to Wellington. Jesse Marston saddled up at the family farm at Oxenbold and rode off. Along the way he may have joined up with Charlie Jones at Haughton and Tom Robins from The Croft. Tom and Jesse were classmates at the Grammar School.

Many young troopers found to their delight that they were to be billeted in public houses. The publicans were generous. They could afford to be generous, the regiment was footing the bill and naïve young officers readily accepted the claims for accommodation and drinks provided. This state of affairs did not last long, by the end of the month the regiment moved to Brogyntyn Park, near Oswestry.

The weekend soldiers had to be turned into professionals. To bring the regiment up to strength new recruits were called for. There was no shortage of volunteers although some were turned away because they could not clear the first hurdle, they couldn't ride!

Fresh horses, harness and equipment and was issued. Bundles of tunics arrived at the camp. This did not suit everyone. The yeomanry were better fed and stockier than the average soldier, some of the troopers had difficulty squeezing into their new uniform. Jesse's was a perfect fit.

The training at Brogyntyn was intensive. Within a month the regiment was at full strength and ready for overseas service. Instead, they were sent to East Anglia – It was rumoured that the Germans were planning an invasion. Throughout the summer of 1915 the Shropshire Yeoman continued to practise the skills and strategies employed by their forebears, but they were not called upon to use them. It was becoming clearer by the day that the cavalry, that had played such a vital role in in the Boer War, on the dry open plains of South Africa, could not be used in the sodden fields of Flanders.

The Army needed infantrymen. None of the Yeomen liked the idea of being dismounted and turned into foot soldiers, but if they wanted to join the fight so be it. If they agreed to do so they were awarded an Imperial Service Badge, and waited to be transferred. The 10th Battalion kept their mounts and were shipped to Egypt to fight the Turks at Gaza, Charlie Jones from Haughton went with them. Tom Robins and Jesse Marston joined the 6th Battalion KSLI and crossed the Channel. They landed at Boulogne in July 1915.

Trench 'familiarisation' was arranged for them at Fleurbaix which meant getting used to the idea of being shelled and shot at. Then followed involvement in a number of minor skirmishes. Their first real success came in 1916 at the Battle of Mount Sorrel. Fighting alongside the Canadians they took the high ground.

The Shropshires soldiered on to collect more battle honours on The Somme – at Delville Wood, Guillemont and Fler-Courcelette. There was no respite, good men continued to be sacrificed. Tom Robins died at the Battle of Transloy Ridges in October 1916.

The Germans lost ground in 1917, they retreated, withdrew to the heavily defended Hindenberg Line. A key objective for the 6th Battalion was Langemark, a village taken by the Germans in 1915 and held for two years. The Shropshire Light Infantry, Oxford and Buckinghamshire Light Infantry, and the King's Royal Rifles formed up for the attack on the 15th of August. Captain Dugdale had been busy laying out white tapes to mark the assembly areas. This was not easy, working in the dark, in the pouring rain with shells bursting all around. The Battalion lay exposed in open ground from midnight until quarter to five.

At zero hour the Royal Artillery opened up and laid down a curtain of fire. Whistles blew and the boys rose up in waves. They advanced to the attack through a hail of bullets in perfect order as if on Salisbury Plain, so said the war diaries. Au Bon Gite was a block house that had resisted earlier attacks, it was taken and fifty Germans made prisoners. They pressed on crossing the Steenbeek, a narrow stream. Now the only way to progress over the sodden ground, churned and pitted by the artillery, was for the troops to move in small columns threading their way between deep pools of mud and water. The Battalion Commander, with Captain Dugdale on his heels, sank up to his waist in mud. Many of his men found themselves in a similar position.

Steenbeek – Bleak Landscape

© Imperial War Museum

Despite all the difficulties 6th KSLI took all their objectives, cleared the shattered village of Langemark and captured many more Germans. They advanced ahead of the battalions to left and right. Without protection on their flanks they were forced to withdraw. They held their ground until relieved by the Welsh Regiment. This had been a costly action. Three officers were dead, three more wounded. In the ranks 147 had been wounded and thirty-nine had been killed in action. Lance Corporal Jesse Marston and four others were 'missing'.

A fortnight later a letter arrived at Oxenbold Farm and prepared Edward and Caroline Marston for the worst. It was then confirmed that their son had been killed in action. Jesse and his gun team were moving forward to occupy one of the enemy trenches when he was shot through the head and died instantly. Lieutenant Banks had been a witness.

He was speaking to me two minutes before it occurred, and I feel very sorry to lose such a good man. He was the best man in my platoon and full of courage.

Another officer added words of praise,

A more efficient, cheerful, hard-working NCO never existed. We have lost not only a splendid soldier but one of the best fellows I ever met.

His body was never recovered, he is remembered on the Tyne Cot memorial, in his home town, and his old school.

Six months after the end of the war families of the fallen began to receive a gratuity. Usually this went to a parent or the widow. It seems that the whole of the Marston family were considered 'next of kin' because they all had a share, father mother, their five surviving sons and two daughters. They all received a little over one pound each.

Of all Edward Marston's sons Charlie was the one nearest in age to Jesse. He served as a gunner in the Royal Garrison Artillery, survived the war and returned to the family farm. They had shared interests and were much alike, unlike the Dyer boys who were as different as chalk and cheese.

Setting a Fine Example

© BES Library

Harry Dyer was born in Bridgnorth, the son of the Baptist minister, the
Reverend William Dyer. He applied himself to his studies at the Grammar
School and won the Careswell Scholarship to study mathematics at
Corpus Christi College. On graduation he taught first in Cardiff, moving
in 1912 to Giggleswick School, North Yorkshire. In addition to his
classroom duties, he had responsibility for the Officer Training Corps
attached to the school. He prepared senior boys for military service, and
watched them leave at the outbreak of war. Within a year some were on
the battlefield.

Early in 1916 Harry Dyer joined the Duke of Wellington's Regiment 'under an urgent sense of duty' and by November of that year he
was serving in France. The boys at Giggleswick School remembered 'his
delightful sense of humour' – and he seemed to have lost none of it, even
in the trenches. His Captain commented on 'quiet cheerfulness'. It was

201

this quality that kept up morale and endeared Lieutenant Dyer to his men.

The Battle of the Somme had been a costly exercise that the winter of 1916 brought to an end. In the New Year General Haig began to plan another offensive to take the high ground around Ypres. He faced opposition from Lloyd George, the British Prime Minister, General Foch the French commander, and some of his own staff. Nevertheless the Third Battle of Ypres began in July, with an artillery barrage that poured four million shells into the enemy lines. This only served to turn the battlefield into a quagmire; men drowned in shell holes filled with liquid mud, as they advanced. A key objective for these hapless troops was the village of Passchendaele, another name that would go down in history as a place of senseless slaughter.

As days passed the list of casualties grew. William Dyer was informed that his son had been seriously wounded and was receiving treatment at No 7 Stationary Hospital, near Boulogne. William and Emma took the train to the coast and crossed the Channel to be with their son.

In preparation for a raid Harry had gone out into no man's land to lay the guiding tape. Returning to the safety of his own trench he was hit by a bullet in his right arm. The bone was shattered and an artery severed. With all speed he was moved to the Base Hospital. At first it was believed that his arm could be saved, but after a fortnight it was amputated. The whole sad story was told in the Bridgnorth Journal in September 1917...

> *However, amputation became necessary and although the operation was so far successful, loss of blood and extreme weakness disabled him from throwing off the septic poison in his system and this was the cause of his death.*
>
> *His mother and father were with him at the end, having crossed over ten days before, when he was reported to be dangerously ill, and their visit was of much comfort to him.*

Another good man, a good humoured schoolmaster, who could have done so much for future generations, was dead. It was left to his brother to carry on the family tradition.

Before the war Arthur Dyer had taken up a teaching appointment at King Edward VII Grammar School, King's Lynn. Apart from his classroom duties he was also a housemaster responsible for forty boarders, this was useful experience. The men who served under him in France were little more than schoolboys. He did occasionally travel home to Bridgnorth, and met up with old friends from the cricket club. He was useful with the bat, long remembered for the record opening stand of 212 runs he made with Syd Richards.

Arthur was drafted into the 3rd (Special Reserve) Battalion of the KSLI. This pleased him.

He wrote in the School Magazine.

> *I begin my work next Monday with a course of training at the School of Instruction at Milford Haven, Pembroke Dock. I believe that the Reserve Battalion is the shortest route to active service.*

The 3rd Battalion was a training unit which fed men into front line battalions. He was obviously keen to see action. Arthur arrived in France sometime in 1915. The following year he was invalided home with trench fever.

> *While in France he was in a warm place in the line and took an active part in the Big Push of mid-July.*

Arthur's best efforts did not mean that the Battle of the Somme was a success. Once recovered from his illness he returned to France and survived the war.

Recovery, for all the nations of Europe following the Great War, was slow and painful, so many families were in mourning. Added to this there was unemployment, and industrial unrest. Men with the drive and talent to bring about a speedy recovery had been lost and this was felt in schools as much as industry.

Arthur Dyer did not have his brother's personality, he was a 'plodder'. He made his way steadily up the career ladder until he was appointed headmaster at Thame Grammar School in 1929. Standards had been falling and it was Arthur's mission to bring about change and this he did, slowly. Brother Harry had been noted for his 'quiet cheerfulness', Arthur had a 'conservative and dour approach to schooling'. He was 'not someone who injected a sense of fun into daily activities'. The brothers had different personalities, but both had a sense of duty to their country. Both had a calling – to teach, to pass on knowledge and values to the next generation.

Harry Dickinson was also dedicated to the same cause.

REV. HARRY DICKINSON, CHAPLAINS' DEPARTMENT – ATT. 28TH BTN. LONDON REG. (ARTISTS' RIFLES)

Harry Dickinson certainly looked more comfortable in an academic gown than he did Army uniform.

Academic & Soldier

© BES Library

Nevertheless, this classics master made the change from the classroom at the Grammar School to the battlefields of Flanders. He did his best to give spiritual guidance and practical comfort to men enduring hellish conditions. He was given the equivalent rank of Captain in the Army Chaplain's Department and attached to the 1/28th Battalion of the London Regiment (Artists' Rifles).

This was a prestigious regiment. Artists of the pre-Raphaelite Brotherhood had been founding members. Men such as William Holman Hunt and John Millais. In the first week of the war 5000 men applied to join, including poets and painters of the day.

The Artists' Rifles were dispatched to France almost immediately and established a training unit at Baillet. In April 1915 they moved to St Omer where more young officers were prepared for front line service. The Shropshire war poet, Wilfred Owen, and the artist Paul Nash were among those who trained with the Artists Rifles.

In many ways the duties as a chaplain were more difficult than those of a fighting man. The chaplain had to attempt to explain the underlying reasons for war. All decent values seemed to have been discarded. How could men show compassion for their enemies? Difficult philosophical questions to be considered. On a practical level Harry Dickinson had to prepare himself for the task of consoling the families of men lost in battle. He was familiar with the conduct of a funeral service, in a peaceful country churchyard in England. In France he was charged with arranging hasty burials within the range of enemy artillery.

The training role of the Artists' Rifles ended in June 1917 when they were transferred to a Royal Naval Division. There had been a surplus of naval reserves at the outbreak of war, men who could not be found a place on board any ship. There were enough of them to form two divisions. After retraining they fought as infantry and proved to be as fearless on land as they would have been at sea.

By a happy coincidence the 4th Battalion Kings Shropshire Light Infantry were assigned to the same brigade, and it would have been surprising if Harry had not taken the opportunity to meet with a few old friends. These Shropshire lads had sailed from the Far East to join the war, they arrived in tropical kit. After a brief spell of training they were billeted at Maroeuil near Arras, and for the first time heard the sound of guns in action.

Royal Fusiliers, Bedfords, Shropshires and Artists' Rifles all assigned to the Naval Division worked together on the front line during a few weeks of relative calm. Individual companies and platoons were sent into the trenches for a few days to gain first-hand experience. The Artist's Rifles attracted many men with a public school and university background who joined as Private soldiers. At the end of June sixty were commissioned as 2nd Lieutenants and transferred to other infantry regiments.

In July preparations for battle became more urgent, troops were issued with respirators to be used in the event of a gas attack. The Reverend Harry Dickinson went through the same training as the fighting men, he was on duty every day of the week, not just on Sundays. After Divine Service on July 8th half a dozen officers, including the commanding officer, went into the front line for 48 hours, two men were wounded. The following week four were wounded and a man was killed. The chaplain, Harry Dickinson, conducted a simple burial service, close to the front line.

At the end of the month Artists' Rifles and the Bedfords relieved one of the Royal Navy battalions at Railway Cutting, four were wounded and three killed – Harry had more painful duties to perform. They moved back to Aubrey Camp in August, still within range of enemy guns. Following Church Parade on the 12th eight men were wounded. Four days later when they went into the line to relieve the Nelson Battalion seven men were killed and more wounded.

There were no casualties recorded in the war diary for the first two weeks of September, although they did lose another seventy men promoted from the ranks to serve as officers. Back in action by the end of September, patrols were sent out to probe the enemy's front line almost every night. This was not without risk, one man was captured, another killed and a third wounded. The anxiety and stress that men were under was too much for some. Second Lieutenant Lightfoot was sent back from the 'Red Line' suffering from shell shock. We do not know what sort of help Harry Dickinson could offer him. Some young officers were little more than teenagers, yet they were expected to lead a platoon of men on the most dangerous of missions.

There was some respite when they retired to La Compte. New men were welcomed, their training began at once. No sooner was the Church Parade over than they went straight to the rifle range for some practice.

The conduct of war was something that ordinary soldiers could not concern themselves with, they were concerned with their own survival. They were often not sure where they were exactly. The generals consulted their maps, prodded them with their fingers and whole battalions moved. Artists' Rifles marched away from La Comte boarded a train to Cassel marched on to Dombre Camp, rested, and marched on again to Reigersberg. The place names meant nothing to men heavily-laden, tramping through mud. Irish Farm, Railway Cutting, Albatross Farm, names created by officers who had drawn up the trench maps, these were the memorable places.

The Germans had been battering the town of Ypres since the beginning of the war. The First Battle of Ypres ended in November 1914, the Second Battle of Ypres ended in May the following year. In October 1917 the Artists' Rifles, the Royal Naval Division and a hundred thousand men of the Canadian Corps were all engaged in what they called the Battle of Mud and historians called the Third Battle of Ypres.

Incessant rain and shelling from 3,000 guns had reduced the battlefield to vast cratered bog where hundreds of abandoned bodies lay unburied. The battle, begun at the end of July, had been raging for two months when the Artist's Rifles took over from the Nelson Battalion at Irish Farm on 27th of October. They went 'into the line' at Albatross Farm the following day. Headquarters was set up and a day spent preparing for the attack, checking equipment, rifle and bomb and bayonet. Harry Dickinson didn't carry arms, he moved among the men encouraging and comforting in any way he could, helping with letters home, and sometimes praying with individuals.

The company cooks worked miracles with the field kitchen producing a piping hot meal. The Quartermaster Sergeant gave orders for an extra ration of rum to be given in the early hours of the 30th of October. Whistles blew and the attack began at 5.50. They battled on for a day and a half until relieved by the sailors of Nelson Battalion.

At Irish Farm the war diary was brought up to date, there was no mention of the weather, the ground conditions, or the territory gained, and no precise figure could be given of the whereabouts of a number of casualties. The handwriting was neat and precise – 124 men were missing, 130 wounded, and seventy dead. Four officers had been wounded and six killed.

A clearer account was given by a noted war correspondent, Sir Phillip Gibbs, who witnessed the attack.

The Artists' Rifles, Bedfords and Shropshires were trying to get forward to other blockhouses on the way to the rising ground beyond the Paddebeek, a small stream that had turned into a morass. No doubt the enemy had been standing at his guns throughout the night ready to fire at the first streak of dawn. As soon as the first companies emerged from their trenches into a deep sea of mud they came under intense machine-gun fire. Rifles and machine guns became clogged and were rendered useless within minutes with the wounded drowning in mud as they fell. It was a tragic time for our men struggling in the slime.

Old Enemies Sharing a Fag

Many of those who died on the day were not laid to rest until the war was over. Over a thousand of those brought from battlefields nearby and buried in the New British Cemetery at Passchendaele were unidentified. The majority had died in the autumn of 1917.

Placed along the far wall of the cemetery are seven special memorials. One is for Alexander Hewitt who gave his occupation as lithographic poster artist. Another is for The Reverend Harry Dickinson, both of the

Artists' Rifles. They died together on the same day.

The village of Passchendaele was finally taken by the Canadians after three months of bitter fighting. During this time the battle front had moved barely five miles forward at a cost of a quarter of a million casualties. There was no breakthrough and the Germans still held the Channel ports, the bases for their U-boats that continued to inflict crippling losses on the shipping bringing in vital supplies.

Chapter 14

Brothers in Arms

The Hinkesmans were an enterprising family, farming and trading in Shropshire since the time of the Civil War, well over two hundred years. They were always willing to take a chance and travel further afield. Thomas Boycott Hinckesman went off to Africa to do some prospecting, changing his trade from corn merchant to miner. He was killed, in 1896, at Tati, during an uprising that historians later called the Second Matabele War. His son, Richard, was ten years old at the time.

Richard Boycott Hinckeman grew up, made the most of his Grammar School education, graduated from Oxford University and travelled to Canada to take up a teaching post. He returned to England at the outbreak of war, he died in France in October 1915.

Thousands of 'colonials', young adventures who had gone out to South Africa, New Zealand, Australia and Canada returned to defend the 'old country'. They proved to be some of the most daring troops to set foot on any battlefield. In October 1917 Canadians took over the ground below Passchendaele Ridge from the Anzacs (Australian and New Zealand Army Corps). The majority of these men were British born, like Richard Hinkesman and his cousins, Charles, George and John.

A very unusual event occurred at Aston Bottrell in September 1890. On the sixth day of the month Marian Hinckesman gave birth to a little boy, John – and nine days later she gave birth to a slightly bigger boy, Charles. It would have been better for all concerned if the twins had arrived on the same day. Two years later another little boy, George, appeared on his own. They were all fine boys and grew up to be fine young men.

At the Grammar School the learning was from books – all the boys were keen to learn and get on in the world. They received their practical education from their uncle at Deuxhill Farm. On the 12th of October 1907, two seventeen year olds, John and Charles Hinkesman, sailed to Canada, on board the *Corsican* to stake a claim on land at Penticton, in the wilds of British Columbia. They saw at once that this was a place where a good living could be made, and returned to England to make preparations for settlement.

This was a time of turmoil for Marion Hinckesman, she was widowed and her sons were planning a new life far away. She moved from Aston Bottrell to Severn House, Eardington.

In 1910 John and Charles returned to Canada, boarded the *Empress of Britain* at Liverpool and arrived at Saint John, New Brunswick two days before Christmas. Alongside their names on the ship's manifest a rubber stamp announced 'British Bonus Allowed'. This meant that part of the fare was paid for by the Canadian government to encourage immigration. Farmers and ranchers were particularly welcome.

Atlantic crossing was the easy part of the journey. As 'Charlie and Jack' travelled the railroad from Montreal to British Columbia, they began to understand the vastness and variety of the land: the Great Lakes, the Prairies, and the Rocky Mountains. The end of the line for these young farmers was Kamloops, there was still some way to go.

The road to Vernon on Okanagan Lake was rough, but at least there was a road. Here they boarded a paddle steamer which carried settlers to their holdings on the lake shore. Finally they arrived at Penticton. Their land, close to the American border, was particularly suited to fruit growing. Now they had a plan, the pair returned to England once again.

According to the census records of 1911 Charles was 'learning fruit farming', preparing for their new enterprise in Canada. They crossed the Atlantic yet again on board the *Empress of Ireland*. This time they were described as 'Returned Canadians'. Crossing the vast nation from the docks at Montreal they returned to Penticton. Brother George had gone ahead.

At the time the town had a population of about a thousand, but that would soon change. Penticton was ready to boom, within a year the Kettle Valley Railway carried the first passengers into the town. The Hinkesman boys had land, the climate was ideal for fruit growing, they were ready to 'make a go of it'. Then came the war.

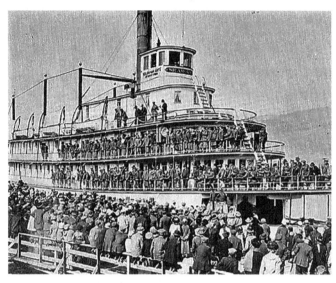

There was no shortage of volunteers. John and George took the Okanagan ferry, reported to the recruiting office in Kamloops and joined the Canadian Expeditionary Force in December 1914. Charlie was left to take care of the ranch. Within a year John was on the battlefield.

LIEUTENANT JOHN WILLIAM HINCKESMAN – 47TH CANADIAN BATTALION

John Hinckesman sailed to England with the Expeditionary Force. Completed his infantry training and served in France and Flanders from September 1915. He was singled out for promotion and commissioned the following year.

The 47th Canadian Battalion war diaries for October 1916 were carefully written: acts of heroism, details of the wounded and those killed in action, troop movements, and the weather were all neatly recorded. By contrast the diaries for October 1917 appeared 'scrappy', completed in a hurry. Certainly the whole Canadian Corps was under great pressure at the time, they were engaged in the Third Battle of Ypres. The objective was to take and hold Passchendaele, a village on the ridge above the town. The battle lasted for three months.

Persistent rain and constant bombardment, from both sides, reduced the battlefield to a vast bog of bodies and shell craters, filled with liquid mud. The ridge remained in German hands, all attempts to dislodge them

© BES Library

failed. General Douglas Haig, commanding the British Expeditionary Force, ordered in the Canadians to deliver victory. Sir Arthur Currie commander of the Canadian Corps objected, he estimated that he would lose 16,000 men, killed or wounded. He had no choice, he had to 'obey orders'.

In mid-October the Canadians arrived at the front to relieve the weary Anzacs. They set about repairing gun pits, building new roadways and bringing forward hundreds of thousands of shells. Gunfire from above on Passchendaele Ridge poured down on them as they toiled, hundreds were killed or wounded. When preparations were complete General Currie launched his attack on the 26th of October.

On the 27th Haig sent a telegram to the Canadian Corps to say, "The success gained by your troops yesterday under such conditions are deserving of the highest praise."

213

In a dugout on the front line Captain Milne wrote a note to Eva Hinkesman, John's wife in Greenock.

Kindly allow me to sympathise with you in your great loss, which came to us all with such suddenness. He was in my estimation one of the finest chaps I ever met, and the best officer this battalion has ever had, and we certainly miss him very much. Kindly accept these few words, as I can't express just how I feel.

These men were very close. More distant was Major Carmichael. He gave a more practical account of the circumstances of John's death. He might have spared the family some of the details.

He was touring the line in the course of his duty, when he was struck on the lower part of the jaw by an exploding bullet, rendering him immediately unconscious. He died two minutes afterwards. In his death the battalion has sustained a great loss... He was looked upon as a thoroughly efficient, courageous and reliable officer and the men of 'B' Company, with whom he was more familiar, felt his loss particularly...

Several men from John's Company volunteered to carry his body from the battlefield, across three miles of open country but heavy shelling by the enemy made this impossible. He was buried hastily where he fell.

The Major went on to explain the practicalities; he advised John's widow on the return of personal effects, how to contact with Estates Branch, and the Graves Registration Department, it was all impersonal, he clearly did not know John Hinckesman. How John and Eva Male met we may never know, but certainly she came from an enterprising family, her father was a building contractor from Birkenhead. When her mother was widowed she took her three daughters to Canada, in search of a new life perhaps. They sailed back to Liverpool in January 1916, later that year John and Eva were married at West Kirby. She was widowed within a year. John was finally laid to rest in Tyne Cot Cemetery.

Eva had lost her husband and Marian Hinckesman had lost her blue-eyed boy – George had hazel eyes.

CAPTAIN GEORGE FREDERICK HINCKESMAN –
2ND CANADIAN MOUNTED RIFLES

Just before the Christmas of 1914 George Hinckesman enlisted as a Trooper with the Canadian Mounted Rifles and joined other recruits at Willows Camp on Vancouver Island.

The weather there could be very unkind during the winter months. George shivered for four days in January, he was in hospital suffering with 'la grippe', a touch of 'flu.

For six months they trained for war and on the 12th of June 1915 sailed for England. The accommodation was just the same, lines of tents at Caesar's Camp near Aldershot. The Mounted Rifles were converted to infantry, George was given specialist training and transferred to the Machine Gun Section. The 2nd Battalion landed in France on the 22nd of September 1916. In December George was granted ten days leave, an opportunity to spend some time with his mother in Hadley. George re-joined his Company on the 23rd of December. There was little to celebrate at Christmas, for Marian Hinckesman, her three sons were all serving in a dangerous place.

The conduct of war changed in 1917. The Germans withdrew to the Hindenburg Line, heavily fortified and more easily defended. A key feature in their defences was Vimy Ridge, high ground that overlooked the Allied lines. An assault by the French had failed.

The Canadian Corps was ordered to seize the ridge in April. On the 9th they launched the assault over what was described as an 'open graveyard', littered with the bodies of French infantrymen. Fifteen thousand Canadians were involved in the attack, well over three thousand died. The battle ended after five days of bitter fighting – a triumph for the Canadians.

Sergeant George Hinckesman was out of action. He was admitted to No 7 Canadian General Hospital at Etaples on the 2nd of April and then transferred to Cayeux. His treatment lasted for a month.

While his comrades were dying on Vimy Ridge, he was suffering from PUO, Pyrexia of Unknown Origin. This was a common complaint, severe headache, high temperature, and fever – Trench Fever. At the time the 'origin was unknown', the culprit was eventually identified – it was body lice that carried the bacteria that put a million men out of action. One of the after effects was depression. George may well have suffered with depression, with a feeling of guilt that he has let his comrades down on Vimy Ridge.

There was still plenty of fighting to be done and young leaders would be needed. George was sent to England for commissioning, at Seaford camp on the Sussex Downs. Sergeant Hinckesman returned to France as a Lieutenant.

In a desperate effort to win the war the Germans launched their Spring Offensive in 1918, the Allies were pushed back but they held their ground, gathered their strength and went on the offensive. In August the Canadians retook the village of Bouchoir, held by the Germans since March. The 2nd Canadian Mounted Rifles lost over a hundred men, half of them on the 10th of August. George lost a friend, a fellow officer, Balfour Palmer – they had attended a Lewis Gun course together a month earlier.

The regiment came out of the line for a well-earned rest, they could relax a little. German troops were surrendering in droves; it was clear that victory was in sight.

Anyone wounded at this stage of the war did not expect to go back into action. George was admitted to the Stationary Hospital at

Wimereux on the 17th of September. An X-ray revealed that his ankle was broken. This was not the result of enemy action on the battlefield, George had been stretchered off the football field. From Wimereux he was shipped home.

After treatment at Whitley he ended the war at a convalescent hospital for Canadian officers at Matlock Bath in Derbyshire. He spent almost a year at the regimental depot in England before sailing back to Canada and return to farming at Penticton with his brother, Charles.

Lieutenant Charles Henry Hinckesman – 72nd Battalion, Seaforth Highlanders of Canada

George and Jack had volunteered to join the Expeditionary Force before the Christmas of 1914. Charlie was already in uniform, a part-time soldier with the 102nd Regiment, (The Rocky Mountain Rangers). He waited, saw out the Spring and Summer at Penticton – he could wait no longer. In November 1915 he took the steamer north and at the recruiting centre at Kamloops he transferred to the 72nd Battalion, Seaforth Highlanders of Canada.

It was almost a year before the battalion sailed to Europe. The *Mauretania* left Canadian shores on the 25th of October 1916, and arrived in England six days later. Sergeant Hinkesman and his Company continued their training at Bramshott Camp, in Hampshire. When leave was granted the Hinckesman boys could visit their mother who had moved on again from Severn House Erdington to Hadley Village near Worcester.

John was dead, George had been in France for nearly two years and then in February 1917 Charles was on his way to the battlefront – these were anxious times for Marian Hinckesman.

Charles arrived at Le Havre with a new draft of the 72nd Battalion. He had to earn his stripes. Sergeant Hinckesman was reduced to the ranks, but in no time he was promoted once again and ended the war as a Lieutenant.

The brothers were typical of a generation of men with a pioneering spirit who were prepared to lay down their farming tools and take up arms in the defence of freedom. They deserved some reward. Charles had shown an interest in 'fruit farming'. He returned to Penticton to do just that and died there when he was ninety-one, a contented man no doubt.

George on the other hand had inherited the Hinckesman's restless spirit. He survived the war unscathed – apart from a sport's injury. He did return to the farm at Penticton but could not settle, he crossed the Atlantic Ocean and the American border a number of times. In 1935 George, with his wife Violet, sailed on the *California Express* from Vancouver to San Pero, Los Angeles. They settled in California, a state noted for fruit growing – maybe that was why he finally settled there.

Captain George Hinckesman died at Cambia, in 1972, he was nearly eighty.

Hinckesman is not a common name and neither is Skelcher, only thirty appear to have served in the Great War and three of them came from Badger.

PRIVATE (87262) FREDERICK JAMES SKELCHER – ARMY SERVICE CORPS & MACHINE GUN CORPS

How a man of modest means could afford to send any of his boys to the Grammar School is something we will never know. Perhaps a generous employer paid the fees. Charlie Skelcher was a gamekeeper and at least one of his three sons also had the same love of woodland and wildlife. All of them had learned to handle a shotgun. This may explain why Fred was drafted into the Machine Gun Corps and Robert and Walter were gunners in the Royal Artillery. The first to take up arms in the Great War was Frederick James Skelcher.

Fred was certainly well prepared. He had already served for four years with the 2nd Volunteer Battalion Light Infantry so he knew something of the risks involved with soldiering. He was a technician, he had trained as an electrical fitter and was working for a company with premises in the centre of Oxford. The recruiting office was nearby and for a year he watched young men pass by to sign on for 'the duration of the war'.

A fortnight before the Christmas of 1915, Fred went into the same office and pledged to serve King and Country. Twenty-three year old Fred Skelcher had a lot to lose, a family and a secure living. He married Francis Turner in 1910, the following year Bessie was born and two years later a son, named Frederick James, after his father.

Initially he was drafted into the Army Service Corps and billeted at

Osterley Park, before being transferred to a reserve battalion at Isleworth. His skill as a fitter and his knowledge of firearms must have been noted. In March 1917 he completed training at Belton Park near Grantham, and joined 143 Company of the Machine Gun Corps in France in August of the same year.

The Germans were making a tactical retreat to the more secure positions on the Hindenberg Line. Fred's Company was in pursuit. They failed to dislodge the Germans who held the town of Peronne until the Australians drove them out in September 1918.

Earlier Private Skelcher was treated to a change of scenery, the Company 'entrained' for Italy in November 1917 and combined with other companies to form the 48th Machine Gun Brigade, a formidable force.

A single machine gun had the equivalent firepower of at least sixty riflemen, probably nearer eighty. In a fixed position the Vickers machine gun was most effective, but it was heavy, difficult to handle requiring a six to eight-man team of men to operate it effectively. The Lewis gun was lighter, could be carried by one man and advance with the infantry, this became the preferred weapon of the Machine Gun Corps.

Take That

© Imperial War Museum

Fred Skelcher preferred to have an electrician's screwdriver and pair of pliers in his hands, and if he wanted to fire at anything, a rabbit maybe, he preferred to use a twelve bore shotgun.

The war ended, he got his wish and returned safely to his wife and family at New Botley near Oxford.

Younger brother Robert, spent longer in uniform; he too was also declared 'fit' when he was finally discharged from the army in May 1919.

LANCE BOMBADIER ROBERT SKELCHER – 21ST HOWITZER BATTERY, RFA

Robert was a territorial soldier, within a month of the outbreak of war he joined his comrades at Shendish Farm in Hertfordshire, where the 21st Howitzer Battery, Royal Field Artillery began preparations for service in France. For 'live firing' they went to the ranges on Salisbury Plain, 'There is one thing about the Howitzers, you can't help seeing the big shell bursts.'

Bob and his Battery landed at Le Havre in March 1915, over the next three years they must have lost count of the number of shells they fired over no-mans'-land. These were mighty machines, Howitzers had a range of well over five miles.

Robert seems to have managed to stay 'well out of harm's way'. After a year in France he was granted a week's local leave. He then benefited from a reorganisation within the brigade. The command pay-master recognised his ability with figures and he was transferred out of the firing line to the Ordnance Workshop.

He was granted two spells of local leave, but did not come home until October 1918 returning to France three days before the Armistice. The process of demobilisation was slow, it was four months before the Skelcher family was reunited, even then it was not complete.

LANCE CORPORAL (155179) WALTER SAMPSON SKELCHER –
ROYAL FIELD ARTILLERY

When the time came for Walter Skelcher to join he, like brother Bob, also joined the Royal Artillery. He was just nineteen when preparations were being made for the Third Battle of Ypres. His battery was set up to support the infantry manning the trenches opposite St Julien. British troops had held this village in 1915 but were driven out by the Germans.

Poison gas was used here for the first time in the war.

In the last week of July 1917 the artillery poured thousands of shells down on the German trenches, and enemy gunners replied with almost equal numbers. There were casualties even before the battle began. The barrage served only to churn up the battlefield and create a sea of mud.

Both sides had detailed maps of each other's defences. To practise for the forthcoming battle some battalions dug trenches identical to those opposite that they were preparing to assault.

In the early morning of the 31st of July anxious men were offered porridge and hot tea laced with rum. Many had lost their appetite for porridge and war. The guns were silent for a while, Walter Skelcher carried forward more shells, closer to the guns ready to give cover to the advancing troops. German gunners opposite continued to shell the British front line and the Royal Artillery batteries to the rear.

So began the Battle of Pilkem Ridge the first of a series of battles that together made up the Third Battle of Ypres. The Battle of Lanagemark raged for two days in mid-August. More good men died for little gain. There was no rest for the survivors, including Walter Skelcher. In mid-September the Battle of the Menin Road began, in the first week of October Polygon Wood was attacked. The Allies advanced, pressing on towards Passchendaele.

The first attempt to take the village on Passchendaele Ridge began on the 12th of October. The same tactics were used once again. The battle began with a heavy bombardment to soften up the enemy and destroy their defences, it had little effect. The infantry advanced, threading their way around shell craters filled with mud. German machine gunners emerged from their trenches and cut them down. Artillery batteries at the rear were targeted by enemy gunners, no one was safe. Lance Corporal Walter Skelcher's luck ran out, he was badly wounded.

An overwhelming number of casualties were being evacuated to the dressing stations. Despite the best efforts of doctors and their orderlies, many of the wounded did not survive. A cemetery was established near the St Julien Dressing Station, this was where Walter Skelcher was laid to rest. He died of his wounds on the 18th of October.

Spring came to Badger Dingle and Charlie Skelcher, stepped out to patrol his beat.

With permission from Vicki Norman

It was the season of rebirth, fresh green leaves began to appear; bluebells and primroses added more colour, and the bracken revived. The woodland was busy with nest-building birds. Charlie was there to help hen pheasants feed and protect their chicks. The stoat and buzzard were his enemy.

Did he ever think when he set his sights on a living thing and pulled the trigger that this was the way it was in war? That this was the way his son and thousands more had met their end.

Skelchers and Hinkesmans sent six sons to war and two were lost.

The Gadsby boys were the lucky ones, all three returned unharmed.

The sign above Ryder's shop on Waterloo Terrace announced to the public that this was the 'Friendly House'. From the doorway Amos Ryder could survey the High Street and watch customers visiting several of the most important businesses in the town. On the right was Beaman's the butchers and The Swan Hotel. On the left were the premises of Burton's the grocers and Whitefoot's, wine merchants. Steward's 'Medical Hall' was conveniently close to Doctor Thursfield's surgery and then there was Gadsby's.

Amos Ryder and his sons liked to keep an eye on the Gadsbys and the price and quality of the goods they were offering the public. Shirts, trousers, straw boaters, and bolts of cloth hanging outside the door of Ryder's 'Friendly House' all carried a clear price tag. These two families were rivals in business but when the war came there was much common ground. Stewards, the pharmacists, were not competitors, the only cloth they handled were rolls of cotton bandages.

In February 1916 there was good news and bad news, mostly bad. The good news was that Frank Gadsby had been given another 'pip' to sew on his sleeve, he was promoted from 2nd Lieutenant to Lieutenant.

The bad news, given to the Ryder family, was that Alf had received severe gunshot wounds to his left hand and was recovering at No 22 General hospital at Wimereux. His stay was short, he was soon back with the 5th Battalion KSLI with severe scars to his left hand. He pulled the trigger with his right hand so the Army reasoned he must be fit to fight.

Amos and Sidney Ryder still kept an eye on the rival business across the street. Harry Gadsby was on his own now, all three of his sons had gone to war. Two of the Steward boys were in uniform, which left only George to help his father in the pharmacy.

LIEUTENANT HORACE SPENCER GADSBY – WELSH REGIMENT

Horace Spenser Gadsby was well prepared for the conflict. He was a Corporal in the Territorial Reserve and transferred to the 14th Royal Warwickshire Regiment when war began. Known as the '1st Birmingham' they were formed by the Lord Mayor in September 1914. Within a year Corporal (14/654) Gadsby was sailing from Southampton to Boulogne to get a taste of battle. During 1916 the 14th Battalion were in action at High Woods, Guillemont, Morval and Le Transloy. Horace Gadsby must have done well because he was selected for officer training and joined the Worcestershire Regiment as a 2nd Lieutenant early in 1917.

The Third Battle of Ypres, was in reality a series of battles between July and October 1917. The guns hardly fell silent, troops were in constant danger. It was a costly affair for the British Expeditionary Force, over 300,000 casualties, one of them was Horace Gadsby. He was wounded by a gas shell on the 12th of September. A lucky man, on home leave, recovering from his wounds, he married an exotic lady from Philadelphia, Dorothy Viola Venus Danby. They could celebrate Christmas together.

The Battle of Ypres had ended in October while Horace was safely home in Kidderminster. The fighting was fiercest at Polygon Wood. Over a thousand British troops died there. Horace recovered and ended the war with the Welsh Regiment. A draper's assistant no more he moved to Great Yarmouth and then on to South Glamorgan where he died peacefully in 1956.

2ND LIEUTENANT WALTER NEWMAN GADSBY – WORCESTERSHIRE REGIMENT

The youngest of the Gadsby boys was nineteen at the outbreak of war, like many local lads he had been 'playing soldiers' with the Yeomanry. They were called up immediately and very soon they who be asked to dismount and fight as infantry.

A Company that kept their mounts was sent to join the Egyptian Expeditionary Force and Walter Gadsby was one the lucky ones. In March 1916 he sailed from Southampton to Alexandria on board

Arcadian. The Turks had made an early attempt to take the Suez Canal, they were repulsed and now British and Anzac forces were ready to push them back into Palestine.

To keep the horses well fed and watered and comfortably stabled in this hot and dusty land proved to be extremely difficult and it soon became clear that many of the mounted regiments would have to be dismounted. The Yeomanry were recalled from Shekira to a camp near Cairo and amalgamated with the Cheshire Yeomanry to form the 10th King's Shropshire Light Infantry.

When the reorganisation was compete they returned to Kantara in April 1917 to prepare for the Second Battle of Gaza. The attack on the 15th was only partially successful; mercifully only two men were killed, Captain Jones was wounded. The 10th Battalion dug in and stayed on Mansura Ridge for a month.

The Khamsin, a hot wind laden with fine particles of sand, made life uncomfortable. Added to this there was an uncountable number of flies, a shortage of water and a lack of fresh vegetables which resulted in an outbreak of septic sores. This made the time spent on Mansura Ridge memorable. The Turks, dug in less than two miles away, showed little enthusiasm for war. They sent over just a few shells; battalions to left and right suffered casualties but not the Shropshires.

In July they marched away to 'Regent's Park' on the shores of the Mediterranean, five miles from Gaza. General Allenby took command of the Egyptian Expeditionary Force which was unfortunate for Corporal Gadsby and boys enjoying rest and recuperation at Regent's Park. Allenby decided that instead of a rest period they would have 'strenuous training of every description'. However, exercise sea air, better food, and saltwater bathing worked wonders on the health of the troops. In August they marched ten miles inland over sand dunes, 'somewhat trying'. It was worth it, they camped in a fig grove.

Training continued day and night. It soon became clear that General Allenby was planning to 'put on a show'. The next move was to Khan Yunus, a camp known as the 'Dust Bin', which described it well. After a brief period of misery they were back in Regent's Park. Parties of men went up to the front line to strengthen the defences and a group of officers were sent to survey the terrain that the battalion were to advance over on the way to Beersheba.

The 10th KSLI were on the move on October 30th, Beersheba fell on the 1st of November. A new front line was established. The battle was not only against the Turks. Everyone suffered in the intense heat and there was little water to quench the thirst. The battalion held one outpost through a sandstorm for 24 hours without food or water before they were relieved.

They marched on to capture Gaza and then set off on the road to Jerusalem. General Allenby led 229 Brigade to the gates of the Holy City and drove out the Turks before Christmas. Walter Gadsby and his platoon spent the festive season three thousand feet above sea level in and around a grubby little outpost called Beit Izza. The weather here was atrocious, torrential rain and bitterly cold. Back in the desert Walter would have given anything for a glass of cool water now he dreamed of hot punch by a blazing fire. To continue the advance to Jericho road-making had to be done. The 10th Battalion were allocated a stretch they called Offa's Dyke. Corporal Gadsby left them to it, he was on his way home to train as an officer. He was commissioned in the Worcestershire Regiment in May 1918, he ended the war in Europe, transferred to Royal Flying Corps and returned to civilian life in 1920.

The Gadsby boys had all survived after service in deserts and mountains and mud. The war had turned boys into men, they were not childish schoolboys anymore. Walter recalled the way 'clowns' performed in the school yard. The same old joke was repeated and Walter must have grown tired of hearing it.

"Tell us again Gadsby, what's y'r big brother do for a livin'? I heard he travels in ladies underwear."

Walter would shake his head too disgusted to make any reply, although there was some truth in it. Frank was a commercial traveller, 'embroidery and trimmings' were his speciality. Some of the trimmings may well have been for ladies underwear. By the end of the war Frank was a Captain, he had fought in France and Italy and been decorated for bravery. There was no more mention of travelling in ladies' underwear.

CAPTAIN FRANCIS LEONARD GADSBY, C D G –
1/7TH WORCESTERSHIRE REGIMENT

A Territorial Battalion of the Royal Worcestershire Regiment assembled in Kidderminster in the month the war began. Frank Gadsby was living at

26 Chester Road at the time and joined immediately. The Battalion were in France within a year. Frank stayed at the depot at Maldon in Essex. He completed training as an officer in 1915 and joined the regiment in France in the following year.

The 'Worcesters' played their part in France and Belgium in battle against German forces, the line was held. In the mountainous border country between Austria and Italy the enemy threatened to break through. Italy had entered the war in May 1915. She was ill prepared and poorly led. Nevertheless they held back the Austrians until 1917 when Germany sent extra troops to back up their allies. A joint force drove back the Italian armies across the Asiago Plateau and Venice was threatened. The enemy advance was checked at the Piave River.

The decision was made to send five Divisions of the British Army, serving in France, to the Italian front. This included the 1/7th Worcestershire Regiment and Captain Frank Gadsby who was now acting as Battalion adjutant.

The train journey was long and slow. At Tincques near the battle front at Arras trains pulled out of the sidings and steamed south. Officers had a relatively comfortable ride, the 'men' were in cattle trucks. It was November but they were going south and by the time they reached the Mediterranean coast they were beginning to enjoy the ride. Frequent stops were made along the way. At Ventimigla 'A' and 'C' Companies stretched their legs and marched through the town 'amid cheers and showers of flowers'. At Bologna 'the troops made merry with the populace on the platform'; the regimental diary did not go into detail.

By December General Plummer had assembled sixty battalions along the battle front. Christmas was celebrated quietly by both sides, there was little actual fighting. The Worcesters kept up their fitness with sporting events and route marches through the pleasant Italian countryside, trying out the local food and picking up useful bits of the language.

The front froze, literally, and there was little activity until February 1918. The war was not over yet but when spring arrived spirits were lifted.

There was no comparison between the muddy, waterlogged trenches of the Somme the gun pits carved into the mountain sides of the Dolomites. In the Eugenean Hills near Padua Frank's battalion were given some training in mountain warfare and took up a position behind the Montello. Worcestershire troops compared it with Bredon Hill. Shells could be seen bursting along its summit. Austrian and German forces has pushed the Italians back onto the Asiago Plain they were held on the banks of the Piave It was astonishing that war-weary troops of every nation could still show any enthusiasm for battle, they must have hoped that the next battle would be the last.

The Worcesters and the Gloucesters were on the move again. Marching through the city of Vicenza. 'Flowers rained down on us, from balconies above beautiful ladies threw down roses as fair as themselves'. They marched on, onward and upward. It was spring, it didn't feel like it as they trudged 4,000 feet up the slopes of Granezza through driving sleet. By the time they reached the summit the blizzard was passed and the full moon was shining brilliantly, flooding with white light the snow covered trees. It was a land like no other they had seen. Captain Gadsby led his Company forward into the trenches, good trenches cut or blasted out of solid rock. They held the position for two months, then moved back down onto the plain.

The artillery had set up a huge 'dump' of shells ready to take on the enemy. The combined force of German and Austrian troops struck first. The 7th Worcesters were roused in the early hours of the 15th of June by a great explosion, the dump was hit. The front line collapsed Warwickshire and Gloucestershire infantrymen were overwhelmed. Men of Worcestershire were sent forward to counter attack. They had battled in France over mud ploughed up by shell fire the only shelter isolated tree stumps.

They advanced in the early hours into dense forest without artillery support, fighting at close quarters with rifle and machine-gun. In the gloom it was hard tell which side had the upper hand. The battle continued all day long. Men died, Captain Prescott of 'A' Company was wounded and so were all his Lieutenants. By the end of the day ninety men of the battalion were casualties. There were three hundred Austrian casualties.

Lieutenant Gilbert Holiday, a well-known war artist captured the scene of The Battle in the Woods, Captain Frank Gadsby's last battle. Medals were awarded for acts of bravery during the battle. The Italians awarded Frank their 'Croc di Guerra', the Cross of War.

Frank came home to be reunited with the family and carry on as a commercial traveller 'specialising in embroidery and trimming', revisiting his old customers.

Service in France and Italy must have broadened his horizons because after two years he took ship to Canada, sailing on the Melita to New Brunswick. He was described on the passenger list as a 'tourist' and allowed to stay for three months. He must have made some useful contact because two years later he was back again, the passage paid for by his employer and with a hundred pounds in his pocket (a considerable sum in those days). On his return he married. His wife, Muriel must have been an understanding woman because within a year he was off again on another business trip this time to America. He travelled on from New York and crossed the border into Canada to visit customers in Montreal. It was now time to settle down, he was forty-one. Frank made one last trip across the Atlantic on the Empress of Australia from Southampton to Quebec and back to Muriel waiting at 'Belle Vue' in Chaddesley Road Kidderminster.

Chapter 15

Talent Wasted

The winter months of The War should have been quiet months, conditions on the battlefields of France and Flanders were impossible. In November 1914, following the First Battle of Ypres, both sides dug in, protected their trenches with barbed wire and machine guns and created No Man's Land. Two years later the great Battle of the Somme ended on the 18th of November. Yet men still died at sea and in other lands. Coastal towns in England were attacked with bombs and shells from air and sea – women and children died. It wasn't a one-sided affair, German troops were dying daily, their grieving families going hungry.

Painfully aware that the fresh American forces were building up and preparing for battle, the Germans made a tactical withdrawal to the Hindenberg Line, well-fortified and more easily defended. At least one Old Bridgnorthian, Tom Wilson, was among the forces snapping at their heals as they retreated.

2ND LIEUTENANT THOMAS WILSON – KING'S SHROPSHIRE LIGHT INFANTRY & TANK CORPS

New House was a fine three-storey house, a prosperous farm in the parish of Sutton Maddock. The Wilsons employed labourers in the fields, servants in the house, a cook, and a nurse to look after the children. From the nursery window little Tommy looked out over a patchwork of fields and paddocks – cattle grazed, shire horses, freed of their harness after a day's work, kicked the air and galloped free. In the distance, beyond the green fields was Windy Hill. This was the scene of a happy childhood.

With permission from Roger and Anabel Baylis

Adam Wilson wanted the best for his boys. Thomas began his schooling at the Grammar School in Bridgnorth. To complete his education he went to Trent College. In 1911 he was boarding with twenty-five other 'scholars' at Long Eaton.

Tom Wilson didn't have time to consider a career. He was eighteen at the outbreak of war and, along with other keen young men, made his way to Shrewsbury. Tom Nevett from a neighbouring farm joined with him. The 5th (Service) Battalion of the King's Shropshire Light Infantry was formed in August 1914. For training they moved to Aldershot and on to Chiddingfold in March 1915, and back to Aldershot, briefly, before they sailed for France. On the 20th of May they landed at Boulogne, ten days later they came under fire at Ypres.

For a year Private (130560) Thomas Reginald Wilson was in and out of the front line. The Battalion saw some of the worst fighting of the war in the Ypres Salient in 1915, around Bellewaerde and Hooge. The following year there was more heavy fighting on the Somme at Delville Wood and Flers- Courcelette.

The Battle of Flers-Courcelette was the first battle in which tanks were used in warfare. Forty-nine Mark 1 tanks took part. The terrain was rugged and the crews not fully trained. General Douglas Haig was warned against the early use of the tanks. Many broke down. A second attack failed, harsh weather and huge casualties brought the battle to an end.

First Lord of the Admiralty, Winston Churchill, remarked,

"My poor 'land battleships' have been let off prematurely and on a petty scale."

With improved design, better training and tactics, army commanders recognised the potential in this new weapon of war. Tom Wilson may have spotted it too.

Tom began his soldiering as a Private, but he was soon singled out for promotion. He had an excellent school and college record, he was a fine athlete, he had proved himself on the battlefield, he was the ideal candidate for a commission.

Second Lieutenant Wilson celebrated Christmas at home, wearing a smart new uniform. He was a new breed of soldier, a tank commander, taking a new weapon of war into battle. The view from New House Farm was little changed. Tom's view may have changed, perhaps he imagined how he might manoeuvre across the lanes and ditches, avoiding the pool and wet ground to climb the slope of Windy Hill.

At Elveden Camp tank crews trained with their 'land battleships'. There were male and female versions, the male had heavier armaments. Both were difficult customers to manoeuvre. A Daimler engine drove the tracks through three gearboxes, three drivers were needed. The tank commander was a junior officer, the rest of the crew were gunners, usually four in number. Conditions inside were appalling, they worked in an atmosphere of heat, noise and exhaust fumes.

The Tank Corps had been formed from the Heavy Section Machine Gun Corps and rapidly expanded; A, B, C and D Companies became Battalions. Finally an 'E' Company was formed intended for service in Palestine.

2nd Lieutenant Wilson was assigned to 'E' Battalion and took command of 'Exquisite'. All the tanks in the battalion were given names beginning with an 'E'. Had the battalion gone to Palestine Tom may have been reunited with his brother Cyril who was serving there with the Machine Gun Corps; instead Tom went back to France and the battle-front near Arras.

Cold, wet weather in April 1917 meant poor conditions for the tanks. They broke down and were bogged down, unable to play their part in the battle plan. Without their support Australian infantry suffered heavy casualties at Bullecourt. The reputation of the Tank Corps was severely damaged and did not recover for some time.

Mark IV tanks appeared in the summer and were deployed in the Third Battle of Ypres. Again they attempted to slog through deep mud; they sank in trenches and shell holes and were battered by artillery. The infantry had no confidence in the tanks; they gave no protection because they attracted enemy fire. Tank Corps morale was low; they needed, fair weather and firm ground to show what they could do.

Cambrai was where the Tank Corps made military history, where they proved their worth on the battlefield. An 'all arms' operation was planned – the Flying Corps, artillery, infantry and tanks would all have a part to play.

To position three hundred tanks on the front line without alerting the enemy proved difficult, it was done under cover of darkness. The Flying Corps flew numerous sorties to keep the skies clear of German spotter planes that might give the game away. Tanks and infantry had not worked well together in earlier battles; new methods were tried out in training. Instead of advancing 'in line' foot soldiers were going to 'worm' their way forward protected by the trundling tank. Large scale attacks had been heralded by massive artillery barrages, the enemy knew what was coming. This time the Allied guns stayed silent until the day of the battle.

On the 17th of November 1917 the artillery moved into position. The next day the tanks assembled and were concealed in Havrincourt Wood, in the evening the infantry arrived nearby at Metz. Highlanders preparing to fight alongside Tom Wilson's 'E' Battalion took over the front line trenches. The last task of the men they relieved had been to build causeways across their trenches for the tanks to cross into 'no man's land' the next day.

In the early hours of the 20th of November the tanks took up position on a taped white line. Hot meals were provided for all.

As dawn broke on this misty November morning Tom Wilson and other youthful tank commanders surveyed the battle front. They had seen maps and models that showed the complex trench system built by the Germans. Through 'field glasses' they examined the pill boxes and gun emplacements they were about to attack. The village of Flesquieres stood out on a ridge to the north east. It had been fortified and formed part of the third line of defence for the Germans. To get there the tank crew could expect a bumpy ride. The 'going was firm' over the chalky fields, they were ready for 'the off'.

Lieutenant Wilson patted the side of 'Exquisite' and climbed in. He examined his watch, looked back at a young Corporal and nodded. The engine roared into life, the 'ship' shuddered, thin blue smoke drifted around the feet of the gunners, the tracks were engaged and they moved over the white tape and into battle.

Shortly after six in the morning the Germans on the Hindenburg Line were woken by a thousand guns of the Royal Field Artillery. A hundred aircraft appeared in the sky, some flying so low they could call to the Highlanders waiting in the trenches for the whistle to blow.

The first wave of twelve tanks, the 'Rovers', ploughed through the tangle of wire in 'no man-land'. The German defenders opened up with machine guns and hurled stick grenades in the path of the tanks bearing down on their trench. The Rovers turned aside and returned fire, a manoeuvre they had practised many times. The second wave of tanks arrived with bundles of timber on top, this was rolled into the trench ahead of them and they crossed over. The kilted Highlanders, shielded by the tanks, set about clearing the trench. They had a fearsome reputation; the Germans called them 'the ladies from hell'.

Surprise and a little fog helped. Smoke screens and a rolling barrage of shells sent the enemy reeling back ahead of the Tank Corps and advancing infantry. However, in the centre, 'E 'Battalion was held up. The battalion war diary described the event.

All went exceedingly well until the tanks appeared over the crest of a hill east of Flesquieres. As they came over the ridge they presented a fine target to the enemy and were knocked out one after the other by a gallant German officer who stuck to a field gun until he was killed by advancing infantry.

The village was taken by the Scots before nightfall. The Tank Corps had shown that they could play a decisive part on the battlefield. General Haig and his staff rejoiced. The enemy had been pushed back further this day than in any previous battle on the Western Front. Celebrations were short lived and this small victory came at a cost. Casualty figures were not precise. On the Allied side at least twenty thousand were wounded and around eight thousand died on the day, a similar number were made prisoner or were listed as missing.

A Bleak Prospect

© Imperial War Museum

Thirty-five tanks of 'E' Battalion had taken to the field on the morning of the 20th of November, by the afternoon eighteen had been destroyed by enemy action. Twenty-nine men had been killed, sixty-four wounded and thirty-one could not be accounted for.

An article in the Bridgnorth Journal reported that Tom Wilson was missing, implying that there was still the possibility that he would be found. There was also a report on the progress of Archie Brown, another Old Boy, from Highley.

PRIVATE (59163) DAVID ARCHIBALD BROWN –
6TH BATTALION CHESHIRE REGIMENT

Archie enlisted in November 1916, he had spent less than a year in France. Most of the time he did not bear arms, he was selected to act as a stretcher bearer. These were men who went unprotected onto the battlefield to recover fallen comrades. Injury and death were part of the job, and Archie was one who had already been wounded.

He was wounded a second time on the 28th of October, 1917, 'a bullet passing through his head'. This was incredible. 'He became quite blind at the time, but it is satisfactory to know there is hope that the sight will return to one eye.'

Archie Brown was treated at the Princess Club Hospital in Jamaica Road, Bermondsey. He never fully recovered and was discharged six months after the end of The War, his reward, a Silver War Badge, some called it 'the wound badge'. Archie's wound must have been obvious, there was no need for a silver badge.

The mood at New House Farm was gloomy, it wasn't just the weather in late November, although that was bad enough. Adam Wilson and his wife Kate had been informed that their son was among the 'missing'. There was still hope that he would be found, or that 2nd Lieutenant Thomas Reginald Wilson would appear on a list of prisoners.

When Tom's commanding officer wrote to Adam Wilson he got straight to the point,

> *Your son was a very gallant boy and he died doing a magnificent thing.*

He went on to describe the action that cost Thomas Wilson his life and concluded,

> *Your boy's name will be put forward for a posthumous VC. I shall do all in my power to add weight to any such recommendation.*

Leading the attack on Flesquieres Ridge, 'Exquisite' was knocked out by a German Howitzer. Tom and those members of his crew who were not wounded scrambled out. Bearing 'small arms' he led them forward to attack the enemy at close quarters. He was cut down before he reached their lines. Captain Richard Wain of 'A' Battalion also died on the 20th of November 1917. He was awarded a posthumous VC for a similar act of gallantry.

That he had 'died well' was small comfort to a family who had lost a lad with a promising life before him. His body was carried from the field of battle and buried nearby at Ribecourt. The cemetery was close to the front line and was shelled later on in the war, Thomas's grave and eighty others were destroyed. These men are now commemorated on special memorials within the cemetery.

Medals were struck for all. Four years after the end of the war a packet was delivered to New House Farm. It contained the '15 Star, War Medal and Victory Medal. The family had moved away, to leave the land for others to farm. Had Tom survived the war it would have been very different. On wet days when it was not fit to work the land he might have stood at the nursery window, rain running down the glass blurring the view, and recalled the battlefields of his youth and the Tank Corps motto, Thorough Mud and Blood to the Green Fields Beyond.

Windy Hill

© Graham Jones

Tom Wilson never reached the green fields that lay around Windy Hill and the parish church of St Mary's at Sutton Maddock. He is remembered within on an indestructible plaque.

© Graham Jones

The moto of the Yorkshire Regiment was 'fortune favours the brave'. True for some but not for Douglas Spurway.

CAPTAIN DOUGLAS SPURWAY MC – ALEXANDRA, PRINCESS OF WALES, OWN YORKSHIRE REGIMENT

Douglas was a boarder at BGS for six years. He was, by all accounts, a very popular boy, described in the School Magazine as ' the best type of schoolboy, distinguished in work and play, bringing honour to The School by his scholarship and winning laurels for her in sport'.

Sharing the dormitory at School House were other boys with the right talents to make a mark in the world, often choosing the same profession as their fathers. Victor Dayus came from a generation of veterinary surgeons, and Rudolph Dawes, the headmaster's son, himself became a grammar school headmaster. John Spurway practised medicine and Douglas planned to do the same.

Douglas was only fifteen when he passed entrance examinations to Birmingham and London University and won a scholarship to study medicine at Saint Bartholomew's Hospital. Any spare time from his studies was spent with the Officer Training Corps. He did not complete his studies, the call of duty was too strong. In 1915 he was commissioned in the 4th Battalion Yorkshire Regiment, the following year he was serving in France and

© BES Library

swiftly promoted to Captain. He was mentioned in one of General Haig's dispatches and awarded the Military Cross. He was also mentioned in the School Magazine, 'Douglas is in the thick of it and obviously enjoying himself'.

His cheerful character made him a very popular man, respected by the bluff Yorkshiremen of his Company and a great favourite with his brother officers. A sprinter at school, a dashing soldier in battle.

The Spurways were living in Kilburn, North London but when Douglas had home leave but he always came back to the town to meet old friends.

Before returning to France in 1918 for the last time he joined other Old Boys on the football field in a charity match against a Town team to raise funds for KSLI Prisoners of War, some he must have known.

Desperate for victory, the Germans planned the 'Spring Offensive' on the Somme, in what would be the final year of the war. They had some initial success. The Yorkshire Regiment was in retreat, they were holding a position near Hancourt on the 23rd of March.

"The Battalion fought a rear-guard action all the way back until

239

they reached high ground near Le Mesnil-Bruntel. Here Captain Spurway was ordered to hold the German advance while other battalions got over the river Somme. Major Brown and Captain Spurway led their men into battle. Fortune did not favour the brave, cut down by rifle and machine-gun bullets seventeen men and both officers died.

In North London, Doctor John Spurway and his American-born wife, Mary, received the news of the death of their eldest son.

One of Douglas Spurway's fellow officer wrote to say, "He died heroically, leading the men he loved".

His body was never recovered, his sacrifice is remembered on the Pozieres Memorial, Panel 31, under an arch at 'Bart's' Hospital, and in the school he referred to as his 'Alma Mater'.

Three years his junior, Cedric Spurway had been awarded a scholarship to study at Oxford University instead he went to the Royal Military Academy and in June 1918 he was commissioned in the Royal Engineers. These were anxious times for the Spurways and the nation. The war was not yet over, more good men would die.

CAPTAIN HAROLD WALTER GIBBS – 158 BATTERY ROYAL FIELD ARTILLERY

Bank Clerk and Gunner

Harold's father was the colliery manager at Billingsley. The Powell Duffryn Company, in reality a collection of rogues, took over the mine in 1908 and then sold it to The Highley Mining Company in 1915. This was not the sort of industry that Frederick Gibbs could recommend to his son.

On leaving school Harold chose a truly white-collar job, a clerk with Lloyd's Bank at Sparkhill, far removed from the dust and grime of a coalmine. That did not mean he was afraid to get his hands dirty. Serving part-time with the Shropshire Royal Horse Artillery he was in uniform from the first day of the war, but did not serve on the front line until 1917.

He arrived on the 24th of May and within a week one of his battery, Gunner Cooper, was wounded. A month later they were heavily involved in the Battle of Passchendaele.

In the spring of the 1918 Lieutenant Harold Gibbs and 158 Battery were moved to the Channel coast. They were preparing to support an amphibious operation intended to land forces to the rear of the German positions. Orders were changed and they moved south to set up the battery near Arras. The experience at Passchendaele had prepared them well for what was to follow. On the 21st of March they were on the receiving end of the heaviest artillery barrage of the war. Over a million shells were fired by German gunners in the first five hours of 'Operation Michael'. The principal targets were signals centres, railway stations and artillery emplacements. Then came the assault by German storm-troopers. Helped by foggy weather they broke though south of Arras.

After two days the German infantry were exhausted and the attack faltered. Allied forces regrouped and prepared to counter attack. German gunners continued to shell communication and supply facilities. On the 25th of March Captain Gibbs was supervising the loading of a wagon train with ammunition. He was walking back to the battery office when a shell exploded nearby. Badly wounded he was evacuated and taken to the 41st Casualty Clearing Station at Douai.

A war artist had been commissioned to capture the scene at 41st CCS, a tented camp, in green fields with patches of woodland not unlike an English country park. The artist's early painting conveyed an atmosphere of calm efficiency, a surgeon surrounded by nurses and orderlies attending a patient, another of an empty ward, a long, long tent and beds with pure white sheets. In later works his brush strokes were more hurried and when he came to paint the ward again the beds were full of men, still in battle dress, the sheets caked in mud and soaked with blood.

A Bloody Mess

Harold did not recover from his terrible wound, he lived for just three hours, and he was buried nearby the following day. The graves of those buried close to the battlefield were marked with simple wooden crosses, officers were given a more distinctive cross than those of the 'other ranks'.

Confirmation of his death and letters of sympathy arrived with apologies for the delay. The adjutant said he would have written earlier but he had had 'a busy time', a huge understatement. The letter from him and Harold's commanding officer and the battery sergeant all expressed the same sentiments: sad day for the battery...died like the brave soldier he was...admired for his spirit of cheerfulness...wasn't afraid to give his all for King and country...a worthy example of what an officer should be – all comments made by men who knew him well.

An impersonal telegram arrived at Billingsley from Buckingham Palace.

The King and Queen deeply regret the loss you and the Army have sustained by the death of your son in the service of his country. Their Majesties truly sympathise with you in your sorrow.

This was one of thousands of identical messages sent to grieving families. It was true however that the country did lose a whole generation of talented young men who could have done so much to 'get the country back on its feet' after the war.

The Gibbs family left Billingsley in 1918 and moved to London. Frederick Gibbs took up a post at the Admiralty and then at the India Office. On retirement Fred and Mabel moved from Streatham to Westcliffe-on-Sea. In the decade that followed the Great War memorials were set up everywhere, some large elaborate structures, some simple and personal. In Billingsley church a marble plaque was set in the wall as a memorial to Harold Gibbs, the only man from the village to die in The War.

When the wooden crosses were replaced by stone in the war cemeteries there was no distinction between the ranks. Few families made

In Honoured Memory

arrangements to have the original cross sent to England, but the Gibbs family did. This cross is the focus for the Remembrance Day service in the parish church every year.

Harold's medals were sent to his parents' home in Westcliffe-on-Sea. Fred and Mabel Gibbs were living at 102 Valkyrie Road, they may not have understood the significance of the address.

In Norse mythology the Valkyries were goddesses, they decided who would die in battle. Lovers of heroes, they would escort their chosen ones to Valhalla, hall of the slain. Harold never married, one of the Valkyries was his bride.

In the 1970s Harold's sister, Vera, visited Billingsley for the last time to stand before the cross and the marble plaque.

Chapter 16

Michael And Georgette

Innocent sounding names, Michael and Georgette, which a loving parent might give a new-born child – these were code-names chosen by the German high command for the first two assaults of their Spring Offensive of 1918.

The Russians were out of the war, German divisions were released from the East and transferred to the Western Front. Allied forces were then outnumbered in some sectors. Fresh American troops were not yet considered battle-ready. This was the last chance for the Germans to break through, encircle the British Expeditionary Force and bring the war to an end.

The build-up of troops in the trenches opposite did not go unnoticed, and perhaps more efforts should have been made to strengthen the defences. The Germans were planning a different strategy that involved specially trained shock troops. Weak points were to be attacked, a hole punched through the lines, isolating well-defended gun emplacements and pressing on to cause confusion in the second line of defence and beyond.

At just before five o'clock on the morning of the 21st of March 1918, ten thousand German weapons opened fire on a forty-mile front. The assault began behind a creeping barrage of smoke and gas shells. There was no lack of heroism on the part of the defenders, they were simply outnumbered. Ten thousand Germans were killed, the British Empire lost more, and at least twenty thousand were made prisoner.

Battle continued, but the German advantage could not be maintained. The advancing enemy could not match the pace of the retreating battalions. Lines of supply were extended and exhausted shock troops ran out of steam.

Casualties on all sides were high, over a hundred thousand Allied casualties, and seventy thousand lost as prisoners.

The next phase of the Spring Offensive, Operation Georgette began on the 9th of April, it claimed the lives of three Old Boys.

Private (57187) Harold Glenn – 1st/10th (Scottish Battalion) King's Liverpool Regiment

The Glenns lived comfortably at Danesford Lodge. The family had moved from Leek in Staffordshire. Samuel Glenn had special skills as a colour- mixer and calico printer. Wardle and Company had taken over the Pale Meadow Works in Hospital Street, an easy bike-ride from Quatford for Sam Glenn.

Little Harold began his learning at St Mary's Elementary School. He must have been a bright lad because when he was given a place at the Grammar School, the governors granted exemption from tuition fees. Samuel and Esther must have been very proud of their only child.

On leaving school he found employment as a clerk. Too young to be recruited at the beginning of the war, Harold joined his regiment in France in 1917. The 1/10th King's Liverpool Regiment had been fighting on the Western Front for three years, some of his comrades may have been over the top half a dozen times, they had plenty of battlefield experience, Harold had none.

In the Spring of 1918 all soldiers on the Western Front: new recruits, veterans, Private soldiers, Generals all knew the situation was desperate. Operation Michael had caused chaos and confusion and, although they failed to break through, the enemy had advanced twenty miles.

The Germans launched Operation Georgette with the same tactics, a heavy artillery barrage with smoke and gas shells followed by waves of shock troops in the early hours of the 9th of April.

The King's Liverpool Regiment were in the front line near Estairies.

'1/10th repulsed the attack, heavy casualties' was the brief entry in the war diary.

Defending the front to their right was a Portuguese battalion. By eight o'clock on the morning of the first day of battle they had collapsed. The flank of the King's Regiment was then exposed; they held on for a while, counter-attacked and then withdrew. Together with Lancashire Fusiliers they took at least four hundred German prisoners with them.

The Germans advanced and captured Armentieres. Two days later Field Marshall Douglas Haig issued his 'backs to the wall' order of the day.

There is no other course open to us but to fight it out. Every position must be held to the last man; there must be no retirement. With our backs to the wall and believing in the justice of our cause each one of us must fight to the end.

Private Harold Glenn did not heed the call. He died at Estaires on the first day of battle.

The struggle continued for three weeks. It was a tactical defeat for the Germans, even though they had retaken much of the ground won by the Allies a year earlier. Casualties on both sides were high.

It was a month before Major Munro found time to sit down and write letters of condolence.

It has been impossible, under the circumstances, to inform you earlier. We all realise the anxiety you have been suffering, and extend to you the heartfelt sympathy of all the officers and men of the Battalion.

His platoon commander, 2nd Lieutenant George Hughes wrote to Harold's parents and said, among other things,

Your son was an excellent soldier, and one of our best Lewis gunners. I deeply sympathise with you in such a loss.

Harold seems to have impressed all who met him, particularly Launcelot Raymen. The Captain said, "I think that Harold was one of the finest types of men I have ever come across, I was very fond of him indeed. I will do my best to find out any information about him, and will write you later on".

There was nothing more to add, a popular boy of nineteen, an only child had died. Like many more who fell when Georgette was unleashed he is remembered on the Loos Memorial (Panel 27–30).

Thousands of young lives were lost, many too young to have

the vote. They took no part in politics, their fate decided by old men. Travelling the road from Danesford to Bridgnorth, Esther Glenn would pass the church at Quatt and could visualise her boy, a choirboy, a picture of innocence.

Not all of those who died in battle were made to be warriors. Farm-hands, navvies, coalminers, these men were used to hardship, for clerks and errand boys life in the trenches must have been a shock but they 'did their bit'. Not wanting to 'let the side down' some were underage and some 'unfit for service' but still willing serve. Such was the case of Alan George.

2ND LIEUTENANT ALAN LEE GEORGE – ARTISTS RIFLES AND 15TH ROYAL WARWICKSHIRE REGIMENT

As a boy, Alan George could watch the world go by from any one the windows above his father's grocer's shop in the High Street. Carriers brought in vegetables from market gardens outside the town, and bottles of wine, brought up from the railway station, rattled in crates as the carts drew up on the cobbles outside the shop door.

Where is everyone?

© John Groome of Kinnerley

248

Alan learned a lot from his parents, customers in the shop, and playmates on the street. The family business prospered and the Georges moved to 'Fernhill' in Oldbury. Alan carried on learning and masters at the Grammar School must have been pleased that their efforts had borne fruit when 'young George' began his studies at Birmingham University.

When war was declared Arthur George, Alan's father, was quick to react. He could foresee that there would be hardship. In a letter to the Bridgnnorth Journal he offered to set up a food sharing scheme.

Alan graduated from Birmingham University as a Bachelor of Commerce. He returned to the town to work as a clerk in the Recruiting Office. He was now ready to make his own contribution to the war effort. He filled in his own application form and Lieutenant Cooksey (another Old Boy) signed it. The process of enlistment had begun.

In November 1915 he travelled to Shrewsbury to complete Army Form B178, a simple record of the medical history of every recruit. For most this was a formality – height, weight, vision, etc.

Alteration had to be made to Alan George's record before he could be declared 'Fit Class A'. The eye examination revealed that his vision was poor, 6/9. This was changed to 6/6, normal vison. Chest measurements were enlarged. Alan had suffered from rheumatic fever as a child, and this was enough for the medical officer to state 'so is unfit'. That was not the end of it, a second opinion was called for. Two days later Lieutenant Bookley added a comment to the effect that he had considered the rheumatic fever, and he overlooked the 'weak ankle' in the 'congenital peculiarities' section. Notes were made in red ink and Alan's fitness to serve confirmed with more red ink on a rubber stamp. Alan was content for the process to continue, he wanted to serve, to do his duty, even if he lacked the physique of an athlete.

He was nearly twenty-one In August 1916 when he applied to join the Artists Rifles. Recruits in the 28th London Regiment (Artists Rifles) were specially selected, they had the education and background expected of an officer.

Two months later at the London Regiment headquarters in Duke Street the application was approved. At last he was on his way. He had completed the paperwork for scores of lads in the Recruiting Office in the High Street and now he was going to join them in France. The ferry crossing of the Channel was usually completed in no more than a few hours. Alan's passage from Southampton to Le Havre took two days – a U-boat problem, who knows?

Private (761625) Alan Lee George began his training in France at Bailleul near the Belgian border. Training for officer cadets was made as realistic as possible with visits to the front line, this was called 'familiar-isation', a friendly word for a dangerous exercise.

In August 1917 Alan was given his commission and took up his duties with the 15th Battalion Royal Warwickshire Regiment. He served with them in France for a year. The battalion then moved to Italy to strengthen Italian resistance. They returned when the situation on the Western Front deteriorated.

Travelling by train from the South of France to the battlefields in the north, Lieutenant George and his company watched the countryside roll by: mountains and pastures, grazing cattle and waving children, valleys and streams, tea and warm pies on small-town railway platforms. It felt like a holiday, but when they thought back they recalled only too clearly the year spent on the Western Front.

The 15th Battalion reached their destination on the 6th of April 1918 and were welcomed by more 'Warwicks' struggling to hold back the enemy. For three days they faced the full force of Operation Georgette. The Allied front line buckled, and German forces swept down the valley of the Lys. Fortunately they ran out of steam near Hazebrouck, an important rail junction. After three days of heavy fighting troops on both sides were weary. The German advance was held but there was still a grave threat.

Officers of the Royal Warwickshire Regiment appeared to have followed Field Marshall Haig's instructions to the letter; 'each one of us must fight to the end'.

The Chaplain of the 15th Battalion, noted in a letter to Alan's father, 'Your son was the last officer of his Company to be hit. He was badly wounded by a shell.'

The wounded were carried from the battlefield to 13th Field Ambulance to receive emergency treatment. Those fit to be moved were transferred to a Base Hospital and the lucky ones shipped home. Alan George died. The first burials in the war cemetery at Thiennes took place on the 10th of April, less than a week later Alan Lee George was laid to rest there. Since his return from Italy Alan George had been at the front for less than a fortnight.

A plot in the cemetery was set aside for the Royal Warwickshire Regiment. During the months that remained to the end of the war many more were buried alongside Alan George.

Colonel Miller, commanding the 15th Battalion, had many letters of condolence to write, he must have repeated the same phrases several times,

I very much regret the loss of your son as an officer, he was very conscientious and hard-working, and both on former occasions and on this occasion had proved himself reliable in action.

The letter from the Chaplin sounded more genuine,

I have known him ever since he joined the Battalion and here he worked hard and did well. It may be some small comfort to you to know that he fell in an action that was a quite remarkable bit of fighting when the men fought against big odds and brought off a fine thing, but an important one, the influence of which it is really difficult to overestimate… We are all sorry to lose so gallant an officer, and send our deepest sympathy in your sorrow.

This letter was something Arthur and Edith George could treasure, more important to them than the telegram from Buckingham Palace.

The King and Queen deeply regret the loss you and the Army have sustained by the death of your son in the service of his country, their Majesties truly sympathise with you in your sorrow.

Hundreds of grieving families received identical telegrams. Their Majesties had simply approved the words of a civil servant.

'Passed Fit in Class A', stamped in blood red ink on the Medical History, Alan Lee George had sealed his fate.

There was some business rivalry in the High Street, but not between the George family and the Beamans, butchers and grocers complimented each other. The news of Alan George's death was shocking to all who had known him and particularly disturbing to George and Annie Beaman. Percy Beaman was home on leave at the time of Alan's death but soon to return to the battlefront.

Private (S/255908) John Herbert Percy Beaman – Royal Army Service Corps

When Annie Beaman's little boys got under her feet she could always send them out to 'see what was going on', and there was always something. Secure behind the iron railings of Rock Cottage they could peer down onto the Shifnal Road. Carters carrying goods in and out of the town, waved and greeted them. Traps carrying the gentlemen farmers to market trotted by. Across the road the engine in the pumping station thumped away steadily. Cattle in the meadows along the river bank grazed quietly. Occasionally they looked up when the white sail of *The Spry*, one of the last Severn Trows, glided past on its way to Bristol. Clouds of smoke issued from the Gas Works and from the stack of Southwell's Carpet Factory. In the distance, more steam and smoke followed the train as it rattled towards the tunnel under the town and hooted at the entrance.

Rock Cottage had one of the best views of Bridgnorth. Standing out on the skyline was the tower of St. Leonard's and the dome of St Mary's and the 'white elephant' that was the New Market Hall. Built by the Town Council in the 1850s, traders in the town refused to use it, choosing instead to set up stalls in the High Street as they had done for seven centuries. igh Bridgnorth was a lively market town, there were business opportunities.

George Beaman, master butcher, set up shop in the High Street in 1890, intending to provide a good living for his family and generations to come. With seven children in the family George and Annie had to plan for the future. Their plans were put on hold when war broke out.

Young men disappeared from the High Street, from every street in the town, and from the surrounding villages, they returned in uniform. Percy Beaman joined them.

Like most of them he dressed up in uniform for a studio portrait, these were photographs the family would treasure forever. Many of his friends were infantrymen, Percy was a Private in the Army Service Corps. These were the men who were part of the supply chain carrying food

© BES Library

and ammunition by road, rail, canal, mule, by any means, from ports on the French coast to the front line.

A great letter writer Percy, never lost touch with friends and family. His letters home revealed that he was more concerned with the fate of his brother Fred, the standard of cooking in the canteen and life at home, than with the conduct of war.

> *"Would you mind sending me some views of Bridgnorth the next time you write?"*

> *"When has Fred to join up? I'll bet the first two or three weeks he's in he'll wish he was out of it as it's not like being at home by a long way,"*

> *"Roast beef or a stew for dinner, always a pudding or fruit and custard afterwards."*

"We have been making a football field this afternoon so it seems we will be stopping here for a while."

"I have not heard from Fred Miles for nearly three weeks but I expect he is in the trenches again."

The Beamans and the Miles were rivals in the butchers' trade but friends when they shut up shop.

Fred Miles had been in the trenches in Gallipoli. His experience there was something he would not have wished to repeat in France. In a letter to Percy he wrote:

I have had typhoid fever, gastro-enteritis and a scrape in my side from a bullet.

I am able now to tell you something of the times I've had on the Peninsular, it has been a very rough and exciting time… We went up in the trenches on the Friday, a thousand of us made a charge… I lay with some wounded till dark… I was glad to come in. the ground next morning was strewn with our dead, they lay there for weeks after, you dare not fetch them in. In about three days the sun turns them black and then like a cinder and don't half stink.

I was a different climate in France in February 1918, cold and miserable. Percy described the conditions.

It has been very cold these last few days. The frost broke down nearly all the telegraph wires around here so you can tell how cold it is, it's even broken branches off huge trees.

Percy was spared the worst of it, his Grammar School background helped him get a job as clerk in the Company Office. He ended one letter on an optimistic note.

I will let you know in a day or two when I expect to come home on leave, the sooner the better I think. But I really don't think the war can last much longer, another few weeks will do it.

He began his fourteen days leave in early March 1918. He must have spent his time between Rock Cottage and the High Street, meeting old friends, chatting to customers and Miss Nellie Trow. George Beaman had taken on this cheery young woman to serve in the shop, she 'lived in' at number 46.

Earlier, Percy's father had written to remind him to write, 'if only a postcard', and also to tell him that Nellie had received some bad news and some good news. After three years everyone was used to hearing bad news. Nellie's brother was fighting in France and was reported 'missing', this often meant that the body could not be found. Then she learned that he was a prisoner and greeted the news with joy.

Percy and Nellie must have talked of war, but more important were tales of romance and town gossip. Leave came to an end, time to say good bye. Nellie was not there. Later she wrote to explain.

Dear Percy,

I guess you are thinking I am a jolly long time writing to you as promised. Well! How are you? I suppose by this time you are back in harness and quite climatised to work again, I expect it would go down rotten the first few days. Did you have a good journey without sea sickness?

Do you know I was mad having to stay in bed that last Sunday of yours at home but I had developed such a rotten cold and felt altogether off the hooks. I should very much have liked to have seen you to have said goodbye but just my luck of course. Well never mind better luck next time, eh!

I went to the pictures on Thursday night with Mary H, they were not very good, a lot of love and sloppy nonsense of course, ah well, that's the stuff to give 'em, but perhaps it is better to see that than the picture of some blood-thirsty villain trying to steal someone else's sugar card or something of that sort.

Miss Hawkins said she would like to have seen you very much, I think she is still going strong with the wounded boy I told you about, he has sent her his photograph. Coming on! you will say. Yes! say nothing, she'll get off this season. What! What!

Well Dear, I don't think there is much news to tell you this time. B.North is looking about the same, the only excitement we get is an aeroplane or two occasionally... I should very much like to hear from you when you get a chance to write but I think it will be wisest for you to address it to my home and they can enclose it in another envelope and send it on. This is my address:

The Grove, Rock, Bewdley, and remember to put Miss N. Trow or it may get opened.

So now I will say Good bye, With Kindest Regards, Your Sincere Pal, Nellie.

PS. Drop the formal (Miss Trow) in letters, it sounds too soft for anything. Don't you think? Try and commandeer me one of those photographs there's a sport. Au revoir.

Percy must have read and reread Nellie's letter, read every word and read between the lines. Was this the beginning of a long romance?

It was said that when Spring came 'a young man's fancy turned to thoughts of love'.

The German generals were not the romantic sort, even though they changed the codename of their April Offensive from George to Georgette. Harold Glen had died on the first day of battle, and Alan George before the end of the month. A supreme effort by British Empire and French troops halted the German advance but the situation was still desperate throughout the month of May.

The Germans re-doubled their efforts, more casualties on both sides. At the end of May Percy Beaman was gravely wounded, a shell fragment had torn into his stomach. He was brought to No.3 Canadian Stationary Hospital at Doullen for emergency treatment. He died on the 28th of May and wasburied nearby in Extension No2 of the Communal Cemetery, he was twenty years old. Next of kin were informed.

Percy had written home regularly, describing life in the trenches. He sent a letter to the family before the fateful day. The postman delivered this, his last letter, to Rock Cottage after his death. His mother read it over and over again, hoping perhaps that there had been some mistake, that the letter from his commanding officer and the telegram from the King were just scraps of paper, with an official stamp. Percy's letter was real, Annie knew by the handwriting, she waited, hoping for another to arrive, it never did.

It was more than a year before his 'personal effects' were returned to the family. Among the souvenirs of battle were the postcards of Bridgnorth, the collection of letters from mother, father and brother George, from Fred Miles and Nellie Trow, the girl who would always regret that she never said goodbye.

In time the family received a scroll and plaque with the name of their loved-one cast in bronze.

He Died For Freedom and Honour

With permission from Frederick John Beaman

257

Chapter 17

The U-Boat Menace

Letters to boys in the trenches usually made light of troubles at home, but inevitably some mention had to be made of local tragedies and hardships. In the town – 'Another lad from Bernard's Hill has gone'. In the country, as always, the complaints were about the crops and the weather – 'We've had some sort o' rain, it's been a poor harvest, I don't know 'ow we shall manage'. There was no disguising the fact that there was suffering on the home front, and it wasn't the weather to blame it was the U-boat.

In the four months from October 1916 to January 1917 U-boats sank nearly 500 ships. In December 1916 the Germans initiated 'unrestricted U-boat warfare' in an attempt to starve Britain into submission. If losses had remained at the January level this would have been achieved within six months.

Some lads from Bridgnorth had never seen the sea until they crossed the Channel for France. Even before they reached the battlefield there was danger from the torpedoes and mines laid by German U-boats. The Royal Navy to the rescue. Most Bridgnorth Boys chose to do their fighting on dry land.

Surgeon Lieutenant Richard Thursfield RN had sailed round the coast of Africa on *HMS Astraea*. In the first week of the war he witnessed the firing of warning shots aimed at the German garrison on Zanzibar, they wisely surrendered. *Astraea* sailed away to West Africa and moored off the coast of Cameroon. Here the most serious threat to life was the malarial mosquito. The health of the crew was Richard Thursfield's responsibility.

He had more serious work to do during the last year of the war patching up sailors in military hospitals at Plymouth and Portsmouth.

Sub lieutenant Awdry Peck was in a better position to take on the enemy in the North Sea.

Lieutenant Commander Geoffrey Awdry Peck – Royal Navy

At least a hundred and fifty folk turned out for the wedding of Naomi Peck and William Dickinson at the Catholic Apostolic Church (the Castle Hall today). The Bridgnorth Journal gave all the details, the list of guests and the presents they gave the newly-weds. There were the usual things, picture frames to put away in the attic, hideous cushions to put in the dog's basket, 'smelling bottles' to revive swooning aunts, and one or two useful cheques.

Miss Maynard gave them a copy of 'The Ancient Mariner' which would have been of interest to Naomi's father. Awdry Peck was a retired doctor who claimed to have once been a Naval Surgeon. In uniform on the day of the wedding was Geoffrey Peck, wearing a white sailor's suit. He marched down the aisle sharing the duty of train-bearer with his sister Geraldine.

Geoffrey did not complete his studies at the Grammar School. He went straight from the classroom in Bridgnorth to *HMS Conway* moored on the Mersey, a floating classroom where cadets learned the ways of the sea.

Heave Ho!

The opening lines of John Masefield's 'Sea Fever' must have inspired many adventurous young lads like Geoffrey Peck,

I must go down to the seas again, to the lonely sea and the sky. And all I ask is a tall ship and a star to steer her by.

Geoffrey may not have read this but he certainly knew about the exploits of local hero, Captain Mathew Webb from Dawley. Every schoolboy knew that he was the first man to swim the Channel and, like Geoffrey, probably learned to swim in the Severn. Webb, Masefield and Peck all had something in common, they all learned the basics of seamanship on board *HMS Conway*.

Young Master Peck arrived on the banks of the Mersey to begin his training in September 1911, not quite sure what to expect. The life of a cadet was hard, it was meant to be, the deckhands they would one day command were hard men.

In the summer of 1913 when Geoffrey came home on leave for a few days, he had something to tell the family. King George, 'the sailor king', had visited Liverpool and been given a tour of *RMS Mauretania*, Cunard's finest ship, the fastest merchant ship in the world. A hundred 'Conway' cadets formed a guard of honour for King George and Queen Mary, and Geoffrey Peck was one of them.

He said goodbye to his shipmates on the Mersey in May 1914 and came home for a month before he joined the crew of the *SS Mongara*. Midshipman Peck put theory into practice on a voyage to India and back. The Mongara docked at Liverpool in February 1915. Things had changed, Britain was at war.

After a month at the Gunnery School at Devonport, Midshipman Peck began his active service on board *HMS Alsatian*. On the 4th of June, while the *Alsatian* was 'coaling' at Birkenhead, Geoffrey joined the crew. A week later they were making for the open sea. There was a lot of traffic in the sea lanes, fishing boats, cargo vessels of every nation, warships of the Royal Navy, every craft was noted in the ship's log.

It was the task of *Alsatian* to investigate anything suspicious in the water, and intercept any vessel that might be carrying materials helpful to the enemy. Of greater concern was not what they spotted on the surface of the ocean but what lurked beneath.

Geoffrey remembered well his trip to India on the '*Mongara*', it was her maiden voyage, and his. She sailed on carrying goods and passengers from Calcutta to London until she ran across U-28. Crossing the Mediterranean from Port Said to Marseilles she was sighted by the Austrian U-boat and *Mongara* came under attack. A torpedo was launched and missed, the captain ordered a change of course, the second torpedo hit home and *Mongara* sank half a mile off the port of Messina. Remarkably, there was no loss of life. There were few U-boat attacks that had such a happy ending. Submarines were a new weapon of war and might have determined the outcome of the war.

The great naval Battle of Jutland In May 1916 was inconclusive. The German High Seas Fleet had a better score, they destroyed or damaged more ships. However they withdrew and gave control of the North Sea to the British Grand Fleet. The German naval commanders believed that the war could be won with the 'Unterseeboot'.

The most ambitious and daring young officers of the German Navy were encouraged to join the growing fleet of U-boats, which had shown themselves to be most effective. From bases at Ostend and Zeebrugge U-boats mined the approaches to all British ports and caused havoc with the merchant fleet. For her part the Royal Navy blockaded German ports and did everything possible to cut off supplies of food and the materials of war.

A certain amount of chivalry was shown in the early years of the war. Before launching a torpedo the U-boat would surface and the Captain give warning to the crew of a merchant vessel, allowing them time to take to the lifeboats.

Germany declared the seas around the British Isles a war zone and all vessels sighted in these waters became 'fair game'. American citizens lost their lives when the *Lusitania* was sunk, and the German government was warned against this declaration of 'unrestricted warfare'. For a while the Germans did comply, but further incidents followed and public opinion in the United States swung in favour of the Allies. Early in 1917 unrestricted warfare was resumed, America broke off diplomatic relations, and a German U-boat sank the US liner *Housatonic*. Both nations had gone beyond the point of no return. In March four more American merchant ships were sunk, in April 1917 the United States declared war on Germany.

This was a turning point in the war at sea. German merchant ships were seized in American ports, and American companies could no longer trade with Germany by shipping goods to Dutch or Scandinavian ports.

Geoffrey Peck and the crew of *Alsatian* spent a winter in the North Sea between Iceland and the Faroe Islands. Conditions here could be very rough. The Royal Navy had a base at Busta Voe on the west coast of the Shetland Isles where they could take on coal and fresh water and shelter from the gales. To replenish stores of food and ammunition they returned regularly to Liverpool. Then Geoffrey had the chance to spend a few days with the family at 15 East Castle Street, and tell tales of high seas.

One fine day, steaming north in the Irish Sea we sighted two destroyers and the battle cruiser, HMS Black Prince. *What a splendid ship, we rule the waves, victory is assured!*

Not his words but perhaps his thoughts. Victory was not assured. As the war progressed the number of U-boats increased, and Allied shipping was being sunk at an alarming rate.

The captain of *Alsatian* ordered extra watches to be mounted from time to time. The main task of the patrol was to intercept all vessels that came their way. Once challenged if a ship failed to stop the gunners fired a few blanks, and usually that was all that was necessary. If they were carrying anything that might aid the enemy two junior officers and a party of armed ratings were put on board and the ship diverted to Lerwick for closer inspection. No matter what flag they flew, Dutch, Danish, French, Norwegian, Russian, the skippers all had to explain themselves, even Scottish fishermen.

Midshipman Peck celebrated his nineteenth birthday in the North Sea. The months he spent there were the foundation of a long career. He had a glimpse of what being an officer in the Royal Navy was all about at Scapa Flow, the vast natural harbour in the Orkneys. When *Alsatian* made her way to her moorings she passed the dreadnought battleship *HMS Iron Duke,* flying the flag of Admiral Jellicoe, the commander of the British Grand fleet.

Alsatian sailed away and continued with her given task, inspecting every vessel and sinking suspicious objects. Scanning the waves through his glasses the officer of the watch spotted a large grey object. This was alarming, it could not be clearly identified by any of the officers on the bridge. Gunners were alerted and Royal Marines checked their weapons. The first volley hit the target, no sign of sinking, a second volley was fired, it did not explode and it did not sink, it was a dead whale.

During his tour of duty in the North Atlantic the schoolboy from East Castle Street had already begun a collection of memorable experiences. He had paraded before the King at the port of Liverpool, and sailed past the most powerful fleet in the world at Scapa Flow. He had witnessed natural wonders, the Aurora Borealis, shimmering curtains of magnetic light illuminating the long winter nights. He had seen icebergs capable of sinking the largest vessels afloat, and mighty marine mammals. Perhaps the most marvellous sight of all was to see breaking waves lit up by a billion tiny organisms, each one glowing like a firefly. Even the Captain, who had spent many years at sea, still noted these events in the ship's log.

A Danish vessel, *Fox II*, sailing from Invigtut in Greenland, and bound for Copenhagen, was intercepted by *Alsatian*. The hold was full of cryolite. This mineral was used in the process to extract aluminium from bauxite. The only source of this vital chemical was Invigtut. This shipment was destined for Germany. Geoffrey Peck led a boarding party to take control of the ship. He was accompanied by a second officer

HMS Erin

and a number of armed ratings. *Fox II* was directed to Lerwick and impounded. This was one of Geoffrey's last duties before his transfer to *HMS Erin*, in August 1916.

This must have been a proud moment for Midshipman Peck. *Erin* was a dreadnought battleship, 'brand spanking new', and had given a good account of herself at the Battle of Jutland.

Geoffrey must have made a good impression, Vice Admiral Stanley thought he was an 'Excellent young officer who shows great promise'.

Serving at sea until the end of the war and promoted to Sub Lieutenant, Geoffrey Peck fired torpedoes from '*Vernon*', laid mines with '*Apollo*', chased U-boats, and escorted convoys with '*Cockatrice*'.

Chasing and destroying the U-boats across vast stretches of ocean was an almost impossible task, but inevitably they would have to return to base to rearm and take on supplies. The ports of Ostend and Zeebrugge had been taken by the German invaders in the first months of the war, attempts to retake them failed. Both were bombarded by the Royal Navy in 1917. Plans for an overland assault were made, and this time gunners of the Royal Artillery would play a part in Operation Hush.

2ND LIEUTENANT RALPH BOURNE – ROYAL FIELD ARTILLERY

Ralph, John and Margery Bourne were all born in Buenos Aires. Argentina was booming, European investors had brought wealth to the country and this was where the Bournes had made their fortune.

At the turn of the century Arthur and Edith Bourne brought their children to England. This must have been a thrilling experience for them. In May 1899 they boarded the *Orellana* in Buenos Aires and steamed across the River Plate to pick up passengers at Montevideo, before they sailed out into the Atlantic and turned north along the coast of Brazil. More passengers joined the ship at Recife. Out at sea on the way to Lisbon the adults were very silly, they dressed up in carnival costumes and tried to shave a man with a big wooden razor. They tried to explain to the children that they were 'crossing the line', the equator. There was no line, there was sea all around, it was all very confusing. As they journeyed north it became steadily cooler. The ship docked at Lisbon, people got off, and more got off at La Corunna on the north coast of Spain. Finally they set off across the Bay of Biscay, this could be a rough passage. The family landed safely at Southampton. Ralph Bourne's first adventure was over.

The children spent some of their early years living comfortably at Hilderstone Manor in Staffordshire. Head of the household was granny Bourne. Her 'private means' was enough to afford help in the house, a cook, a governess for the children and four housemaids. Ralph was living in a woman's world and it must have been a welcome change when he was enrolled at Bridgnorth Grammar School in 1908. Ralph was completing his education in 1910 and missed the Centenary Exhibition in Buenos Aires. On display were the latest flashy cars from Europe, yachts, aeroplanes and locomotives, just the sort of 'toys' that schoolboys were interested in. The Bourne family, with a manor house in Staffordshire, a residence in a fashionable district of Buenos Aires, and a ranch, were certainly the sort of people who could afford such things.

Edith Bourne, with children John and Margery, sailed from Southampton on the *Avon*, back to Buenos Aires, in 1913. Arthur Bourne and Ralph followed later.

The next we hear of Ralph Bourne is from the Army. In June 1916 he began his training as a Gunner (Private 105971) at No 7 Artillery School near Bordon. On joining he gave his trade as 'clerk' but when he applied for a commission he claimed to be 'manager of a ranch in Argentina'. This was true, his father had died, his mother moved back to set up home in Bedford.

Ralph was commissioned as a 2nd Lieutenant. In April 1917 his battery (2/1st Shropshire RHA) was part of 158 Brigade of the Royal Field Artillery. On the 7th of May they assembled at West Down on Salisbury Plain for extra firing practice. A fortnight later they were on the move, Folkestone to Boulogne by sea, to camp at St Martin, and on to Bailleul by rail. Here Shropshire Royal Horse Artillery were given more instruction by New Zealand gunners in preparation the Battle of Passchendaele, 158 Brigade were going to put on a 'side show'.

The battle to take the ridge above Ypres began on the 7th of June, Ralph certainly heard the 'big bang' when nineteen mines blew up under the German lines. The artillery continued to pound the enemy positions, but Messines Ridge remained in enemy hands.

In July Ralph and his battery were in position at Zillebeke Lake, not as tranquil as the name suggests, German gunners were returning fire and there were casualties.

Next the Brigade moved by lorry to the coast, preparing for their part in Operation Hush. They arrived at Malo-les-Bains near Dunkirk on 13th of July. Three days later Ralph Bourne's battery sailed up the Yser on a canal barge to protect the bridgehead surrounding Nieuport. At the time they were unaware that Operation Hush had been called off. Had it been successful it would certainly have shortened the war.

The Germans had occupied most of the Belgium coast. Operating out of Ostend, Zeebrugge and Bruges, submarines and surface raiders were a constant threat to vessels in the Channel. The ports were heavily defended against attacks by sea and air. Operation Hush, an amphibious landing on the coast, was planned, supported by a breakout attack from Nieuport. Success on the coast depended on success further inland at Ypres. If Allied forces had broken through at Ypres, German forces would have been withdrawn from the coastal defences to plug the gap.

Although preparations for Operation Hush were conducted in great secrecy the Germans anticipated the British manoeuver and struck first on the 10th of July. The British infantry, supported by gunners on the ground and air gunners flying dangerously low held their ground at Nieuport- les-Bains. Artillery exchanges continued for over a month.

Makes a Change from Mud, Fritz

© Imperial War Museum 050665

The Battle of the Dunes, as it was called, was a 'side show'. Even so, British casualties, killed, wounded and missing, totalled more than three thousand. Ralph Bourne was one of them. He died on the 10th of September 1917 and was buried about 10 miles behind the front line in the Coxyde Military Cemetery, still within the range of the German artillery.

Every family with a son on the front line half- expected tragic news. Men were dying every day. Such was the scale of events that the War Office closed the file of each man with a few slips of paper. In London Edith Bourne received a telegram at the 'town house' on St George's Square, details of Ralph's final resting place were sent to her home in Bedford. A few personal effects were returned from his battery and his pay brought up to date. Edith acknowledged receipt and by the end of the month there was nothing more to be said. She was one of thousands who had lost a son.

An equally determined attempt to deny the U-boat crews a safe haven was made in April 1918.

WIREMAN OLIVER JOHNSON SCHOOLCRAFT – ROYAL NAVY

It could be very confusing, a custom imported from the United States, giving the first-born son the same name as his father.

Oliver J. Schoolcraft Jnr. completed the 1911 census form for the whole family and signed it. He was sixteen, a scholar at the Grammar School; Esther, Dolly, Henry and Albert were all at school too. Lily Rose Schoolcraft was twenty when she started her family, Oliver Johnson Schoolcraft Senior was forty-one, he appeared to have married late. The census form did not tell the whole story, although it did reveal that Oliver Schoolcraft was born in New York, and that did help to explain why his son had been given the same name.

Oliver Senior had attended an academy which prepared young men for service in the US Navy. He was not military-minded, he was fair-minded, and this characteristic caused him considerable distress. The exact sequence of events is not entirely clear, but it seems he travelled to England in 1880. He intended to study for the Church, but he was led astray, he met Eliza Isabella Beauchamps on the streets of London. Believing he could 'save her from sin', he whisked her away to Jersey, and they were married at St Helier in 1881.

Oliver had friends in Heidelberg, he wanted to introduce his wife to polite society and sent her to art school, hoping this would help. She ran away to London. He wrote to her and she returned to Heidelberg, only to 'misbehave' with university students. She was a hopeless case, and yet her loving husband did not give up. He gave her a generous allowance, and she repaid him by sailing to America.

In Chicago Eliza moved in with William Ruhmor, 'Wild West Bill', a man more to her liking than kindly Ollie Schoolcraft. Oliver travelled to America in 1889, his mission to save his wayward wife failed, divorce proceedings began, and Oliver returned to begin his studies in theology at St John's College, Cambridge. In 1890 he was ordained and he began his ministry in Lambeth. The divorce became final in May 1893, and in September of the same year he married Rose Lily Tupper, twenty years his junior. The newly-weds moved to Herne Bay where Oliver Johnson Schoolcraft Junior was born. This was a happy event, followed by four more happy events. The Reverend Schoolcraft retired. The family moved to 'Spring Holme' on the outskirts of Bridgnorth. They lived comfortably. Oliver had 'private means', all the children attended school, he had found happiness at last. Then the war came.

Oliver Jnr. had spent his early years at Herne Bay. Merchant ships carrying goods in and out of the Port of London passed by every day. Sharp-eyed little boys scanned the horizon for a glimpse of battleships of the Royal Navy, the most powerful navy in world. When war came Oliver Jnr. joined the Royal Navy.

So far from the sea, men of the Midlands in navy blue stood out in the streets where most were wearing khaki. Oliver Schoolcraft caught the eye of Harriett Letticia Bourne from Droitwich. The young lovers were married at Portsmouth in 1916, where everything was navy blue.

Britainia ruled the waves, she had the largest fleet of ships, and yet they could not stop the U-boats sinking merchant ships, battleships, liners and even hospital ships. To counter the U-boat threat the Royal Navy were fighting fire with fire, employing the latest technology, and this required technicians with special skills.

Oliver Schoolcraft applied the maths and science learned at the Grammar School to the mechanics and electrics of the torpedo. To distinguish him from other ratings he wore a torpedo badge on his arm and was given the rank of 'Wireman'. These were the men who checked, repaired and primed the weapons.

It was no secret that the ports of Ostend and Zeebrugge were bases for the U-boats that were causing such havoc in the Channel. Several plans had been drawn up to capture or block these ports, but it was not until 1918 that one was put into action. A force made up largely of volunteers was assembled, to 'put a cork' in the canal basin. This proved to be no easy task. The entrance was protected by a mile-long mole, with shore batteries at intervals, stretching in an arc out into the North Sea.

The invading force assembled at Swin Deep, south of Clacton, few were aware of their target. On the 2nd of April they set off for Zeebrugge. The success of the raid depended on smoke screens, the wind direction changed and seventy-seven vessels had to 'turn about' in the dark and return to base. They were at anchor for three weeks – battleships, cruisers, ferry boats, minesweepers and submarines.

On board *HMS North Star*, Wireman Schoolcraft patted the sides of his torpedoes, confident that they were ready to strike a blow for Britain. On the 23rd of April they set off once again.

HMS Vindictive faced heavy fire when she approached the Mole, she pressed on and drew alongside. Held in position by Mersey ferryboats *Iris* and *Daffodil*, landing parties swept ashore from her decks.

A Hostile Reception

Scores of Marines were casualties before they had advanced more than a few yards. At the same time the cruiser *HMS Thetis* was escorting the block ships *Intrepid* and *Iphigenia* into the channel entrance. They were scuttled, but not precisely as planned.

Offshore, Wireman Schoolcraft and the crew of the destroyer *North Star* were throwing everything they had at the enemy. The whole operation should have had the protection of a smokescreen, but an unfavourable wind meant they were exposed. *North Star* was hit. Her sister ship, *Phoebe*, came to the rescue and managed to get a line across to tow her out of danger. The ships drifted apart, the engine room and boiler room of *North Star* filled with water, and the extra strain caused the cable to snap. *Phoebe* drew alongside to make another attempt to tow the stricken vessel to safety. *North Star* was struck again by several shells, blowing her capstan overboard and killing and wounding many men. *Phoebe* cast off, set up a smoke screen, and lowered her boats to pick up survivors. It was past midnight, but the tragic scene was lit up

Stirring Stuff

270

by German searchlights, making the rescue operation hazardous in the extreme.

The *North Star* sank at two o'clock in the morning. The body of Oliver Schoolcraft was never recovered from the North Sea. Harriett Schoolcraft, married less than two years, was now a widow. Lily and Oliver Schoolcraft had lost their son; Esther, Dolly, Henry and Albert had lost their brother.

Ten thousand sailors had been 'swallowed by the deep'. To honour their memory a memorial was built at Portsmouth. It was in the form of an obelisk, to serve as a leading mark for shipping. On a panel at the base the name of Oliver Johnson Schoolcraft may be found, but he is almost lost among the sea of names. He is better remembered in the Old School Library, among his old school friends.

Over forty years later school boys were still reading of the heroic action at Zeebrugge.

Chapter 18

The Final Hundred Days

Elizabeth Vaughan must have needed some help in the house – between 1894 and 1901 she gave birth to five boys. Lillian Maskell, an eighteen year old 'domestic' lived in at Westbrook Manor, and other servants living locally no doubt helped with the daily chores. William Vaughan was a gentleman farmer and could certainly afford it. In 1906 he went some way to solving the problem of noisy boys about the house by sending David and Reginald to board at Bridgnorth Grammar School, and the following year Richard and Cecil were admitted to the school.

The eldest boys did not return to the farm when their schooling was complete. The British Empire was at its mightiest then and there were opportunities for adventurers worldwide. Reg and David chose Canada as the place to stretch their wings. David began farming in Manitoba and Reg settled seven hundred miles to the west, in Alberta. They were reunited by war.

PRIVATE (2114899) REGINALD ALFRED VAUGHAN –
10TH CANADIAN INFANTRY
PRIVATE (312026) DAVID THOMAS VAUGHAN –
DIVISIONAL AMMUNITION COLUMN

In March 1916 David Vaughan left his farm at Foxwarren, Manitoba, and made his way to Winnipeg with other local lads to 'sign on' and serve with the 106th Regiment, Winnipeg Light Infantry. In the week before Christmas of the same year Reg Vaughan completed the formalities that changed his occupation from 'motor driver' to soldier with the 103rd Calgary Rifles. Winnipeg Light Infantry and Calgary Rifles were combined to form the 10th Battalion Canadian Infantry.

Serving in France David and Reg would have had identical battlefield experiences. This was most appropriate because although there was a three-year difference in age both brothers were 5'8" tall and had with same dark hair and blue eyes.

They may have arrived in France just in time to take part in the greatest victory of the war for the Canadian Corps. The Germans had taken and held Vimy Ridge since 1914, the British and the French had attempted to dislodge them and failed. Careful planning by the Canadian staff officers and the heroism of their men paid off. The 10th Battalion played a part in this great drama that began on the 9th of April 1917. They reached all their objectives within three hours but at the cost of 374 casualties. Their reputation as 'shock troops' was made on Vimy Ridge.

In the middle of August 1917 the 10th Battalion were back to full strength. They led the way in a diversionary attack on Hill 70 overlooking Lens, an important rail junction for the surrounding coalfield. Hill 70 was captured, Private Harry Brown was awarded a posthumous Victoria Cross. A total of eighty medals for gallantry were awarded to the Battalion, more than any awarded to a single Canadian combat unit in a single action during the Great War.

Reg and David Vaughan must have been proud to be in such gallant company. A year later they prepared to do battle again at Amiens.

The German Spring Offensive of 1918 had failed, their advance halted at Amien. It was now the turn of the Allies to launch the Hundred Days Offensive that would end the war. A strong team took the field: the British, French, the Americans, and leading the charge, Australians and Canadians.

They set off in dense fog on the 8th of August, protected by a creeping barrage, and advanced so quickly that they captured a party of senior German officers eating breakfast. A fifteen mile gap was punched through enemy lines, the Canadian Corps ahead of the rest. Demoralised German troops surrendered in droves on the 'Black Day' of the German Army.

Success came at a cost, 'D' Company of the 10th Battalion lost Private Reg Vaughan, killed in action on the 9th of August. He has no known grave. His brother David fought on.

The 10th Battalion had already collected a dozen battle honours, and in the final year of the war collected half-a-dozen more, including

273

Passchendaele, Hindenberg Line and Canal du Nord. The Hindenberg Line was the last line of defence for the German Army in the Amiens campaign. During the Battle of Cambrai the 'Fighting 10th' finally made a successful crossing of Canal du Nord in late September, this was their last major operation, there were heavy losses.

David Vaughan was a survivor, there is no record of any wound, and by all accounts he came away without a scratch. To commemorate the heroism of the Canadian forces, land was donated by the French government and over a ten year period a memorial was built.

One of the few official functions conducted by Edward VIII was the opening of the Canadian Memorial on Vimy Ridge in 1935 to honour the memory of those who had no grave. Eleven thousand names are carved on the memorial, among them is that of Private Reginald Alfred Vaughan.

Vimy Ridge

© Commonwealth War Graves Commission

Cecil and Richard Vaughan were just too young to serve in the Great War, for this Elizabeth Vaughan was grateful. David was far from home, farming on the Canadian prairies, her other blue-eyed boy was lost.

Her grief was shared by Sophia Price and Edna Gregory. The Bridgnorth Journal of 14th of September 1918 reported the deaths of their sons, both had died of wounds within three days of each other.

LCPL (52557) REGINALD CHARLES GREGORY – 1/7TH LANCASHIRE FUSILIERS
PRIVATE (31837) HORACE CYRIL PRICE – 1ST DEVONSHIRE REGIMENT

Reg and Horace, Don't Spend Much on Razor Blades

© BES Library

These boys knew each other well, baptised in the same church, taught in the same classrooms, familiar with every street in the town. Their fathers would have known each other, Bill Gregory worked for a local wine merchant and Dick Price was a baker in the High Street.

As a boy Horace may have been spoilt, he was something special, something of a surprise to Richard and Sophia Price. His sister, Ethel was thirteen years old when Horace was born in 1899. She worked alongside her father in the family bakery during the day. In the evening she could play with Horace, she was of an age when playing with a baby was every girl's dream.

It was a similar story for Reg Gregory, he also had a sister called Ethel and another, Francis, and an elder brother. The Gregorys were practical people, Reg's sisters were dressmakers, his brother Harold a housepainter.

With a Grammar School education Reg might have looked for a white-collar job. Instead be began work at The Bridgnorth Garage, at eighteen he was claimed by the army. He enlisted at Ironbridge in 1917.

At the same time Private (8/9003) Horace Price was joining the Devonshire Regiment, the 53rd (Boy Soldiers) Battalion. This was one of three battalions created in late 1917 to train and prepare young recruits for active service. Horace was given a new service number (31837) when he was drafted into the 1st Battalion Devonshire Regiment.

The 1st Devons seemed to spend their time 'holding the line', filling a gap. In November 1917 they were sent to Northern Italy where the Italians had been routed at Caporetto, here they held the line near Vicenza.

In the Spring of 1918 the Germans launched a series of attacks, in a desperate attempt to end the war before Americans arrived in strength to tip the balance in favour of the Allies. British troops bore the brunt of Operation Michael launched in March. They were taken completely by surprise and forced to make a fighting retreat. The 1st Devons recalled from Italy in April returned to the Somme. They held their position at Nieppe against repeated German counter-attacks.

The enemy were forced back, the Hundred Day Offensive was underway. During ten days at the end of August more than two hundred Germans were taken prisoner by the Devons, but those ten days cost them 263 casualties. Every yard won from the enemy came at a cost.

Private Horace Price was still fighting fit. The weather was awful and there were gas attacks, but the Germans were retreating, surely the war would end soon. His old school chum Reg Gregory must have felt the same way.

Lance Corporal Gregory wasn't far away, also on the Somme, serving with the Lancashire Fusiliers. Reg was in good company they had fought well at Passchendaele a year earlier. Surrounded by men who had survived this battle was some comfort to him when the 1/7th Lancashire Fusiliers went into action at Arras. They then prepared for the Second Battle of Bapaume. In March the Germans had taken Bapaume, New Zealanders liberated the town in August. Fighting continued into the first week in September.

Although the Germans were beaten this was still a dangerous place to be. Enemy artillery continued to shell the Allied front line. On the 5th of September Reg Gregory was hit and evacuated to No. 3 Canadian Casualty Clearing Station, he died the same day. His parents were living at 13 Innage Lane when they received the news.

The regimental chaplain wrote a letter of sympathy to William and Edna Gregory. He might have spared them the details, 'wounded in the head and thigh, and only lived a short time' – 'died of wounds' would have been enough. Lance Corporal Gregory was buried nearby in Varennes Military Cemetery, honoured by comrades of the Lancashire Fusiliers and remembered in his home town as a boy whose 'genial and kindly nature at all times won him many friends'.

The report in the Bridgnorth Journal also outlined the tragic end of one of his 'many friends', who had died three days earlier.

Mrs Richard Price, 75 High Street Bridgnorth, has been officially informed that her son, Pte. Horace Price, died at 46 Casualty Clearing Station, France, on the 2nd inst, of wounds received that day. The deceased was the youngest son of the late Richard Price and Mrs Price.

Horace was buried in Bac-Du- Sud British Cemetery, Bailleulval, less than a dozen miles from the final resting place of Reg Gregory. Had they lived they might have shared stories of trench-life, or perhaps, like so many others, it was something they did not care to recall.

The painful details of the final hours of these boys' lives was something that Annie McMichael could understand. She had watched her son slowly die in the same week as Horace Price and Reg Gregory.

PRIVATE (514997) COLIN JOHN WYLD MCMICHAEL – 14TH LONDON SCOTTISH

'JW' McMichael completed his studies at the Grammar School, but instead of joining his father Colin in the family business in the High Street he began his training as a bank clerk at Shipston-on-Stour, not far from Stratford-on-Avon. He took a room at The Old White Bear, a coaching inn in the heart of the town.

In December 1916, a month before his eighteenth birthday, he made the short journey to Pershore and presented himself for medical examination at Norton Barracks. He was declared fit for service. Back in Shipston-on-Stour the bank manager wished him well, 'JW' packed his bags and said goodbye to his landlord, stepped out into the street and looked up at the gently swinging sign of The Old White Bear, for the last time.

© BES Library

Although news from the battlefields was grim in the dark days of December there was still a festive air in Bridgnorth High Street. Colin McMichael, grocer and stationer at number 23, was doing a brisk trade in tasty treats and cards for Christmas.

Along the street in the Agricultural Hall the recruiting officer was completing the paperwork for young men ready to serve King and country. Lieutenant Frank Cooksey checked the details, 'JW' took the oath of allegiance and the process was complete. On Christmas Eve he was officially on the army reserve, a soldier at last. For just over a month he went about the town talking to old school friends, or anyone who could tell him what it was like 'over there'. On 14th of February he was 'mobilised', which meant a train journey to London and an interview at Alexandra Palace. Captain Smith signed at the bottom of the Attestation Form and the bank clerk and 'Old Boy' of BGS was now a Private (514997) in the 14th Battalion of the London Regiment, The London Scottish.

At the outbreak of war construction began on a vast camp outside the village of Owslebury near Winchester. Private McMichael arrived at Hazeley Down Camp to begin his training. He had hardly got used to wearing his kilt and glengarry when he 'reported sick'. His eyes were sore and inflamed and did not respond to treatment, he was referred for specialist treatment at the Central Hospital in Winchester. He was suffering from a severe case of iritis, an inflammation of the iris. It is a painful condition that today would be treated with steroids. Eventually he began his training.

The villagers were by now used to hearing strange voices; Welsh gunners came and went, Canadians arrived, followed by the 'Cockney Jocks', the London Scottish. Pipes and bugles sounded, rifle fire could be heard miles away, and new recruits let out terrifying screams as they sunk their bayonets into bags of straw. At the end of their stay new drafts, destined for France, took the train from Shawford Station to the coast. For some who sailed away this would be the last they would see of England.

Private McMichael spent his last Christmas on home soil in hospital. His eye trouble had flared up again. His treatment lasted fifty-five days. This boy should never have been sent to the battlefront, but at this stage of the war every man was needed and he was a willing lad.

The London Scottish had fought hard from the start. In their first encounter with the enemy at Messines near Ypres nearly half the battalion, six hundred men, were casualties. Fresh men were continually being sent from England to strengthen the 14th Battalion. Three hundred young men, including Colin McMichael, landed on French soil on the 19th of March. They were given two weeks training behind the lines at Mont St Eloi and joined the Battalion on the 2nd of April.

Private Colin McMichael mingled with men who had been tested in battle. They told of their experiences on the Scarpe River and Tadpole Wood, and how tanks had helped to push the enemy back. Everyone was beginning to believe that the tide would turn, the Germans would be forced to retreat and the war would soon be over.

On the 10th of April the London Scottish marched from the relative safety of their dug-out billets near Arras to the front line. Their first encounter with the Germans was most successful. The weather was in their favour.

London Scottish and 4th London advanced with the wind at their backs during a particularly vicious hail storm. The Germans were sheltering in their trenches and the sentries were barely able to see the Scots bearing down on them. Prisoners were taken and the advancing 'Jocks' now considered the next objective, a pill box. An assault was mounted in the evening but a forceful counter-attack sent the London Scottish back into the newly won trenches. An artillery duel followed. So ended Colin McMichael's baptism of fire.

For the next four months the London Scottish remained in the Arras region, either in the front line or in support, and at other times resting and training, in preparation for the 'big push'.

The 23rd of August 1918 was a fateful day for Private Colin McMichael. It was the day he should have died. The day began early, at five minutes to five, and after twelve minutes bombardment on the ruined village of Boiry-Becquerelle the 14th Battalion advanced. With the Royal Scots on the left and the 4th London on the right they surrounded the village. With a tank and supporting infantry they took a hundred prisoners and eight machine guns. In less than an hour they had secured a line of German trenches. Five hundred yards to the rear was a second line of trenches still held by the enemy. Each of the front line companies sent out platoons to continue the advance. They were caught in the open and several men were cut down by machinegun fire. The Germans put on a spirited defence of their position. The 'Scottish' took cover in captured trenches and the ruins of the village. The Germans kept the attackers pinned down, they pounded the Scots positions with high explosives and gas shells.

Liquefied Mustard Gas was delivered in shells marked with a yellow cross. It was the weapon most feared by frontline troops, for there was no defence against it. When the shell burst an oily liquid, the colour of red wine, spread everywhere. The area could remain toxic for weeks. Food, clothing, water, soil were all contaminated. In small doses it caused blindness and had a blistering effect on flesh, it even corroded metal armaments. The gas was heavier than air and settled in hollows. A trench was the worst place to find shelter, inevitably there were casualties. In the early evening an assault was mounted by 'A' and 'C' Company of the London Scottish. About a hundred German infantry surrendered and the fighting was over for the day.

In total over two hundred and fifty prisoners had been taken. The German dead were not counted. Among the Scottish casualties were forty-four soldiers and two officers all suffering from the effects of mustard gas.

The Tommies referred to it as 'Hot Stuff'. Earlier, during the Spring

Offensive, men blinded by the gas were photographed standing in line holding on to the shoulder of the man in front. This image moved the war artist John Singer Sargent to paint a large mural that now hangs in the Imperial War Museum.

Lean on Me Old Friend

©IWM ART1460 & © IWM Q 11586

The casualties were treated at the scene of the battle and moved with all speed to the rear, to a Casualty Clearing Station. Private McMichael and others who had received a heavy dose of the Hot Stuff were assessed at the CCS, and the next day moved to No 25 General Hospital at Hardelot-Plage, and into the gentle hands of Australian nurses.

The pain must have been extreme. Breathing was difficult. The gas strips the mucus membrane from the bronchial tubes causing internal bleeding. Colin's back was covered with huge mustard coloured blisters. His condition was so serious that he was shipped home to receive more specialist treatment at the Bevan Military Hospital at Sandgate. For the 'walking wounded' this was a very pleasant spot overlooking the sea. A flight of broad steps led down to the sandy beach and the Channel that separated them from the horrors they had witnessed.

Colin McMichael was made as comfortable as possible but the outlook was bleak. In similar cases the unfortunate casualty took four or five weeks to die. Annie McMichael, Colin's mother, took the train to the south coast to comfort her boy.

Colin's medical notes described 'very extensive burns extending over the entire back and chest and partly over limbs, profuse discharge'. To clean and sterilize the wounds boric acid was used and Vaseline to provide some comfort. For a little over a week they did what they could to save him, but in the early hours of 6th of September 1918 he died. His heart failed, perhaps the pain was overwhelming. Now the pain was gone.

A telegram was sent to the headquarters of the London Scottish and 'next of kin were informed'. It may even have been a relief to Colin's mother. He was still her little boy, Annie McMichael knew that, had he lived, he would never have enjoyed the full and active life she had planned for him.

Christmas was no longer a time of celebration for the family. Christmas 1916 - Colin was at home and on Christmas Eve received the news that he was being transferred from the reserve and would soon begin his training with the London Scottish. Christmas 1917 - Colin was in Winchester Military Hospital suffering from Iritis, inflammation of the eye, a condition now believed to be stress-related. Christmas 1918 - The nation rejoiced, the war was over. The McMichaels mourned the loss of their nineteen year old son. He was home at last, buried in the town cemetery.

Chapter 19

Heroes All

Peace at last, there was rejoicing in every town in the land, the air was filled with hope and the peel of church bells. The joyful sound from the belfry of St Chad's in Shrewsbury echoed along the Town Walls, cheering the Perkins family at Sabrina View House. Their eldest boy, Christopher, would soon be home.

Across the river The Abbey bells rang out. Folks in Monkmore Road came out to greet their neighbours, shake hands and smile. A telegram boy knocked at the door of number sixty-nine. Harriet Owen knew by his face that he carried bad news.

Her son Wilfred Owen had been killed in action a week earlier on the 4th of November.

On Armistice Day she learned of his death.

Lieutenant Wilfred Owen had been with the 'Manchesters' since the outbreak of war – Private Christopher Perkins served with the same regiment. Owen spent most of the war in France, Perkins spent a year in Scarborough, and this was where their paths crossed. They may have crossed earlier, of course, in Shrewsbury town.

Owen was making a name for himself as a poet. He was one of the great poets of the Great War. He did not glorify war. In *Strange Meeting* he describes a dark cavern, Hell, where he encounters one of the enemy, 'I am the enemy you killed my friend… Let us sleep now.'

Only someone who had experienced hand-to-hand combat could fully understand the horror.

At Scarborough, while recovering from the stress of battle, Owen wrote *The Ghost of Shadwell Stair* – a dark poem, set in the London docks, written by a troubled man.

Along the wharves by the water-house
And through the cavernous slaughter-house
I am the shadow that walks there.

Lieutenant Wilfred Owen returned to the battlefield, to the 'slaughter house', and the real possibility that he would die, Private Perkins stayed on in Scarborough.

Crossing the Sambre-Oise Canal, Wilfred Owen was killed on the 4th of November.

A month earlier he had been recommended for the Military Cross… 'for conspicuous gallantry and devotion to duty in the attack on the Fonsomme line on 1st/2nd October 1918'.

He never knew that he had been honoured for his bravery, the award was not confirmed until after his death.

Eleven Old Boys of Bridgnorth Grammar School received the Military Cross. The final tally for the school was impressive, a Distinguished Service Order, Distinguished Flying Cross, Air Force Cross – several received the Croix de Guerre from the French.

Croix de Guerre

The Egyptian, Serbian and Italian governments awarded decorations to three who had fought alongside their troops.

Tom Wilson's parents placed a memorial plaque Sutton Maddock, he was killed when leading his men in the Great Attack on Cambrai, November 20th 1917. His commanding officer recommended him for a posthumous Victoria Cross. The medal went to a fellow officer who died in the same action. The only Old Boy to receive a VC, the highest award for gallantry in the face an enemy, was Hugh Rowlands. He was one of the first. His VC was awarded during the Crimean War, in 1854 after the Battle of Inkerman.

Victoria Cross

Not everyone could be a hero, Christopher Perkins, simply 'did his bit', and may have saved a few lives.

PRIVATE (75135) CHRISTOPHER PERKINS –
5TH MANCHESTER REGIMENT & RAMC
Sound schooling and a good qualification that was what Christopher's

father must have believed in. He was a chemist and made a good living, enough to pay for all three children to have the best education. When Christopher had completed his studies at the Grammar School he became apprenticed to his father, also Christopher. The family moved from their modest house in Bank Street, Bridgnorth to Sabrina View House on the Town Walls of Shrewsbury, they were going up in the world.

For three years the Perkins's, and the rest of the nation, watched with alarm as the casualty lists grew longer and gloom spread across the land. Would the war never end? In August 1917, two months short of his eighteenth birthday, Christopher walked into the recruiting office in Shrewsbury to 'attest', to swear that he would serve King and Country for the duration of the war.

A month later, in September 1917, he went before the medical board. Christopher's vision was perfectly normal, '6/6'. Physical development was 'V. Poor', he was short and he was slight, he had the physique of a twelve year old boy. He was not 'A1', but he was passed 'Fit B1' and assigned to the Manchester Regiment.

The 5th Battalion was a reserve battalion. When Private Perkins joined them they were in barracks at Scarborough. Some men drafted in were recovering from wounds, or in the case of Wilfred Owen, mental scars.

Owen returned to the battlefield, others were hoping to sit out the war at the seaside, even if the weather could be wild on the Yorkshire coast. Private Christopher Perkins had hardly settled in when he was admitted to the hospital suffering with tonsillitis, he was discharged after a fortnight, only to be readmitted five days later, and put on 'light duties'. He was not the stuff that warriors were made of.

Private Perkins did have something to offer, a knowledge of medicine. In the final year of the war he was transferred to the Royal Army Medical Corps and posted to Aldershot.

Within two months of the end of the war, tens of thousands passed through the process of demobilisation. Private Perkins was not released, he served on for further twelve months. The victims of war, the sick and wounded, were still in need of care and treatment. Christopher Perkins training as a chemist was put into practice.

He was seventeen when he joined the Manchester Regiment, the same age as Jack Ransom, whose courage on the battlefield was recognised.

CORPORAL (96230 AND GS/84244) JACK LESLIE RANSOM DCM –
LONDON REGIMENT

For Henry Ransom, Jack's father, it was an easy walk to work from Montrose Villas to the Highley Pit. He was one of the few men in the village who could go to work in a collar and tie. When his neighbours climbed into the cage that took them underground to hew coal, Henry went to his desk in the office to deal with the paperwork.

Jack began his studies at the Grammar School in 1911, there was no question of him ever working at the coal face, quite the opposite. When he was just eighteen he joined the Royal Flying Corps, as an Officer Cadet (93099).

Perhaps he was frustrated by the long training and was anxious to 'see some action'. Whatever the reason, on the 5th of November 1917, Jack requested a transfer to the Middlesex Regiment for posting to the 19th Reserve Battalion London Regiment.

He was not in reserve for very long, there was a desperate need for new blood to hold back the Germans who had launched their Spring Offensive in 1918.

They had swept through the British lines in March, and if they had carried their advance to the Channel coast British forces would have been cut off from their French allies.

North of the Somme, the enemy had taken Bapaume and advanced along the road to Albert, and here they were held. British forces regrouped and steadily advanced, every yard of the road to Bapaume was fought over and cost lives. At Pozieres, two years earlier, thousands had died. The village was heavily fortified, the Germans still held on for nearly six months.

Corporal Jack Ransom arrived with the 2/2 Battalion, London Regiment in September 1918.

This NCO pushed forward with ten men and two Lewis guns, and under intense machine-gun fire established an isolated post on the far side of the village, where he put out of action two hostile machineguns and several snipers. After five hours, when his ammunition was spent and he was almost surrounded he withdrew to Tottenham Post (16. 1. 19)

Eighteen year old Jack Ransom was awarded the Distinguished Conduct Medal for 'great courage' at Pozieres on 10th Sept 1918. A more satisfying reward for men like Jack was a happy marriage, good health, and 'peace at the last'. Jack married Violet Mountford in 1924, and passed away fifty years later. A DCM was also awarded to John Valentine Hasler. The Military Cross was awarded to a handful of other Old Boys, certainly the most decorated were the Westrop brothers.

Brigadier Sidney Albert Westrop CBE DSO MC – KSLI and Machine Gun Corps

Studying Engineering at Birmingham University, Sidney trained part-time with the Officer Training Corps, he was commissioned in the 5th KSLI. His training as an engineer made him a very suitable candidate for transfer to the newly created Motor Machine Gun Service. After attending a course at the School of Musketry, he joined the 8th Battery of the Motor Machine Gun Service.

By the summer of 1915 he had some experience of trench warfare.

A SWIFT-GOING MOTOR CYCLE WITH MACHINE GUN

In a letter to the editors of the School Magazine he described gore and glory of the battlefield.

Since my last bout in the trenches, when I was there 11days in 13, we have started another instruction class and I expect it will be the end of next week before we go up again. I much prefer the trenches to instructing officers in the use of the machine gun. Since I last wrote I have been up twice, once for two days and the other time for one day only. While I was there I saw men killed and wounded by trench mortars very close to me but I have not been touched yet. The last day I saw a great battle between a B E Biplane and a Taube. They circled up and up and fired at each other from 7.30 to dusk, but neither seemed to win and both sheared off in the twilight.

His enthusiasm and talent as an instructor earned him promotion to Captain in November 1915, the following year he was still in the front line.

Mentioned in Dispatches by Lord French, he was awarded the Military Cross in June. There was more promotion, to Major in July 1916.

The Motor Machine Gun Service was expanded to become the Machine Gun Corps, which in turn was absorbed into the Tank Corps. Tanks were sent into action ahead of the infantry. At Flers-Courcelette they did have some success, although many broke down. They did not perform well where there were deep trenches, shell holes and mud. Battling with these conditions at Arras and Ypres, the reputation of the Tank Corps suffered, but at Cambrai they broke through the Hindenberg Line and the full potential of the tank was recognised.

Major Westrop was also given some recognition. The London Gazette of August 1917 confirmed the award of the Distinguished Service Order.

For conspicuous gallantry and devotion to duty. He commanded his company with marked ability and success. He carried out reconnaissance of the captured ground and it was due to his information that enemy machine guns were located and captured.

Distinguished Service Order

Although Sidney Westrop had been exposed to danger many times he seems to have escaped serious injury. His brother Arthur was not so lucky

Major Arthur Richard Westrop OBE MC CdeG – Royal Field Artillery

Arthur Westrop was more interested in living things than things mechanical. Leaving Grammar School, he began his studies at Harper Adams Agricultural College and went on to do research at London University. Already a member of the Officer Training Corps, he joined the Royal Field Artillery as a 2nd Lieutenant.

He arrived in France with his battery to join the Guard's Brigade in August 1915.

Almost immediately they were sent into action at the Battle of Loos. Throughout the spring of 1916 detailed preparations were made for the great Battle of the Somme. D/61 Battery was spared the carnage of the opening weeks of the battle, but in September Lieutenant Westrop and his gunners had their sights set on High Wood, a key target at Fler-Courcelette.

The entry in his record was brief – *15 Sept GSW High Wood.*

Gun Shot Wound – the gun in question was a machine gun, the wound was in the left arm, the median nerve was damaged and there was a loss of feeling in Arthur's thumb and fingers. Taken first to a dressing station and then admitted to the 3rd General Hospita,l Arthur was transferred to the coast after a week of treatment and sailed home from Le Havre to Southampton. He spent six weeks at Wordsley Hall, a military hospital near Manchester. Home on sick leave at Camden Lodge, he was informed of his transfer to the Scottish Command.

His conduct at High Wood had not gone unnoticed, in the London Gazette of 14th Nov 1916 there was an extract from the citation for his Military Cross.

> *For conspicuous gallantry in action. He carried out his work as observation officer under very heavy fire, with great courage and determination. Later he led a party of infantry to their objective, the second line of German trenches, when he was wounded.*

His stay a Redford near Edinburgh was brief, he was back 'in the field' in January 1917 and in 25 Stationary Hospital in February. There was no bloodshed this time, he was suffering with scarlet fever and out of action for another six weeks. On the road to recovery he was promoted to Captain.

Captain Westrop was kept busy for the next eighteen months, either commanding a battery at the front or attending courses at the Artillery School at Shoeburyness.

Even in wartime there was joy and romance, in the summer of 1918 Sidney Westrop and Eileen Alton were married at King's Norton. The war came to an end and he was lucky enough to be at home for Christmas. There was good cheer, and homes were decorated. Major Westrop was also decorated, a grateful French government had awarded him the Croix de Guerre.

Clara Westrop's boys had proved to be outstanding soldiers – out of uniform they had to make their way in the world. Sidney Westrop sailed back and forth to the coast of West Africa, applying his training as an engineer to mining projects there. His brother, Arthur, an agricultural chemist, divided his time between Malaya and Nyasaland. He died there in 1965. Sidney was over eighty when he died fourteen years later.

Arthur Westrop, agricultural chemist & Sidney Westrop, engineer

Sidney and his young wife were living on Stafford Road, Wolverhampton, when his war medal, victory medal, and '15 star arrived in a small cardboard box. Wolverhampton was a very suitable location for an engineer, the Black Country was a centre for all the 'metal bashing' trades at the time. Sidney did not settle and neither did Arthur.

When Arthur first applied for his medals he gave an address in Normandy, Le Quesnay, he moved on, to 4 Bankshall Street Calcutta. The Westrops must have had family connections, another brother, Wilfred was born there. Arthur was back at Camden Lodge in 1922. The following year he had every reason to settle down, he married Margaret Logan a farmer's daughter from Worfield. Marriage was not the cure for wanderlust for Arthur or Sidney Westrop.

Sidney sailed off to New York just before Christmas 1925, leaving Eileen and his baby daughter at home in Essex. On the passenger list he described himself as a mining engineer, as he did when he travelled back from Lagos the following year.

For the next ten years he sailed back and forth to West Africa – from Takoradi on the Gold Coast, Freetown, Sierra Leone and Lagos, Nigeria on a variety of ships –*MV David Livingstone, MV Accra, SS Apapa.* This was an unhealthy part of the world, Eileen did not accompany him.

Meanwhile Arthur Westrop was also exploring warm lands. The *Grantully Castle* carried him from the Port of London to Durban, and on to Ceylon (Sri Lanka), a land famed for its tea plantations. He became an expert in the cultivation of tea and rubber, tea in South Africa and rubber in Malaya.

Throughout the 1930s he spent most the time in Malaya. He was a sociable man, one of the founder members of the Hash House Harriers, a non-competitive running club based at the Selangor Club in Kuala Lumpur. It became so popular that it quickly spread throughout the British Empire. This civilised way of life changed dramatically when Japan made war on the Allies.

Malaya was invaded from the north, the Japanese army swept south, and Singapore fell in February 1942. Alberto Gispert, one of

Arthur Westrop's old friends, died in its defence. Tens of thousands of British, Australian and Indian troops became prisoners of war. Arthur was no longer in uniform, but along with other ex-patriots he was made a prisoner at Changi Jail.

There was a certain amount of freedom, civilian prisoners had to fend for themselves, they were desperately short of food. It was as if all Arthur Westrop's training and experience had been in preparation for this event. He supervised the planting of a variety of vegetables in every available plot of land. These were desperate times.

When the war ended, Arthur had stayed on to help with the reconstruction programme. The rubber plantations, vital to the economy of Malaya, had been neglected during the war years.

He moved on and applied himself to the cultivation of tea, in Nyasaland (Malawi today). His estate at Magomba prospered and he expressed his satisfaction by writing an autobiography, *Green Gold*.

A staunch supporter of the Scout Movement, he spent time camping on the Mwabvi Game Reserve, tracking the wildlife there. A keen photographer, he became an authority on the bird life of South Africa. For his public service in Nyasaland he was awarded the OBE.

While Arthur was held as a Prisoner of War in Singapore, Sidney was back in uniform in 1940. His skill as an engineer was called for, he was promoted to Brigadier in the Corps of Engineers. He served on the home front throughout the war, and was awarded a CBE in 1946.

The brothers were reunited in 1954 when Sidney, accompanied by his wife and teenage daughter, Caroline, sailed out to Singapore. Arthur Westrop died at Magomba, in 1965.

Sidney Westrop was over eighty when he died in Lincolnshire fourteen years later.

These were exceptional men, the life stories of either of them would fill a book. Other Old Boys might have had equally eventful lives had they not been cut short by war.

The Old Boys who fought in the Great War were all Victorians, born before 1900. This was the age when Britannia ruled the waves and the sun never set on the British Empire. So the young men who flocked to 'join the colours' in 1914 were full of bravado, they would give the Hun a bloody nose. War would be gory of course, but glorious. For some it appeared to be.

Barlow and Boucher, Bill Hutton, Alan Steward and Vic Dawes were all rewarded with a Military Cross. Milner Deighton had an Air Force Cross and at least a dozen more were decorated. French, Italian and Serbian medals were awarded to Old Boys Tom Warburton received something rather unusual.

CAPTAIN THOMAS MARSHALL WARBURTON – 1ST GARRISON BATTALION, KING'S LIVERPOOL REGIMENT

Tom Warburton was a teenage when his father died. His legacy was a love of music all his children, William, James, Tom, Susan and Harold were musicians, either teachers or students of music. When Tom completed his studies there was no time to practise his gift for music, he went straight into the army. He was commissioned in the King's Liverpool Regiment, the 1st Garrison Battalion was formed at Seaford in August 1915, and within a month they were in Egypt.

There was no home leave, Lieutenant Warburton did not see his widowed mother for four years. What part he played in the campaigns in

Knight of the Order of the Nile

the Middle East we do not know but he clearly impressed his commanding officer. In June 1918 he was mentioned in dispatches and promoted to Captain. He was still serving at Alexandria a year after the end of the war and for this he was rewarded with a medal from Sultan Hussein Kamel, the Order of the Nile.

Safely back in England he took up an appointment at Merchant Taylor's School in Liverpool a world away from the Pyramids, dessert sand or the greenery of the Nile Delta. He moved into a house in College Road and lived in that same house until he died, a bachelor, in 1953.

All who served overseas received the War and Victory Medals. Private Perkins' two years of military service was entirely at 'home'. He was not rewarded.

Christopher Perkins, the frail young chemist, who carried on treating the sick for a year after the Armistice and probably saved one or two lives, was a willing recruit. He would have wished that he could have done more.

The schoolrooms of the Grammar School were no different from schoolrooms anywhere or at any time. In every class there were the studious and the sporty, bullies and peacemakers, the brave and the timid, would-be world travellers and stay-at-home boys. Nevertheless, as far as we can judge, there were no cowards, whatever talents they had they gave willingly in defence of their homeland.

Chapter 20

The Red Revolution

The course of the war changed in 1917, the Tsar of Russia abdicated and a Provisional Government was set up under Alexander Kerensky, who pledged to continue the struggle against the Central Power.

This agreement lasted only a matter of months. Kerensky's government was replaced by the Bolsheviks, led by Lenin, the communist revolutionary. He signed a treaty with the Germans that ended Russian involvement in the war. German troops were then transferred to the Western Front to strengthen their forces in France and Belgium.

A 'Red Army' was created to support the new regime in Russia – there was opposition, a 'White Army' was formed and civil war broke out. The War Cabinet in London decided to give support to the White Russians in the faint hope that they would again do battle with the Germans on the Eastern front. Winston Churchill put it more bluntly, "...to strangle at birth the Bolshevik State."

Communism had its followers in all nations. The promise of peace it offered to Germans, Russians and the French was certainly attractive at the time. French infantrymen had suffered appalling casualties, their food was poor and medical care second-rate. Mutinies flared up in the rest camps that were no more than military slums. Men refused to return to the front line. The mutineers staged protest marches, they waved red flags and sang the *Internationale,* the Communist anthem.

Churchill was among those who feared the spread of Communism. He was the driving force behind yet another campaign that critics described as 'Whitehall's Folly'. This would involve at least two Old Boys.

Doctor John Spurway had a medical practice in North London, 79 Brondesbury Road, Kilburn. Born in Kidderminster, he had local connections and decided to send his boys to Bridgnorth for their education. The Reverend Dawes's reputation as a mathematician may have been a deciding factor.

Cedric Spurway began his school life as a boarder in 1911 and studied hard for six years. Every year his examination successes in mathematics, were noted and in 1917 he was awarded a place at Worcester College, Oxford, instead he went to the Royal Military Academy. He was commissioned in the Royal Engineers the following year. Second Lieutenant Spurway then transferred to Signals Service.

Signallers were often the first on the battlefield providing intelligence to the advancing troops. In the early days the signalling was done with flags. When wireless telegraphy was developed, during the Great War, more skilful men were recruited to handle the equipment. The work was no less dangerous, laying landlines across the trenches and manning observation posts on the front line.

Lieutenant Spurway did not serve in France, his first experience of conflict was in Northern Russia. The campaign, in support of Russians still loyal to the Czar against the newly formed Red Army of communist revolutionaries, was ill-conceived and unpopular. Men lost their lives fighting for a cause that was of little concern to them. Cedric Spurway served on the banks of the Dvina River where another old Grammar School boy, Richard Thursfield, lost his life. These must have been anxious days for the Spurways. They were still mourning the loss of their eldest boy killed in March 1918, on the Somme.

Cedric returned safely to the family home in Kilburn before the army dispatched him to the North West Frontier of India. This area, on the border with Afghanistan, had been a trouble spot for many years, and is to this day. The British public had become familiar with the names of towns and rivers in continental Europe. Cedric could certainly put his finger on Archangel and Murmansk on the map of Russia, now he had stranger names to learn. He was promoted to Captain and took command of No 2 Signals Company, at Mianwali, near Karachi, on the North West Frontier of India. Captain Spurway soon became familiar with the villages and outposts in the border region.

Afghanistan had remained neutral throughout the Great War, despite pressure from the Germans and the Turks who wanted to cross Afghan territory and invade British India. As a reward for their neutrality the Afghans were promised independence. The diplomats dithered, and trouble broke out on the border, difficult terrain to police and patrol. The Indian Army was greatly reduced, men were demobilised at the end of the war, and many were dissatisfied with British rule.

In 1915 at the Grammar School Senior Sports Cedric had excelled, he was an athlete, not just a prize winner in the classroom. The tracks between the outposts manned by Cedric's signallers were steep and winding, travelling between them was difficult even for the fittest of men. Mules carried supplies to the troops, and dispatch riders, on motor bikes, carried vital messages. To carry out inspections and make sure his men were kept 'on their toes' Captain Spurway travelled the stony tracks on his Enfield motorbike. Those who served here qualified for the Indian General Service Medal with a clasp for Waziristan.

On his behalf, Cedric's commanding officer applied for this and his other war medals, eventually they arrived and were promptly returned, to Godden, Holme and Ward, solicitors in Old Jewry Street, London. Captain Spurway was dead, killed in a motor-cycle accident in March 1924. There appeared to be on 'next of kin'.

Doctor John Spurway had died in 1920, Douglas Spurway had been killed in action in March 1918. Mary Alsop Spurway had lost everything, her husband, and her sons, who had shown such promise and had a bright future ahead of them.

Another motor-cyclist, Phillip Hutton, was a survivor and success-ful business man. His last duty with the British Army was serving with a force sent to protect oil supplies from the Middle East.

CORPORAL (152377) PHILIP HUTTON – ROYAL ENGINEERS

The School Magazine reported that Corporal Hutton was in France and 'doing well' as a dispatch rider with the Royal Engineers. His medal card confirmed that he had served in Theatre 1, France and Belgium, also on record was – *23rd Dec. 1917* – *Caucasus*. This meant that Philip had been selected to join a rather unusual unit.

Some men who joined the 'Hush Hush Party' were serving in

Mesopotamia, others had proved themselves on the battlefields of Europe. They were men 'of strong character, adventurous spirit, especially good stamina, capable of organising, training and eventually leading irregular troops'. These were the same qualities expected today of Special Forces.

Orders handed to the Western Front 'volunteers' instructed them to report to the Tower of London. They were kept in the dark, kitted out with clothing for cool and warm climates but given no inkling of their mission. They were introduced to an Iranian and a party of Russians. On the 29th of January 1918 they began their journey to the Middle East. First crossing from Southampton to Cherbourg by ferry, then a long train journey across France and Italy to board a steamer at Taranto and sail to Alexandria. They were joined by about sixty Australians. It was a truly multinational force – Canadians, South Africans, and New Zealanders, all with battlefield experience.

As they journeyed on, the Russians offered language lessons, but no more information on the task ahead. An overnight train trip took them to Port Said to board a decrepit transport vessel, *The Nile*, which carried them down the Red Sea, through the Indian Ocean, and up the Persian Gulf, eventually arriving in Basra. Almost two months had passed since they left their units in France and Flanders.

A flotilla of flat-bottomed barges was assembled to carry them up the Tigris to Bagdad, this was a hazardous undertaking, even in peacetime. They had expected to meet their commanding officer, Major-General Lionel Dunsterville, in Bagdad but he had already set off on his mission.

The area south of the Caucasus Mountains was complex territory – Kurdistan, Azerbaijan, Armenia and Georgia. There were rival nations involved – Russia, Turkey, Germany and the British Empire. Added to this there were conflicting ideologies – Islam, Christianity and Communism. And then, as now, oil was a flammable liquid.

Russian forces had held the territory between the Caspian Sea and the Black Sea, they protected the pipeline that ran from the oilfields around Baku to the port of Batum. All this changed when Communist revolutionaries took over in Russia and signed the peace treaty with Germany and Turkey. Turkish forces were then free to invade. The primary objective for 'Dunsterforce' was to recruit and train Kurds and Armenians to fight alongside them and prevent the oil supplies, so vital to the war machine, falling into enemy hands.

General Dunsterville set off on the long journey to Tiflis, a town on the railway line that ran alongside the Baku-Batum pipeline. The advance party travelled in an assortment of Ford vans and touring cars. The first obstacle was the Asadabad Pass, particularly difficult in winter. At the top, one thousand eight hundred metres above sea level, they regrouped at Hamadan before travelling a further 250 miles to Enzeli on the southern shores of the Caspian Sea.

Russian revolutionaries had recently occupied the town. Dunsterville met with the Bolshevik committee and was left in no doubt as to who was in charge, the Russians had 3000 armed men to back up their claim. 'Dunsterforce' withdrew travelling the 250 miles back along the road to Hamadan and there they stayed for three months.

The main force was called up from Bagdad, Canadians, Australians and Philip Hutton. The first seventy miles, by train, were easy, the last 230 miles was on foot – not so easy. Phillip Hutton had a motor bike. Once they had recovered from the journey they began the task of recruiting and training local militia, mostly Armenians.

Straighten Your Backs!

© Imperial War Museum

New Zealanders were responsible for communications, operating the latest wireless technology. When this failed they had to rely on runners, or Philip Hutton and his Lee Enfield motor bike.

With new recruits and reinforcements Dunsterforce was ready to take on the Bolsheviks at Enzeli. They captured the town at the end of June 1918. A smaller contingent sailed up the coast of the Caspian to Baku, but they were never in full control of the port. The Turks counterattacked, 180 men were lost. The Turkish triumph was short lived. Forces of the Ottoman Empire laid down their arms at the end of October. British forces sailed through the Black Sea and occupied Batum in 1919.

The General had earlier described the mission as a 'mad enterprise', and he was right. However, the confusion caused by Dusterforce in the region meant that no oil was pumped from Baku to Batum and as this had been one of the objectives, Lionel Dunsterville could claim some success.

What remained of Dunsterforce withdrew to Bagdad. Canadians and Australians went their separate ways, as did New Zealanders and South Africans, and Philip Hutton came home to begin a new life.

Richard Thursfield had made the navy his career, he would still be a serving officer when the war with Germany was over. He too was called upon to take part in 'Churchill's War' against the Bolsheviks

Surgeon Lieutenant Richard Mortimer Roland Thursfield – Royal Navy

Surgeon Lieutenant Thursfield had been waging war on the mosquito in the Gulf of Guinea, dosing the crew of *Astraea* with quinine for over a year, and only occasionally treating a war wound. It was something of a relief when the campaign in West Africa came to an end in February 1916, with the surrender of the last German stronghold in Kamerun.

HMS Astraea put out to sea, and Richard Thursfield and the rest of the crew had to find their sea legs once again. They had been moored for twelve months and needed to refresh some of their nautical skills. Gunnery and torpedo practice took place as they sailed past the Niger Delta. They called in at Lagos and Accra and finally steamed into Freetown harbour, Sierra Leone.

A few lucky members of the ship's crew transferred to other ships to take them 'back to Blighty', the ship's surgeon was unlucky. Astraea sailed south, crossed the equator, anchored off St Helena for a few days and returned to base at Simonstown, under the shadow of Table Mountain. Astraea took on stores and at last Richard Thursfield was on his way, he crossed the equator once more and sailed into home waters.

A warm welcome awaited him in Bridgnorth. He had much to tell the family and he must have been keen to learn the fate of friends and neighbours, the Stewards and Gadsby boys, Arthur Rhodes, medical officer with the Argyll and Sutherland Highlanders, Walker and White-foot and all the other 'Old Boys' from along the High Street.

Richard Thursfield returned to duty and spent the next two years at the Marine Artillery Infirmary, Portsmouth, doing the work he had trained for. The war was drawing to an end, but not for Surgeon Lieutenant Thursfield. His war began off the coast of Darkest Africa, it would end on the on the Dvina River, fighting alongside White Russians against the Red Army.

To counter the communist threat an intervention Force was formed that involved British, French, American, Canadian, Greek, Italian and even Japanese troops. They established a military presence in the Baltic, the Caucasus, and even in Eastern Siberia, supplying war material and assisting the White Russian armies. British airmen, infantrymen and sailors were all involved.

Richard Thusfield spent a month at HMS Vivid, solid naval barracks at Devonport while *Glowworm* was being prepared for action. She was one of the Insect Class gunboats. Her sisterships, *Cicala, Cricket, Cockchafer and Glowworm* all sounded harmless enough, but they were gunboats and in preparation for active service four Lewis guns were added to increase their firepower, and an anti-aircraft gun for defence.

In October 1918 they set off in convoy from Lowestoft to join the Dvina River Force at Archangel in Arctic Russia. They might have waited a while because they were laid up there throughout the winter months. Come the Spring, the ice melted on the Dvina River and operations commenced. In the Summer *Mantis* and *Moth* arrived to join the flotilla.

The gunboats were in action daily, and in one month fired over 1000 rounds of 6 inch ammunition apiece at targets as varied as enemy cavalry units, entrenched positions and gun barges. It was not all one-sided, *Cicala* and *Cricket* were both put out of action, and towed away for repairs.

bad."   "Humber."   "Cicala."   Seaplane Ba
Dvina River Flotilla, Bolshevik Campaign, 1919.

The gunboats didn't just patrol the river avoiding mines. Landing parties were organised to storm ashore and harass the Red Army. Commander Green took the lead on one raid and was awarded the DSO for an action at Tchamova. Lieutenant Thursfield patched up the wounded.

Overall the campaign was not going well, morale was low. The only soldiers who felt at home in North Russia were the Canadians. The Royal Marine battalion was made up largely of nineteen year old lads led by men who were tired of war. The American contingent had no experience of battle. It was small wonder that there was discontent.

At home, The Daily Express declared that 'The frozen plains of Russia are not worth the bones of a single British Grenadier'. A company of the Durham Light Infantry refused to parade, two sergeants were court-martialled and sentenced to death. They were reprieved but still served a ten year prison sentence.

Everyone taking part in 'Churchill's War' recognised that this was a futile cause. It was rumoured that the crew of *Glowworm's* sister ship the *Cicala* had mutinied, certainly four men were court-martialled for disobeying orders, and were sentenced to five year's imprisonment.

The White troops, they had come to support, became increasingly disheartened and unreliable. By the summer of 1919 it was clear that the Red Army would be victorious in this part of the world. The decision was made to withdraw, Richard Thursfield was to remain.

On the 25th of August *Glowworm* was patrolling on the Dvina when she was called to assist an ammunition barge in distress, fire had broken out on board. The barge was carrying mines and shells. As *Glowworm* drew alongside the whole barge was ripped apart, shells flew in every direction killing members of both crews and even men on the dockside. Nearby on HMS Fox the explosion killed Lieutenant Walter Waganoff, a Russian interpreter. On board Glowworm Commander Sebald-Green and Able Seaman McCoy survived the blast but died the next day. In total eighteen members of the crew were killed.

Lost on that fateful day were Able Seamen, Signallers, a Stoker, a Steward and Surgeon Lieutenant Richard Thursfield. They were all buried in Russian soil, in the Allied Cemetery Semenovka (Breznik Cemetery Extension)

RN SRGN R. M. R. THURSFIELD was placed top of the roll of honour on the Bridgnorth War Memorial, and below him other Old Boys, who died closer to home.

Lost at sea more than twenty years later was Lieutenant John Foxall.

SERGEANT (80116) JOHN FOXALL – MACHINE GUN CORPS & LIEUTENANT – ROYAL ARMY SERVICE CORPS

From the family home in Underhill Street John Foxall could chose a different route to school every day of the week, Cartway, Friars Street, St Leonard's Steps, Rope Walk, Stoneway Steps and along the High Street. There was an uphill climb on every route, for a lively lad this was not a problem.

John completed his studies at Bridgnorth Grammar School in 1916 and on 4th September began his engineering apprenticeship at the Coventry Ordnance Works.

HEAVY ENGINEERING

School friends wished him 'the very best of luck in his career'. He wrote back to say that he was 'pleased with the work and the possibilities it holds'. He could not imagine then where it might lead. Eighteen months later he signed the form that turned him from civilian to soldier.

After recruit training some men waited years for promotion. John 'signed on' at Coventry on the 18th of March 1918 and was promoted to Sergeant on that day. They must have been expecting him because the next day he was sent to Grantham. There was no time to learn marching and saluting, he had experience of handling ordnance, he needed just three weeks practice with small arms before Sergeant John Foxall embarked at Southampton.

After a month at sea they sailed up the Persian Gulf and docked at Basra. Here he joined an Armoured Car Squadron, part of the Royal Naval Air Service that had served in Northern Russian and were now known as 'Duncars'. John and his friends were part of Dustersterforce and he may have met with Phillip Hutton at Hamadam as they prepared to advance towards the Baku in the Caucasus.

Even without battlefield experience John Foxall could see that this was a futile exercise because on the 20th of May he was reprimanded for 'not complying with an order'.

In July the road to the port of Enzeli on the Caspian Sea was cleared, with the help of Russian Cossacks who were at odds with the communist revolutionaries. John Foxall was admitted to hospital for two days, it was probably nothing more serious than a 'touch of the sun'.

The advance party sailed north and landed at Baku on the 4th of August, for the rest of the month troops of Dunsterforce drove or marched from Bagdad to join them. To assist in this venture were about six thousand local recruits, 'The Baku Force'. They were ill-disciplined and untrained. When the Turks attacked they failed to give support to Dunsterforce. There were heavy casualties and General Dunsterville ordered the evacuation. The mission had failed, even the 'special forces' of his team, Foxall and Hutton, could not hold out.

Dunsterforce regrouped at Bagdad and then dispersed. John Foxall sailed home, the war ended, a New Year began and at Prees Heath on 1st of April he was discharged.

The next big event in John Foxall's life was at St Andrew's Church in Shifnal.

Minnie Ford had spent her childhood at the Boar's Head on Morville Heath, her father was the innkeeper, and perhaps John was a regular customer.

At the outbreak of the Second World War John Foxall was forty

years old and he was not obliged to go back into uniform, but he did and he was promoted, Sergeant Foxall of 1919 became Lieutenant Foxall of 1939. He was commissioned in the Royal Army Service Corps.

History was about to repeat itself. In July 1941 Lieutenant Foxall was on his way back to Basra once again. This would give him the opportunity to tell fellow officers of the time he spent with Dunsterforce.

From the pool of London *SS Shahristan* sailed out to join convoy 05-1. As they approached the Azores she left the convoy to make her own way to the Gulf.

Heindrick Driver, the Captain of U-371, had the Shahristan in his sights. He gave the order to launch torpedoes, they struck home with deadly accuracy. Some survivors were picked up by the Royal Navy (HMS Sunflower and Derbyshire) and a Spanish trawler, John Foxall was not one of them. Nearly half the ship's complement was lost.

Lieutenant John Foxall died at sea on the 29th July 1941. He is remembered in his home town and also on a rather unusual memorial at Brookwood, near Woking. On the 1939-45 Memorial are the names of over three thousand men and women, who have no known grave. He shares this memorial with Commandos who went on raids on the coast

of Norway and France and did not return, and Special Agents who died in captivity. There are airmen, and soldiers lost at sea, and even nursing sisters serving on hospital ships.

Left to grieve were John's parents in Bridgnorth, still living at 42 Underhill Street, and his widow, Minnie, in Shrewsbury.

Chapter 21

Odd Bods

Clerks and schoolmasters, farmers and shopkeepers were the trades taken up by many of the Old Boys. There were one two doctors, a vet and a few engineers. There were stay-at-home boys who seldom crossed the county borders, and some who travelled the world.

When Nathan Mindel was introduced to his classmates the master probably hung up the map of Europe to show them were Lithuania was. It was then part of the Russian Empire.

LIEUTENANT NATHAN ISADORE MINDEL OBE – ARMY SERVICE CORPS

The Mindels were from Danilovich, a town near Vilna (present-day Vilnius) in Lithuania. At the time, it was 1890, half the population of Vilna were Jewish, it was a centre of Jewish culture in that part of the world. In the 1880s a series of anti-Semitic 'pogroms' flared up and thousands of Jews emigrated, many to the United States, the Mindels came to London.

The Buckle Street Buildings in Whitechapel were not the most comfortable surroundings for Isaac and Leah Mindel to bring up a family. Conditions were cramped for their five children. Nathan Isadore Mindel was born in Whitechapel in 1891, but was still considered a Russian national. There were dozens of Russian immigrants in Buckle Street, Jews like the Mindels, Sukolskys and the Galablats. The odd ones out were the Connors from Ireland and the Smiths from Wiltshire.

Nathan's father found work as a poorly paid boot finisher. The family worked hard and moved on, away from the East End, and they prospered. The children were given the best 'schooling' the family could afford. Isadore became a boarder at Bridgnorth Grammar School.

In 1911, twenty year old Nathan was living with an older brother in Stoke Newington, and studying part-time at London University. In 1916 he was listed in the School Magazine as one of the 'Old Bridgnorthians with the Colours'.

He had been a cadet with the Officer Training Corps of London University, yet he began his service in the British Army as a Private in the Royal Army Medical Corps. He was an alien, a Jew, a Russian by birth, promotion in the British Army was going to be difficult.

His first experience of active service came shortly after he arrived in Egypt in November 1915, and sailed on to the Greek island of Limnos. Troops withdrawing from the beaches of Gallipoli were arriving at the port of Mudros. The Dardanelles Campaign against the Turks had been a disaster.

From the beginning the priority in the Middle East was the defence of the Suez Canal. This was the supply route for troops, equipment, foodstuffs and materials essential to the conduct of the war. Attempts by the Turks to disrupt the flow of shipping on the canal failed. British, Anzac and Indian forces, helped by some Arab tribesmen, forced the Turks back into the Negev Desert.

Private Mindel of the Royal Army Medical Corps was now serving with the Camel Corps. Hundreds of horses and mules were required to support troops on the move; draft horses to pull the water wagons and forage carts, with mules and pack horses to carry equipment. They were organised in 'trains', doubtless referring to wagon trains. In the desert it soon became clear that the camel, although temperamental, was the most reliable beast of burden.

During a night exercise Private Nathan Mindel suffered a knee injury and was out of action for six months. It was time to consider promotion, he made an application to become a commissioned officer. There were difficulties, there was the question of qualifications, and he was a Russian-born Jew.

His bother went to the Home Office in London, and the records showed that Nathan had become a naturalised British subject in 1912. The Reverend Adler an army chaplain remembered him as a cadet with the London Regiment and gave a character reference. Professor Percy Lord of London University confirmed that Nathan Mindel was a graduate of the university. A telegram was sent to the camp at Abbasia in February 1917, Private Mindel was promoted to 2nd Lieutenant in the Army Service Corps

Meanwhile the Turks were being pursued along the coastal strip towards Gaza. They made a stand and held out for over six months. In March and April determined efforts were made to dislodge them from the town. Only after a ten-day battle at the end of October were they forced to retreat into Palestine. General Allenby gathered his forces and swept on to capture Jerusalem on the 9th of December. The British Prime Minister, Lloyd George, proclaimed that 'This is a Christmas present for the British people'. It was more than that for Nathan Mindel, he had helped to liberate the Holy City, a place of pilgrimage for Jews, Christians and Muslims.

There was a Jewish community already settled in Palestine, families that had fled persecution in other parts of the world, Russia in particular. Western governments felt some responsibility for the injustice they had suffered for so long and now looked favourably on the establishment of a homeland for the Jews. Lionel Rothschild, a wealthy British banker and Zionist activist, received a letter in November 1917 from the Foreign Secretary, Lord Arthur Balfour, in which he explained that the British Government was ready to give their support.

The Balfour Declaration was a modest document. A single sheet of paper. In just sixty-seven words it set out the position of the British Government.

"His Majesty's Government view with favour the establishment in Palestine of a national home for the Jewish people, and will use their best endeavours to facilitate the achievement of this object."

It went on to mention 'existing non-Jewish communities', which meant Palestinian Arabs. At the time they made up 90% of the population. The troubles and conflict that would develop over the years could not have been predicted at the time.

In the spring of 1918 Lieutenant Mindel celebrated the Feast of the Passover in Jerusalem. To mark the occasion Jewish officers and civilians of all ages stood before the camera on the steps of the synagogue with the Chief Rabbi and two British Army chaplains. At the time he was acting as an interpreter.

By the end of the year, after victory had been declared, the process of demobilisation began, and men in uniform looked forward to going

home and beginning a new life. Nathan sailed back to England in January 1919, six months later he returned to duty in Egypt. While politicians debated what to do with the remnants of the Ottoman Empire (France would administer Syria and Britain Palestine) Lieutenant Mindel went about his administrative duties at Kantara and Ismalia. He was in no hurry to return to Britain.

In September 1920 a 'chit' (a document) from the Orderly Room at Kantara informed him officially of his release from the British Army. Mr Mindel stayed on to serve the new Government of Palestine, to help with the birth of a nation. The medals awarded to him for war service were sent to the Immigration Department at Jaffa.

Lord Samuel was appointed High Commissioner in Palestine in 1920. General Allenby predicted trouble, the Arab population would not accept a Jewish administrator. Lord Samuel did in fact win the confidence of all sectors of the population with his impartiality. Immigration was at first carefully controlled to be 'within the absorptive capacity of the country'. This was a difficult job, the responsibility of Nathan Isadore Mindel.

In his memoires Lord Samuel spoke highly of Nathan Mindel, he was marked for promotion. It seems he had all the necessary qualities, Jewish by birth, an officer in the British Army, a naturalised Russian. Many of the immigrants came from Russia, his knowledge of the language must have been very useful. He also spoke Yiddish and probably some Arabic learned during his service with the Camel Corps.

His love of the land he regarded as his spiritual homeland deepened when he met Miriam Weinberg. Her family had been resident in Jerusalem for generations. Still in the uniform of a British officer he proposed to her on the beach at Tel Aviv. They married in 1921.

The flow of Jewish immigrants to Palestine became overwhelming and resentment grew in the Arab community. It was revealed in 1934 that to qualify for entry arranged marriages were conducted abroad by 'unqualified rabbis'. This was yet another factor that contributed to the growing tension between Arab and Jew. The police force was strengthened with uniformed volunteers. Nathan, a respected civil servant now, was issued with a rifle. The 'specials' only served to inflame the situation and they were ordered to hand in their arms. Nathan was incensed, instead of handing over his rifle calmly, as one might expect, he raised it above his head and slammed it to the floor.

The Arab Revolt which began in 1936 lasted for three years. There was a pause in hostilities. During the Second World War nations were united against the fascist forces of Hitler. At least a million Russian Jews took up arms.

The troubles in Palestine resumed in 1945 and British troops did what they could to keep the peace. At the time Nathan Mindel was the Senior Assistant Commissioner, he had served his people and the British Government well, and in 1946 he received the OBE for his part in the creation of the State of Israel. He returned to Britain and settled in North London, a far cry from the East End. He must have been saddened by the continuing conflict between Jews and Palestinians that continues to the present day.

Nathan made one last visit to Israel. Travelling alone in a first-class cabin he sailed from Manchester along the ship canal on board *Pinemore* and arrived at the port of Haifa in October 1958. He died, aged 70, in Jerusalem, Nathan had helped to build a nation.

Frank Sugg had a less distinguished career.

A benefit match between Lancashire and Kent was played at Old Trafford for Frank Howe-Sugg in 1897. Frank Reginald Sugg couldn't remember it, he was only one year old at the time. As he grew up he gradually learned of his father's fame as an athlete and first-class cricketer. He had appeared for Yorkshire, Derbyshire and Lancashire, and for England against Australia in the Test Match of 1888.

Frank Sugg Senior

During the winter months he played football for Sheffield Wednesday, Derby County, Burnley and Bolton Wanderers. Frank Sugg won prizes for rifle-shooting, bowls, billiards, weight-lifting and swimming. Over six feet tall he was an imposing figure, someone to look up to.

Although he grew up surrounded by all the right equipment in the Sugg's sports shop at Walton-on-the-Hill Frank junior could not hope to follow in his father's footsteps in any sport.

When the time came to consider 'schooling' it was decided that

Frank would lodge with his uncle and aunt at 4 Victoria Road and attend Bridgnorth Grammar School. His uncle, John Turton-Smith, was church-organist and music master and handed on his talents and enthusiasm to Frank.

When war came Frank Sugg showed very little enthusiasm for it, unlike many of his old school friends. Lieutenant Sugg,s career in the British Army was set out very simply in two documents, the Attestation (Army Form B 2512) and his Application for a Commission (Form MT 393 A).

Frank attested at the recruiting centre in Liverpool, and was given the rank of Acting Lance Corporal, class 'B', in the Army Reserve, not a particularly brilliant start for a young man with talent. He was studying at Jesus College, Cambridge at the time. With a rubber stamp the Inns of Court administrators in London gave their approval for further promotion to Corporal, in the cadet battalion of the Officer Training Corps – and he was paid for it! He must have reasoned that he would be better paid as an officer and so he completed Form MT 393 A.

Frank was very fond of exclamation marks (!) and used them on his application for a wartime commission. Several of the questions he dismissed with a dash of the pen.

"Are you able to ride?" YES! Of course, all the people I know ride.

"Are you in possession of Certificate A or B?" NO! I'm studying at Jesus College.

"Are you of pure European descent?" YES! My father played Cricket for England.

Whether married NO! I may be considering it.

When asked "What is your occupation in civilian life?" Vocalist was Frank's response.

The response of the interviewer was not recorded. Some men had talents that the army could use – farm hands could dig trenches in any weather – country gents were used to giving orders to unruly men – athletes, like Frank's father, could bound over rough ground like a stag. Could a singer make a serious contribution to the war effort?

Frank was granted a commission. In April 1917, the London Gazette announced his promotion to 2nd Lieutenant in the 3rd West Yorkshire Regiment, attached to the Garrison Battalion of the Manchester Regiment. Frank was not going anywhere dangerous, which suited him fine because in the summer, when his studies at Cambridge were complete, he moved to Newcastle-on-Tyne and married Mabel Coleman.

In June 1919 Frank was relieved of his commission and received a letter that thanked for his 'services in the war and for doing all in his power to bring it to a successful conclusion'.

It seems that Frank never found fame as a singer, instead he found employment as a clerk at the Ministry of Labour. He must have had a spark of ambition because when he was seeking promotion in 1934, he wrote to the War Office requesting details of his army record, which appeared to have been mislaid. His attestation form was probably being used as an example to staff of poor recruiting procedures. How could he have slipped through the net?

He didn't follow his sporting father to bat for England at Lords. Frank Reginald Sugg never made 'the big time' on the stage, unlike one Old Boy he had known. While Frank was seeking promotion in the Ministry of Labour, Cedric Hardwicke was receiving his knighthood from the King, for distinguished work on the stage and in films. Was Frank a little envious?

Lieutenant Cedric Webster Hardwicke – 9th Northumberland Fusiliers & Army Service Corps

Edwin Hardwicke, physician and surgeon, had a modest practice at Lye, in the early part of the century,and he hoped that with a good education his son would go on to study medicine. Young Cedric was sent to the Grammar School, he was a boarder there for three years. He showed a talent for drama, and no interest in medicine. He failed the exams for medical school. The family must have discussed the problem, father listened, and to his credit, paid for Cedric to study at the Academy of Dramatic Art in London.

He joined the Birmingham Repertory Company in 1912 and began to practise his art. The scene in Europe grew dark as the clouds of war gathered; the storm broke in August 1914.

There could be no greater drama than war and Cedric Hardwicke wanted to play a part, even if his would be only a minor role. He began his war service with the 9th Northumberland Fusiliers. They were a locally raised unit and together with others from the North-East formed the 34th Division. They began training near Ripon. In August the following year, 1915, they moved to Salisbury Plain for final training and firing practice.

Now considered to be ready for battle, the troops were advised to make the most of the Christmas celebrations. On the 3rd of January 1916 embarkation orders arrived, and by the 15th the Division had crossed the Channel. They set up base at La Crosse, east of Omer. They were soon engaged in the senseless struggle on the Somme, casualties were many. The 43rd Division remained on the Western Front until the end of the war, not Cedric Hardwicke.

He was promoted to Lieutenant in the Army Service Corps (Horse Transport). This was another job he was not qualified for. He was transferred to the Judge Advocate General's Department where his gift for public speaking could be used to good effect.

Offences tried by courts martial ranged from murder to not shaving in the morning. Not every man who came before the courts was capable of defending himself. They were allowed a 'friend' to defend them. Usually a junior officer was appointed to speak on behalf of the accused. Some lucky lads may have had the services of Lieutenant Hardwicke. He had no legal training but that didn't matter, he could play the part of a barrister. With a stage presence and the ability to captivate an audience there must have been many occasions when the man on trial was relieved to hear, 'case dismissed'.

The war came to an end, but that did not mean an end to the work of the Judge Advocate General and his team. Lawyers do like to tie up loose ends at public expense. Cedric Hardwicke stayed on with the army of occupation until 1921 and claimed to be the last British officer to leave the war zone. He returned to the stage, to the Birmingham Repertory Company.

Cedric made a name for himself as Caesar in George Bernard Shaw's 'Caesar and Cleopatra', this was his ticket to the London stage. He appeared in a string of Shaw's plays.

In 1931 he made his first film, the 'Dreyfus Affair'. Alfred Dreyfus, a captain in the French army was accused of spying. He went before the courts and was wrongfully imprisoned. With years of experience in the Judge Advocate General's Department during the war no one could have played the part of Captain Dreyfus more convincingly than Cedric Hardwicke.

At a time when few actors received honours, Cedric was knighted by King George V. He was introduced to the hard-of-hearing King by a palace aide before the ceremony.

"Arise Sir Cedric Pickwick",

the King announced as he tapped the kneeling actor on the shoulder with the ceremonial sword.

'Joey' Barritt, Bridgnorth Grammar School headmaster, gave everyone the day off to mark the occasion.

Sir Cedric moved to Hollywood. With his resonant voice and aristocratic presence he was much in demand, appearing in a string of major films. His popularity continued for twenty years. In the course of his acting career he shared films sets with some of the most glamorous actresses. Playing opposite Maureen O' Hara in 'The Hunchback of Notre Dame' he seemed to have difficulty looking her in the eye.

They were together again in 'Sentimental Journey'. It must have taken him back to his childhood at Lye, his father sitting at the desk in his surgery, a stethoscope hanging permanently around his neck. Now

he was playing the doctor, Maureen his dying patient. He was lost for words, but often quoted: "I did nothing but look at the handsome bosom of Maureen O' Hara and listen to the murmuring of her heart through a stethoscope."

It seem that he did not pay sufficient attention to his own health. He died in New York of emphysema, the likely cause was smoking. The habit probably began with 'Woodbines' in the trenches, graduated to 'Craven A' and then to more exotic brands (Sobranie Cocktail) when he moved to Hollywood.

His savings were eaten up with hospital expenses, incurred during his final illness, there was nothing left to pay for a funeral. Money was donated by an actors' charity to cover the cost.

He never forgot his old school, he kept in touch and had even offered to help with productions. It would have pleased him to know that one day one of the 'houses' would bear his name.

Chapter 22

No More Letters Home

The Reverend Henry Dawes served as headmaster for thirty-three years. It was most fitting that one of his last duties at The School was to attend the opening ceremony of the Memorial Library. He had known the majority of the forty-three men whose names were recorded on the memorial tablet. He would, no doubt, have approved the inscription: 'So they passed over, and all the trumpets sounded on the other side.'

The quotation, from John Bunyan's Pilgrim's Progress, referred to the last act of Mr Valiant-for-Truth, crossing the River Jordan, a soldier no more.

As a minister of the Church, the Reverend Dawes certainly believed in life after death. Not every Old Boy who fought in the Great War had his faith, but one certainly did. Harry Jones was described as, 'One of God's Faithful Warriors'

Captain Harry Martin Jones – 1/8th Royal Warwickshire Regiment

Harry Jones was a complex character: simple upbringing, studious boy, schoolmaster, and snob.

> *I was awfully pleased to see that so many Old Boys have responded to the call of their country. One is always proud to compare one's Old School with those of one's brother officers on such matters. When one takes the size of The School into account I think we have done as well as any.*

It sounded rather pompous, but whatever his shortcomings there was no questioning Harry Jones' courage and sense of duty.

© BES Library

He must have anticipated the outbreak of war because he was commissioned in the 1/8th Royal Warwickshire Regiment in September 1914. The regiment trained for six months and sailed for France in March 1915. There was a good covering of snow on the quayside when they arrived at Le Havre.

Transferring from the docks to barracks at Harfleur would have been a different experience for Harry Jones and his fellow officers from that of Private Ralph Miller and his mates. Ralph, a territorial and true 'Brummy', had joined with the rest of his footballing friends at the outbreak of war.

When I got to France there was four inches of snow on the ground, and we marched from Le Havre to Harfleur. It was a nasty bloody march with full pack. A slog all the way. The little French kids shouted 'Chocolat' at us.

Within a month the Royal Warwicks were given a taste of the trenches. Harry Jones was full of enthusiasm.

> *A few days ago we were put in the firing line with a regular battalion. It was a very novel experience and would have been quite enjoyable had it not rained the whole time we were in. We only did a 24 hour spell but even in that short time we were absolutely covered in mud. The trenches are really wonderful. The men have their dugouts, and the officers have a small kitchen and mess-room constructed in the walls of the trenches.*

It seemed odd that Harry was so conscious of his rank, and the distinction between officers and men. He had a very ordinary background, his own father was a house painter and his mother a baker and confectioner. Not all Old Boys of the Grammar School applied for commissions, and at least one of the masters, a university graduate, served as a Private soldier.

Serving in the same battalion as Captain Harry Jones was Private Ralph Miller who was more concerned with becoming a 'master at arms' than comparing the accommodation of officers and men.

> *The finest hand grenade of the war was the Mills bomb. It had a pin to pull out, and then you held the lever down, and when you loosed it, it flew up, struck the detonator, and the bomb exploded about three or four seconds after you threw it.*

Harry Jones described the routine of trench warfare that would become a way of life for a whole year.

> *We have a spell of four days in the trenches then we come out for four days. During the four days rest we dig communication trenches from 8pm till midnight. Then we occupy the reserve trenches until 2 am, when we fall back to a wood. We sleep in this wood till 6.30 am and then go back to our billet which is a rather dilapidated farm-house. The men occupy the barn, while we sleep on our valises in the house itself.*

Private Miller was still more interested in self-preservation than the sleeping arrangements.

When you were sniping you set yourself a site, you saved yourself a little space, you got a good view of something and you let go. Aiming at anything that moved. Sometimes you'd strain to look at a tree trunk, and you'd see it move, and the more you stared the more it moved, and you had to be very careful. If you let go at that, there might be one of their snipers having a go at you.

Don't Shoot, It's One of Ours

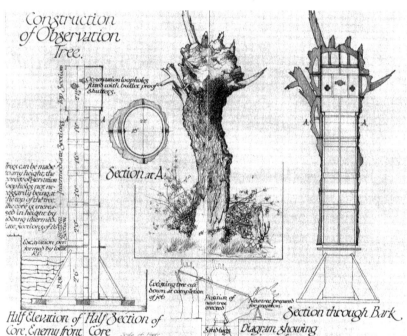

As a relief from the tension of trench life, Ralph Miller and his mates could boot their football about behind the lines and dream of being picked to play for Aston Villa when the war was over.

Home on leave, boots polished and tunic pressed, Lieutenant Jones married Edith Gray in Birmingham. Everyone wanted the war to be over so that dreams could be fulfilled. But first the German front line had been broken. A great battle was planned, for June 1916, which would deliver an early victory, or so the generals believed.

Elaborate preparations were made for the opening days of the Battle of the Somme. To brief the men their officers were given maps of the enemy positions, and airmen were flying dangerously low over the trenches to gather vital intelligence.

The fellows are remarkably plucky and daring. The other day we saw one of our aviators flying over the German lines to reconnoitre for our artillery. The shells from German anti-aircraft guns burst all around him, but he calmly went on with his work and only returned to our lines when he had evidently obtained the required information. It was really a splendid sight.

The portion of the front allotted to the Royal Warwicks lay between the villages of Serre and Beaumont Hamel. Eight hundred yards of open ground separated the front line trenches. Covering no man's-land were machine gun posts and artillery batteries within The Quadrilateral, a heavily fortified German redoubt, which had withstood many earlier attacks. The prospect was bleak.

In the early morning of the 1st of July the battalion moved into the front line. Equipment was checked, inspected and checked again. The artillery poured shells into the enemy positions, while the infantry were served a hot breakfast, not everyone could stomach it. The artillery bombardment intensified. The Germans must have anticipated the timing of the attack because they opened up with machineguns at 7.25. At 7.30 the whistles blew to signal the advance on the enemy positions.

All the officers were in line with the men and each carried three bombs and 170 rounds of ammunition. With their badges of rank obscured, Lieutenants, Sergeants – Captain Jones and Private Miller were now all on an equal footing. Ralph Miller wanted to get on with it.

We got to the point that we thought the quicker the bloody whistles go, the sooner we go over the top, the better. We always said to one another, 'Well it's a two-to-one chance. We either get bowled over, or we get wounded and go home. It's one of the two.' We got so browned off with waiting, to the extent that we didn't care what happened. In fact I was pleased to go over. You can just imagine there were hundreds of fellows, shouting and swearing, going over with fixed bayonets.

The Germans had withdrawn from their front-line trenches and these were quickly taken, although not without casualties. The decision was taken to move the Headquarter's Company forward to the trenches held by the 8th Battalion. This cost the Brigadier his life, killed as he stood in the open, cheering on his men. Casualties among the officers and men were high and there were insufficient troops in reserve to hold the position. The Germans counter-attacked, dead and wounded were left behind as the battalion withdrew. Many lay in shell holes in no man's-land until darkness fell at the end of the first day of the Battle of the Somme.

This was a sorry day for the 1/8th Royal Warwickshire Regiment. The commanding officer, Colonel Innes was dead and so was his adjutant. In all over twenty officers were killed or wounded. Fifty-seven men were dead and over 500 wounded or missing. Private Ralph Miller had foreseen this catastrophe.

We had no chance of getting across no man's-land, there was so much barbed wire. Of my football club from back home, we all went over together, ten out of twelve of us were killed. I wanted a Blighty wound.

I was hit by a shell blast. I didn't know a thing from that moment until I was back in Birmingham. I didn't know who picked me up and saved me. I was hit by shrapnel in my hand, my arm and I lost two fingers on my right hand. When I came round at the University Hospital in Birmingham, I was told my parents had been to see me. I was in a nice comfortable bed – but it was the shock of my life: 'Where am I? What am I doing here?' I asked the orderly. 'You're in Brum he said, and I shook his hand.

Captain Harry Jones was also in Brum, also in a nice comfortable bed, in the officer's ward, of course. His young wife, Edith, came to visit him.

Harry's mother, Eliza Jones, was relieved to hear that her son was safely back in England. From the family home at Northgate, she could look out and imagine how it was when she used to pack Harry off to school, watch him scamper across the street, and disappear up Moat Street. The school boy became a schoolmaster and then a soldier, not an ordinary soldier but an officer. How proud she had been when he appeared in his smart new uniform in 1914 and how cheered she had been by his first letters from France.

Months passed, Harry was moved to a convalescent home, he was still not fit for active service. The war went on for another year. In July 1918 Harry received the Silver War Badge, awarded to men who were honourably discharged. The war came to an end on the 11th of November, Harry had 'done his bit'. Harry died at the end of the month at Pinewood Sanatorium near Wokingham, 'after a long and painful illness, patiently borne'.

His widowed mother read the account in the local paper that concluded, Captain Harry Martin Jones was 'One of God's faithful warriors. His will be done.'

A proud man, proud of his regiment, proud of his school and the Old Boys who had 'responded to the call of their country'. It was up to them now to make their way in the world. The headmaster's son made a simple decision, return to the classroom.

Captain Rudolf Victor Dawes MC MA BSc – Royal Garrison Artillery

The headmaster's son grew up surrounded by 'scholars'. One of Rudolph Dawes earliest memories must have been the clatter on the stairs in the early morning when the boarders rushed down to the 'ablutions' in the backyard of School House.

He would have known schoolboys five or even ten years his senior, men like Percy Nevett. When he in turn took his place in the classroom he studied alongside Douglas Spurway. No one then could have imagined that one day Douglas would do something so heroic that he would be awarded the Military Cross. He was killed in action in France – Percy Nevett died on the shores of Gallipoli.

Rudolf sat the entrance examination at the Woolwich Military Academy in 1915. He came back a changed man, according to the editors of the School Magazine.

...returned with a moustache of the 'I fear no foe' type, positively bristling with martial vigour. On the following Wednesday he gave his commands at drill with such energy and distinction that a wanderer on the High Rock could hear every word.

The following year he was commissioned as a 2nd Lieutenant in the Royal Garrison Artillery. His record shows that he entered Theatre of War No. 1 on 28th June 1916. He was in France, 'where he is busy and delighted with his work'.

As a cadet he had won the Donegal Badge for Shooting. With the 151st Siege Battery, Royal Garrison Artillery he was given a really big gun to play with. These weapons could fling a 90 kg shell up to nine kilometres.

Rudolph must have impressed his commanding officer, after over a year of active service he was promoted to Captain in May 1918. In the final month of the war his 'devotion to duty' was rewarded. The London Gazette of January 1919 confirmed the award of the Military Cross to Captain Rudolf Dawes. As far as we know he survived the war without a scratch.

Rudolph owed much to his father, and followed his example. He studied at Gonville and Caius College, Cambridge after the war, and began his teaching career at Rossall School in Fleetwood. He was appointed headmaster of East Grinstead Grammar School just before the outbreak of the Second World War. He held the position for only a year.

At the outbreak of the Second World War, Rudolph was back in uniform again, promoted to Major (18536) in the Royal Artillery. His contribution to the war effort is not clear, but he may have aided the resistance movement in Norway in some way. In 1948 his name appeared again in the London Gazette – he was awarded the King Haakon VII Freedom Medal.

Out of khaki uniform and back in his black academic gown he returned to East Grinstead Grammar and served there as headmaster for nearly twenty years before he retired.

He lived to celebrate his ninetieth birthday. He was remembered as a man of 'inherent modesty and natural dignity'. There must have been many occasions during the course of his long life when he thought back to his school days and remembered all his boyhood friends – whose who

© BES Library

had suffered a violent end far from home, and whose who returned to pass away peacefully in old age in the land they loved.

Bill Page and his brother Richard certainly had a love of the land. They both fought in France, but they never truly left Manor Farm at Middleton Scriven.

Private (331522) William Page – Loyal North Lancashire Regiment

The initial enthusiasm to join the fight quickly drained away. The war was not 'over by Christmas'. The casualty lists grew longer, there were too few volunteers to fill the ranks and it soon became clear that conscription would be necessary. The Military Service Bill was introduced in January 1916 which provided for the conscription of every man aged between eighteen and forty-one. Unless they decided to join immediately every man was deemed to have enlisted by the 2nd of March 1916. Bill Page had already responded to the call to arms.

On the 3rd of March he sent a postcard to his sister Mary, to say that he would be home at the weekend, and…"then I'll tell you everything."

With permission from Margaret Crawford-Clarke

At the time he was training for war just south of Whitchurch. At the height of the Great War thirty-thousand men were billeted on Prees Heath.

For the next three years he wrote to Mary once every ten days, sometimes more often. The letters were short because paper was short. He made light of his experiences in the trenches. He did his duty but what he wanted most was for the war to be over so that he could return to the family farm. Mary kept him up to date with local gossip, the fate of his old school friends and the details of the farming calendar. She sometimes asked for help with algebra or French, this was important to her. Mary was a boarder in St Leonard's Close, attending the Girls' High School.

Bill came home on a few day's leave in July, he sent postcard to say "arriving on 12.27 train. Don't send a trap if you are harvesting and nobody going to auction".

Many of the boys who served with The Loyal North Lancashire Regiment, passed through the camp on Prees Heath,

The Loyal North Lancs were in the thick of it from the start. Tom Wilkinson of the 7th Battalion was KIA on the 5th of July 1915. His parents lived at Lodge Farm, Dudmaston. Like many local lads he tried his luck in Canada, the land of opportunity. At the outbreak of war he swiftly returned to the 'old country' and was commissioned as a 2nd Lieutenant and appointed battalion gunnery officer. During an attack at La Boiselle he spotted a party of men from another unit retiring without their machine gun. With two of his men he got the gun into action and held up the enemy. He forced his way forward and found another group sheltering behind a wall of earth, pinned down by German bombers. Tom Wilkinson brought up his machine gun and they were dispersed. Soon afterwards he was killed trying to bring in a wounded man.

Charles and Edith Wilkinson had lost their son, his body was never recovered. The only consolation was that his bravery was recognised. He was awarded the Victoria Cross. The Regiment had a reputation to live up to.

A year later Private Bill Page went out to join the 7th Battalion. Like thousands of other lads, clerks, butchers, plumbers and farm boys, once in uniform they all looked the part. On the 5th of November 1916 he sent a studio photograph home for the family to see what a fine soldier he was. This was the day he set off for the battlefields of Flanders.

Mary sent Bill a long letter and a photograph of herself which he thought did not do her justice.

It's time you had it taken again. – Well I'm getting on very well indeed, of course I don't tell you everything about it, I'm at the back of the front yet and hoping to be for some time.

Bill might not have been able to help her with her school work but he sounded confident of his ability on the keyboard of the piano. 'I should like to be able to show you how to play 'Spring Song' but I shan't for a bit I expect.'

This melody by Sibelius was subtitled 'The Sadness of Spring' and Spring was a long way off.

In February 1917 he wrote:

It's a bit cold out here now but we have not had any snow yet. I can't tell you anymore now, it's time to get under the blankets, 1 between 2, we're in billets, barns, it's a change I can tell you but it's not half bad.

Behind the lines football and cricket matches were arranged, in the evening concerts and 'picture shows'. One silent film proved to be enormously popular at home. It seems strange that 'The Battle of the Somme' was shown to troops who were expecting to be back in the firing line within days. General Rawlinson said, 'Some of it was good but it cut out many of the horrors', and Private Page agreed.

Regular letters from home kept up morale. The Army Postal Service was established. This was an astonishing enterprise. Mail bound for troops on the Western Front was sorted in Regents Park on a five acre site, said to be the largest wooden structure in the world at the time. By 1917 nineteen thousand mail bags crossed the Channel every day, half-a-million in the run up to Christmas.

Letters to Mary were addressed to a house she shared with other boarders attending the Girls' Public High School. From 4, St Leonard's Close post cards, photographs, birthday cards, and knitted socks were dispatched to France, letters and packages flowed back and forth and time passed.

Mary must have complained about school meals because when Bill wrote to his sister he said, "You have not got much cause to grouse about the grub you get at school, everything we get here is frozen and we have to thaw the bread before we can cut it, it's as hard as iron. By God, I was never so cold in my life before".

This was a man who was used to working outdoors in all weathers but even he found conditions in the trenches harsh.

Some of his comments were not to be relayed to the family.

We had a pretty quiet time, one shell bust somewhere behind me and blowed my tin hat off my head and nearly upset me but that's nothing, I'm getting used to it, you need not tell anyone at home. You must tell them I'm alright, we're not in the trenches at present, but having another rest and a pretty easy time.

At this stage in the war lads too young to enlist at the outbreak were being called up. In his next letter he mentioned his younger brother, Dick, and an old school friend, Colin McMichael. He had just learned that his 'chum' had joined the London Scottish.

I should like to have a look at him when he's got his kilts on. I hear Dick has had to attest, but father will appeal for him won't he? It will make it very awkward for them if he has to join won't it?

There was understandable anxiety at Manor Farm. Bill was in and out of the trenches near Court Croix, Neuve Eglise, Waterlands Camp or any number of locations that no one in Middleton Scriven had ever heard of. Added to this was the news that the appeal to keep Dick at home had failed.

In March the weather was changeable, fine and warm at the beginning of the month, then six inches of snow. Bill took it all in his stride. He could not understand why the family were suffering from colds and sore throats when he was in the best of health without the comfort of a feather bed and home cooking.

I only wish you could see us cooking Oxo and Quaker oats, it would make you laugh.

Bill reported on the effects of a heat wave in May.

Well, I'm going on A1 as per usual but to give you a bit of an idea how warm it is out here I went to sleep yesterday and wakened up with a jump dreaming the place was on fire but it was only the sun shining on me. Then somebody shouts, 'you didn't come out here to sleep, you came out to work.

He claimed that there was not much going on in June 1917. In fact there was a lot going on. In comfortable country mansions well away from the battlefront the Generals were dining on fillet steaks washed down with fine wines, and planning the future for men like Private Page.

Preparations were being made for the great attack on Messines Ridge. Additional roads were being constructed, light railways were being built to bring up stores and ammunition, and assembly trenches were being dug for the second wave of assault troops. It was difficult to conceal all this activity from the enemy. The Germans held the high ground on Messines Ridge and had a commanding view of the whole area. What they could not see were the network of tunnels and the mines being laid under their feet.

Such was the secrecy of the tunnelling operation that infantrymen, British and Canadian, waiting in the front line were also unaware of the existence of the huge stocks of high explosives buried ahead of them.

The Royal Artillery spent a fortnight shelling the ridge, the Germans knew an attack was coming. When the guns fell silent at 3 o'clock on the morning of 7th of June, they came out of their dugouts to man their machine guns. They were in for a shock. Ten thousand men died when six hundred tonnes of explosives blew the ground from under their feet. Nine divisions of infantry, supported by tanks and aircraft, advanced under the protection of a creeping artillery barrage. Within three hours all the initial objectives had been taken.

Reports of this most successful operation filled the newspapers at home. There was no news of Bill and the Loyal North Lancashire Regiment. Then a letter arrived, dated 18th of June 1917, the envelope bore the stamp 'Passed by the Field Censor'.

My Dear Mary

Thanks for your letter and good wishes, it was on the right day for a wonder and it was a rather lively day for us too, I think about the hottest I've had out here so far but we've had a few different experiences the last week or two, I expect you know as much as I do or perhaps more from the papers about what's been going on. Those mines that went up shook the ground like a boat rolling on a rough sea and then we were away. It was a bit exciting poking the Johnnies out of shell holes and dugouts, poor devils they hadn't got a ghost of a fight left in them after the artillery had finished with them and were only too pleased to be shown the way to our lines. I could tell you a lot more about it but well I'll keep it till the next time we have a tea party at David and Georges', that is if we have the luck to have another there. I've been very lucky so far to come through without a scratch. You should have seen us coming out a few days ago after being about twelve days without a shave or a decent wash or sleep, we looked a nice lot I can tell you. This is a bit of writing paper I picked up in one of the trenches, the owner had started to write a letter but I don't suppose he'll ever finish it now.

Well I'll make a finish now, I'm looking out for that long letter you promised me.
With best Love from your old Brother Billy

A week later Billy wrote briefly to complain about the rain,

We were camped on a slope, the rain ran in one side of the tent and out the other, I wakened up with a pool of water under my back.

At the beginning of July he was complaining about the heat. "Too bally hot to work but we have to do a bit sometimes." At the end of the month he was doing even less. A rash of boils on his legs put him out of action and he was laid up in a rest camp.

I'm at a rest camp and having the softest time I've had out here. I've been doing nothing but eat and sleep the last few days. I shall make it last as long as I can, it's safer here than running after Johnnies.

Wishful thinking, he was soon back with the Battalion and in action once again. Mary had been on holiday on the south coast and from there could hear the sound of gunfire across the Channel.

So you heard the guns firing did you? I only wish I had the chance of hearing from the same place as you did, it would be worth something. If I ever hear anything any bigger than the old double-barrel when I get back you will have to report me missing.

Some families never received news of their sons on the battlefield, many had little schooling and simply could not write. The army provided a Field Service Post Card, to convey information by crossing out a few sentences.

I have been admitted into hospital…sick/wounded and am going on well.

Hope to be discharged soon.

Bill sent one on the 6th of October to say… "I am quite well". This wasn't strictly true because a few days later he admitted,

> *We've had a rather hot time of it lately as I dare say you can guess because you know if there's anything doing round here we're not far from it. Well I've had some of the narrowest escapes I've ever had, shells have been dropping all round us only missing by a few yards. One came through where six of us were with the machine gun, it dropped right at the side of me but it happened to be a dud and did not explode. That's only one instance, I think it is more than luck that has helped us out of it this time.*

The changeable weather was mentioned in almost every letter. "We are having some glorious weather now only hope it will last." The weather changed and Bill's luck changed.

> *We had some rotten weather while we were in and had to keep baling the water out of the shell holes we were stuck in and it came in almost as fast as we could chuck it out.*

On the 19th of October Bill was propped up in bed in the 1st Australian General Hospital, suffering from 'trench foot'.

> *I arrived here yesterday after about twenty-four hours in a hospital train… My feet would have been worse only I had two pairs of socks and dried one on the side of the trench and kept changing them. I shall not want the pair you're knitting for me for a bit I hope but I know lots of lads with the Battalion who'd be glad of them.*
>
> *Thanks for the photos you sent me, that's a very good one of Dick and old Kitty (a pony). I think I've still got all the snaps you've sent me so far.*
> *Best love from your old brother, Bill*

A week later he was lying comfortably in Ward 21 of Wharncliffe Hospital in Sheffield. The journey from Rouen had taken the best part of two days. It began at Rouen where he was carried onto a river barge which meandered down the Seine to Le Havre, a very busy port. The British Expeditionary Force had disembarked here in August 1914 and vessels of every description had been coming and going on every tide since. The night crossing to Southampton was rough, some were seasick but not Bill Page.

Then I was shoved on a train and sent here. I wish I could have been a bit nearer home but this doesn't seem a bad sort of place, better than around Hill 60 where we've been lately, but I'll tell you more about that when I see you.

Hill 60 was a spoil heap on Messines Ridge made from the diggings of a railway cutting before the war. There must have been troops on both sides who questioned if this was worth fighting over. Its value was as a view point. The invading Germans took Hill 60 in November 1914 and held it for over two years, until the opening day of the Battle of Messines Ridge when it was partly demolished by one of the mines that had shaken Bill and his mates.

Bill must have thought about it as he lay with his feet sticking out of the bottom of the bed, where matron could keep an eye on them. Trench foot was a dangerous condition and many men lost legs when gangrene set in. He wrote yet another letter to his sister encouraging her to visit him in hospital. She wrote a long letter back, she had problems at school with Latin, algebra and history. Bill could not help.

Bill's brother, Dick, had still not been drafted, he wrote to Bill more concerned with the running of the farm than the struggle on the Western Front. He told him there was plenty to do at Manor Farm. He closed the letter saying he was off to the Fair in Bridgnorth and hoping for a prize with a pen of cattle. Bill wished him well, wishing he could be there with him.

When he was back on his feet Bill rode the trams around Sheffield, "You can get almost anywhere for a penny". He sent Mary a postcard of the hospital, it was a very impressive building. "I don't think I could get to a better place than this".

He was happy with the treatment and would have been content

to stay at Wharncliffe, he was moved on, back to Prees Heath Camp to attend a medical board.

Parading before two doctors 'the sick, the lame and the weary' lined up with greatcoats over their shoulders and nothing else.

There was a lot marked for active service and one or two discharged, I think I'm still home service.

Bill was called to the company office, he had a pleasant surprise,

A Mr Dutton who has a big farm about 7 miles away had asked for his son, who is in the same hut as me, and myself to go an help him thrash wheat, well we both got off. It was almost like being at home.

He was not so cheery when he wrote from Knowsley Park, a rehabilitation camp for men still not fit enough to be returned to their unit.

This place is alright but the staff here try to make the crippled here fit for France again by bullying them as much as they can. I'm about a mile from Prescott and about seven from Liverpool. The Park is Lord Derby's private pleasure and shooting ground full of deer and game etc.

It was too far away to get home on a short leave pass. The Regimental Depot at Felixstowe was even further away

"You'll see by my address that I've left 'prison' and jolly glad to get away too".

Bill's feet were still troubling him, salt water bathing was recommended. Every evening he was encouraged to soak his feet in a bucket of near boiling sea water.

The letters between brother and sister, which went back and forth between barracks on the East Coast and St Leonard's Close were so regular that they were more like a conversation than correspondence. They talked of visits to the dentist, visits to the playhouse, shortage of writing paper, freezing temperatures, treatment for trench foot, and waiting for leave, waiting to be sent to France again.

337

The Germans did attempt to bring the war to Bill billeted in England. He described a Zeppelin raid on Felixstowe. Early on in the war it was feared that the Germans might attempt an invasion along the coast of East Anglia. After the Battle of Jutland the German High Seas fleet did not venture far from port, there was no longer a serious threat from the sea, but there were still casualties. Bombs dropped from Zeppelins killed soldiers and civilians, and caused alarm. In all five hundred were killed in bombing raids in Britain.

We woke up at one o'clock last Thursday morning, got an air raid warning and had to get out double quick, stayed out nearly an hour and Johnny did not come near us so we got back to bed again and were just getting warm when one comes right over the camp and of course we all had to bale out again. He didn't drop any bombs near though

On this raid bombs were dropped on Coventry, the pilot believed he was over Birmingham. The Zeppelins were slow moving and when flying at low altitude could be attacked with artillery from the ground. They were enormous machines that dwarfed the tiny aircraft sent up to attack them. Some were brought down in flames and made heroes of the young airmen.

I didn't know Milner Deighton was in the Flying Corps, but he always was a bit of a swank…

Bill preferred to keep his feet planted firmly on the ground.

The news is extra the last day or two, Old Shuker is letting them have it with a vengeance. I think he'll be able to finish it off without me, don't you think so?

When Bill joined the Loyal North Lancashire Regiment he was given a regimental number (33152). Just behind him in the line of recruits was 33158, Private Alfred Shuker. They shared good times and bad until Private William Page was shipped home to 'Blighty'.

Alf Shuker could not finish it off single-handed. In March another contingent of the Loyal North Lancashire Regiment was sent out to join him. The troops were given short notice and no leave, there was discontent in the ranks.

Dear Mary

Just a few lines to tell you I'm starting for a tour of the continent again. I should've thought they're making proper fools of us this time sending us on the First of April without leave. Well this is as far as I know. The tour begins sometime tonight via London, then take the boat to Boulogne, one or two nights there then to the base at Etaples, after that up to where the real fun is going on.

I don't know how long the trip is going to last this time, but not so long as last I hope.

It's rotten luck not getting a leave. The General told us the other day that if it had been anyhow possible to give us leave we should have had it. We'd been pretty nearly up to rioting fight all day and at night our Colonel and Officers took the draft to the Playhouse and marched in front with the band just to quieten us down a bit, rather a poor compensation for a six day leave don't you think?

I shall not get your letter tonight as there's only one post today but it will follow me on I expect. Don't write again until I give you my continental address, Will let you have it as soon as I can. No more news now, sorry I've not had the chance of seeing you before going but with a bit of luck I shall soon be back again.

Best love from your loving Brother, Bill

Bill gave his address as 'With the Expeditionary Force' and communications broke down, briefly.

"With a bit of luck I shall soon be back," he had said and indeed he was. He was back in Wharncliffe Hospital with another 'leg problem' (gunshot wound?) Bill did not regard this as a serious condition.

There's lots of folk didn't know there was anything the matter with them till the war started then they suddenly hatched a complaint, me for example, in here with nothing the matter with me...

Bill was soon hopping about and moved to Eden Hall in Kent. This was close enough to the battlefields of France for Private Page. He was assessed regularly and could not understand why he was not being returned to his regiment, yet thankful that he was not.

The grounds of Eden Hall suffered neglect when the staff went off to war. Private Page was given the task of getting the lawns back into shape for tennis and crocket, a job he tackled with enthusiasm. Driving an old horse and the smell of mown grass reminded him of more peaceful times at Manor Farm. Within a fortnight the lawns were fit for croquet, a game that many of the patients could take part in, even the limbless. Teenagers in wheelchairs, some who had lost both legs, took pleasure in friendly competition and forgot for a happy half-hour that their lives had been changed forever. Bill Page was a lucky man. Bill Page had seen how war had maimed so many young men and recognised the futility of it. By now he was 'war weary' and wanted to see an end to it.

Bill returned to the Western Command Depot at Knowsley Park, and was put in the 'leg squad'.

I wish you could see us crawling about at a snail's pace and limping for all we're worth. We had an hour's gym yesterday afternoon with shoes and socks off, you'd just about kill yourself laughing if you could see us, you'd think the Army has gone mad. I think it has lately and we're all going dotty together. They might just have well let me off for a few weeks harvesting as keep me messing about here doing nothing.

Bill was certainly needed at Manor Farm.

Sorry to hear Dick has had to go out, poor kid...

Dick Page and Fred Jones one of the farmhands were with the Light Infantry in Ireland and preparing to sail to France. Anxious and frustrated by events Bill was well aware of the dangers his brother faced. He had lost some of his 'chums' in France and now he was reluctant to make new friends.

340

I went down to Liverpool on Saturday but somehow it doesn't seem the same as when I was here with George for company. I'm having an easy time of it, messing about doing nothing only just filling in the time. I'm about fed up with it all and wish I could be back home again".

Meanwhile in France, Dick, 'poor kid', and the 7th Battalion KSLI were not 'having and easy time'.

PRIVATE (43761) RICHARD WYRE PAGE –
7TH KING'S SHROPSHIRE LIGHT INFANTRY

In June 1918, Dick wrote to Mary to describe the condition around the Old Barracks in Fermoy. He was clearly not impressed by his surroundings.

The people here are a dirty lot and the town is full of dogs and donkeys and such. There's nothing to see here, it's like being at the end of the world.

He went on...

Well we had a miserable week. We were vaccinated on Tuesday and had a double dose of inoculation on Friday and jolly bad it made us, as if anyone touched our left arm there was some cursing. We have got all our equipment now besides rifles and bayonets. We have been doing squad drill under officers up till now with a little gas drill and physical training in between. We have all our meals outside. It would be a puzzle to tell what sort of meat it is, it tastes like anything.

It rained heavily last night and the men in the beds under the window had to shift their beds so you can tell what the windows are like.

It takes ten to fourteen weeks to train men in this battalion and then a ten-day leave.

When home leave was over Dick returned briefly to the Old Barracks in Ireland and then joined the 7th Battalion King's Shropshire Light Infantry in France.

The first taste of battle for Private Page was at Albert on the 21st of August. The objective was the railway line between Bapaume and Albert and the orders for the battalion were simple, 'to reach and hold the railway at all costs'. They made their way forward through heavy mist at 5 o'clock in the morning. Two hours later they were on the railway embankment and fighting hand-to-hand with the demoralised defenders. The Germans fell back. The following day they launched counter-attacks but were repulsed.

The battalion withdrew to Moyenneville to 'reorganise and clean up' and count the cost. Over two hundred Germans had been captured together with their field guns, machine guns and trench mortars. The 7th Battalion were sent a number of congratulatory telegrams, no mention made of the 250 killed or wounded during the month of August. Reinforcement arrived in preparation for the Second Battle of Bapaume.

It was another early start on the 2nd of September. Whippet tanks arrived to help out. The Germans held the high ground. The Shropshires forged ahead and reached their objective ahead of the Scottish regiments to left and right and ahead of the tanks that faltered, most suffering mechanical failure. Forty men died, two hundred were wounded, eight gassed and a number were missing. Private Dick Page was unharmed. Telegrams, from Brigade Headquarters congratulated the Shropshires on their courage and determination.

Newspaper reports at home were full of optimism, the Germans were certainly 'on the back foot'. For troops in trenches there was still death and danger from shells, bullets, bayonets and gas. Another forty men died and many more were wounded at Canal du Nord.

In November Dick and 'C' Company were being 'rested' in billets at Escarmain. It was here that he wrote to his sister for the last time.

My Dear Mary
I hope your thoughts are not troubled concerning me at not having heard for so long, I have been on the move ever since I returned from leave, so you know why I have not written. We started for the line this morning between 7 and 8 o'clock and were met about a mile out with the news that peace was signed so we turned about and came back to billets in a small town.

What is going on in Shrewsbury tonight, I should like to see it?

We stayed in Cambrai one night, it has been a fine town but is knocked about badly.

I have another cold at present but it is only what I could expect roughing it out here.

There has been a football match here today between our Company and 'D' in a ploughed field full of shell holes, our company won 2-0.

The French were returning to their old homes or ghosts of homes.

Well I will be like Jerry now and pack in.

Wishing you the best of luck, I am your loving brother, Dick

This was written on an historic day, Armistice Day, the day everyone had been praying for.

The Page boys returned to familiar fields.

Chapter 23

Home and Abroad

For all who took part, the Great War was a life-changing experience. Most wanted nothing more than to return to the life they had known before the war – John Icke would settle for that.

Quartermaster Sergeant John Francis Icke – Royal Engineers

In the first eight years of marriage Agnes Icke had five children. The family moved from Wrockwardine to Quatt and John Icke worked the land around Little Holt Farm. He must have worked hard, hard enough to pay the school fees for his eldest son, also John.

The Grammar School background must have helped his progress through the ranks of the Royal Engineers. He began his career as a Driver and by the end of the war he was a Quartermaster Sergeant.

John Icke arrived in France in September 1915 to play his part in a war in which technology produced casualties on an industrial scale. Royal Engineers built roads, bridges, railways and tramways to transport the infantry. They built fortresses and gun emplacements and maintained the guns of the Royal Artillery.

Gas was the most feared weapon of war, it was used by all sides. Royal Engineers were responsible for the gas attacks on the German lines.

In the early hours of 7th June 1917 they produced the greatest explosion in history when 600 tonnes of explosives were detonated under Messines Ridge. Tunnelling parties of the Royal Engineers had been toiling underground for eighteen months preparing for this event.

We do not know what part Sergeant Ike played during the conflict. He certainly knew about mining, if only from men working in the nearby pits at Alveley and Highley, or in conversations with his old school friend Harold Gibbs, the son of the Billingsley mine owner.

What we do know is that at the end of the war he found himself in India, a member of a training battalion, handing on what he had learned in France to local troops defending the North West Frontier with Afghanistan.

John Icke came home from India to farm quietly at Little Holt Farm. Another engineer, Ernie Baulk did not settle down.

CAPTAIN ERNEST OSCAR BAULK – 26 FIELD COMPANY ROYAL ENGINEERS

Ernest's father made a move, from Walton in Hertfordshire to Astley Abbots. Charlie Baulk was a gardener by trade and wanted something better for his son. Aged thirteen Ernest was admitted to the Grammar School to complete his education. He gained useful qualifications to begin his training as a draughtsman on the Sussex coast. Little did he know that he would be asked to produce drawings of gun emplacements and shell shelters in France.

At the outbreak of war Ernest was twenty years old, a man with useful technical skills, the ideal recruit for the Royal Engineers. Ernest was used to working in an office, with a large sheet of white paper in front of him, now he was expected to get his hands dirty.

Lance Corporal Baulk arrived in France in August 1916 to join 230 Advanced Tunnelling Company. A tunnelling company was usually made up of about half a dozen officers and two hundred Sappers. The job of the Sapper was to dig saps, narrow trenches for the infantry to crawl forward along, to approach the enemy. This was dirty and dangerous work. Tunnellers of the Royal Engineers also constructed dugouts and shelters, to protect their comrades, and they laid mines under the German positions, to give the enemy an uncomfortable 'wake-up-call'.

One thing is certain, Ernest's Tunnelling Company was not responsible for the mighty explosion on Messines Ridge in 1917. Ernest was England, receiving officer training. He was commissioned in November that year and returned to the front line to join 26 Field Company Royal Engineers.

The Commanding Officer was particularly pleased with the work completed by his men in the month of April 1918: trenching, tunnelling, wiring, demolition, and bridging operations. Without the expertise of the Royal Engineers the battlefront would have remained static. Roads, railways and bridges, built by the engineers made possible the swift supply of food and ammunition, the transport of heavy guns, fresh troops to the front and the recovery of the wounded.

Engineers designed and built machine-gun posts and concrete bunkers. In the open, unprotected, RE Sappers set up barbed-wire defences and laid minefields. Command posts and signals centres had to be given extra protection with Elephant Shelters.

Shelter for One Elephant or Half-a-Dozen Men

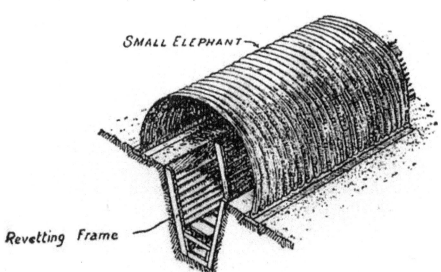

No matter what the project, there had to be a map or working drawing. Second Lieutenant Baulk's skill as a draughtsman was invaluable.

Ernest had arrived at the front at a particularly hazardous time. The Germans had launched their Spring Offensive which they hoped would secure victory for them. They did have some success, but they could not hold the ground and, in the months that followed, were steadily pushed back.

26 Field Company were on the move – Bethune, Ronville, Arras, Selle – with tool carts, cycles, mules, field kitchens, trucks full of mines and coils of barbed wire, horse-drawn limbers carrying all manner of bridging equipment, and at least a hundred spades. At Miraucourt in September they used some to bury German dead.

The end was in sight, at the Battle of Selle hundreds of weary Germans surrendered. The Battle of the Sambre was the final engagement.

The final action for Ernest Baulk was a bridging operation on the Oise Canal. Field guns, tanks, and swarming infantry could not engage with the enemy until bridges were in place.

The engineers went about their task with shells falling around them. It was not until dusk on the 4th of November that 'Lieutenants Baulk and Mitchel between them put in the first trestle of the canal bridge.'

The canal was bridged, infantry crossed under fire, tanks, trucks, wagons and field guns followed. The work of the Engineers was done. 26 Field Company retired to Fresnoy-Legrand for 'a good rest and a clean up'. Within a week, news was received that the Armistice had been signed. There was rejoicing.

A most memorable event for Ernie Baulk was joining the 'March to the Rhine', with the 3rd Infantry Brigade and hearing the National Anthem played by village bands along the way. This would not have been possible if others had not made the 'supreme sacrifice'.

On the 4th of November, the day Ernest Baulk began the task of bridging the Sambre-Oise canal, Wilfred Owen died leading his men across the canal at Ors. He was twenty-five when he died. Ernest Baulk was eighty-nine when he died in Aylesbury.

In time, Owen was recognised as one of the great poets of the Great War. Many of his poems were anti-war, he would not have been comfortable in uniform in peacetime.

Ernest Baulk chose to serve on with the British Army. He married Grace Bennett in 1922. While he was serving in Egypt the Baulks had a home base in England, near Cranleigh, Surrey. Employment prospects in 1930s Britain were not good. Canada and Australia seemed to offer more. Ernest and Grace 'gave it a go' in Australia, but finally sailed home to the port of London in 1931.

Bob Hutton never doubted where he belonged, he returned to Tasmania when there was no more 'soldiering' to be done.

SERGEANT MAJOR ROBERT HUTTON – 'C' SQUADRON,
9TH AUSTRALIAN LIGHT HORSE

Working in Australia at the outbreak of war and keen to see some action, Robert Hutton went straight to the recruiting office in Melbourne to volunteer. When asked if he had any military experience he said he had served with the Rhodesian Imperial Mounted Police. This Grammar School boy had an adventurous spirit and although he gave his trade as 'labourer' he was swiftly promoted. Over six feet tall, he certainly stood out in a crowd.

He joined the 9th Light Horse as a Private soldier, a little over a month later he was promoted to Sergeant.

There was no shortage of recruits, most were British born and eager to return to join in what they believed would be another adventure. On the 11th of February 1915 the 9th Light Horse rode into Melbourne to take ship to Europe. They loaded all the paraphernalia of a cavalry regiment together with enough fodder to keep their horses in shape for the voyage to Egypt. An enthusiastic crowd waved them off from the pier. The mood changed when *HMT Menominee* sailed out of sight and loved ones and old friends turned to make their way home. For some this was the final parting.

A Rough Passage

With the storms of the Indian Ocean behind them the 'trooper' passed through the Suez Canal and docked at Alexandria. With solid ground under their feet and green pasture on the banks of the Nile the horses, at least, soon forgot the misery of life at sea. Among the troops there was an air of excitement, instead of sailing on to Europe to take on the Germans they were preparing to take on the Turks at Gallipoli.

Australians and New Zealanders, French and British troops stormed the beaches on the 25th of April 1915. They did not get very far. Nowhere could they break through the Turkish defences. The Anzacs made valiant attempts to dislodge the Turks from the cliffs around Gaba Tepe but failed. This was not suitable ground to send in the cavalry, the Light Horse regiments were held in reserve in Alexandria. Casualties mounted, reinforcement had to be found.

Sergeant Major Hutton and 'C' Squadron were dismounted, their mounts left to graze in Egypt while they sailed to Lemnos, a Greek island and 'jumping off point' for Gallipoli. They landed on the beaches in May to join their countrymen amid the 'muck and bullets'. This was an unhealthy place, the only ones enjoying the mess were the flies. In the heat they multiplied and went about their business of spreading disease and misery everywhere. One man complained that 'more men were killed by Turkish flies than Turkish bullets'.

At full strength the 9th Light Horse numbered over five hundred, within three months they were reduced to 181 men. A note in the School Magazine mentioned that Bob Hutton had been 'wounded'. This was not strictly true, he had fallen victim to a Turkish fly or flies. Suffering from dysentery, he was ferried back to Lemnos on the *Clacton* and then back to Egypt to be treated at the General Hospital in Cairo. The main building (The Heliopolis Hotel) was a grand affair and the treatment excellent. To cope with the many casualties the grounds were filled with bell tents.

Bob soon recovered and returned to duty, travelling by train back to the coast, to Ras-el-Tein near Alexandria. Sergeant Major Hutton was tasked with training new arrivals.

The Gallipoli campaign failed and all Allied troops were withdrawn by the end of 1915. In February the following year Bob Hutton was back in No. 1 General Hospital this time suffering from enteric fever (typhoid). This was a dangerous condition, over eight thousand British troops died in the South African War from typhoid. Bob recovered and was sent to the Rest Camp at Port Said at the entrance to the Suez Canal.

The Turks had attempted to take control of The Canal early in the war and they were still a threat. Back on his feet again and back in the saddle Bob was promoted to the top job, he was now the Regimental Sergeant Major in charge of training troopers of the 3rd and 9th Battalions of the Light Horse.

From Serapeum, north of the Bitter Lake, patrols went out into the desert to engage the Turks. They were eventually pushed back to Palestine and finally defeated. RSM Hutton ended the war at Moascar and was granted leave. He spent ten days at sea on board *HMT Caledonia*, sailing from Port Said to England. After a month's home leave he re-joined his regiment in Egypt and prepared for the voyage 'down under'.

Joyful that they were leaving, sad that many of their comrades were left behind, the 9th Light Horse boarded the *Boorara*, sailed through The Canal, they had defended for over three years, and out into the Indian Ocean.

In July 1919 they docked at Melbourne Pier. Regimental Sergeant Major Robert Hutton returned to civilian life, and settled back in Tasmania. His brother Tom returned to Minsterley Hall.

Minsterley Hall – Rather Grand

TOM HUTTON – INTERPRETER, ROYAL ARMY MEDICAL CORPS

It was hard to imagine a more peaceful place than Minsterley Hall and the surrounding Shropshire countryside. Working alongside his father at the outbreak of war, they managed one of the estates at the Down, near Bridgnorth, and ensured that fields, hedgerows and cottages were kept in good order. During four years on the Western Front Tom Hutton had see what war could do to farmland in Flanders.

Although Tom had little knowledge of medicine he did have a knowledge of the French language and this was something the army could use. He joined the Royal Army Medical Corps in 1914, and found himself in trouble from the start. The Germans overran Belgium and the British Army was in retreat.

In a letter to the school magazine he wrote:

I have had a rather exciting time, for I had to fly from Belgium during the German advance, came in for the first bombardment of Rheims and, stupidly enough, managed to get myself arrested by the French. Since October I have been working with the Ambulance Americaine, first as interpreter and later as anaesthetist and operation attendant. In the spring of this year I had the luck to be chosen as operation orderly in attendance on Migot, the great French surgeon, and accompanied the Wanamaker Flying Ambulance to the Southern Front. I had a very terrible, although very interesting, experience and am eagerly anticipating my return to work later in the year.

An Act of Vandalism

The destruction of Reims Cathedral provided useful propaganda to show the world just how 'uncivilised' the Germans were. They did enter the city but then withdrew to more easily defended positions. Fresh French troops arrived from Paris in a fleet of 600 taxis.

Americans, resident in Paris, established a hospital there at the outbreak of war to treat the first casualties and the film maker Sam Wanamaker financed what was probably the first air ambulance service.

The Southern Front that Tom referred to in his letter was the mountainous region of Northern Italy, a particularly difficult area in which to operate light aircraft.

We cannot be sure if Tom ever did return to duty, following his 'very terrible, although very interesting, experience'. His service record has not yet been found.

Bob and Tom Hutton had cousins of a similar age in Warwickshire, and we do know more of their activities. Two of them had a lively time during the war.

Captain William Hugh Hutton MC – Royal Field Artillery

How proud his parents must have been when they learned that their eldest boy had been awarded the Military Cross.

Tanks were used for the first time at Fler-Courcelette in September 1916, the final phase of the Battle of the Somme. Lieutenant Hutton was there to lend a hand. The artillery poured shells ahead of the tanks and the infantry followed. The battle came to an end on the 22nd of September, Billy Hutton made a name for himself on the first day, the 15th.

> *Temp. Lt. W H Hutton went forward and established himself in a shell hole on the outskirts of a village and observed from there, repeatedly repairing his telephone wires under fire.*

In recognition of this brave act the Military Cross was pinned on his tunic on the battlefield.

His brothers, Sidney and Phillip, also serving in France, may not have been surprised, he was after all four years older, and they had always looked up to him.

In the years before the war, encouraged by his father, William began his training as a land agent at Brigstock in Northamptonshire, a county famous for its shoemakers. This was a trade that Phillip Hutton, later, showed a keen interest in.

Corporal (152377) Philip Hutton – Royal Engineers

Phillip Hutton's last action was in the oilfields of the Middle East. When Turkish forces surrendered, and the port of Batum, on the Black Sea, was occupied in 1919, Phillip's war was over. He came home to begin a new life.

The Hutton brothers must have discussed the future. The life of a land agent was certainly very agreeable but Phillip wanted a change. The talk turned to Northamptonshire where William Hutton had lodged with Joe and Anne Bellamy in Brigstock. In the surrounding area there were many small shoemakers, producing high quality, hand-crafted footwear.

Phillip was a man with ambition. Backed by family money, no doubt, he moved to Northamptonshire and established the Hutton Shoe Company. The business flourished and by the mid-1930s Phillip was making trips to New York to promote the company products, Hollywood film stars needed something special and the Hutton Shoe Company was more than willing to satisfy their needs.

Phillip had sailed back and forth across the Atlantic, on the *Aquitania* and the *Majestic*. In October 1940 his mother sailed to New York on the *Scythia* with a lady companion. Among the passengers were many Jews who had fled Nazi Germany, and been given refuge in England. They were moving on to begin a better life. These were dangerous times, Britain was threatened, perhaps Anne Hutton had also been advised to 'sit out the war' with friends in the United States.

The U-boat threat was virtually over by March 1945 when Philip sailed from Avonmouth on the *Empire Grace* to New York. Not for the first time, he took a chance. Trade picked up and became very profitable.

Philip must have taken another chance because in 1948 the Board of Trade accused him of making an illegal profit of £1300. He appeared in the Northampton court to explain his bad behaviour. His reputation was restored five years later.

A combination of wind, high tide and low pressure over the North Sea produced a storm tide which produced widespread devastation from the Scottish islands to the Dutch coast. Sea walls were breached in Lincolnshire, flood waters reached two miles inland, and hundreds were made homeless. Philp Hutton's response was to donate dozens of pairs of shoes and he called on manufactures all over Northamptonshire to do the same.

Philip gave up sea travel, for business trips across the Atlantic he took to the skies, flying to New York, Montreal and Chicago. Business boomed. A new generation of Hollywood stars were demanding Hutton footwear. Steve McQueen popularised the 'chukka boots'. They have become collector's items.

Really Cool Footwear

Smarter shoes in the 'Playboy' range were worn to impress the 'Bunny Girls' in the clubs that sprang up in the 1960s, although the girls were more interested in what the guests had in their wallets than what they wore on their feet.

Philip Hutton married Jessie Marriott in 1924, he died in 1974. An adventurer in his youth, he became a successful entrepreneur, and must have considered himself fortunate to have had such a full life.

No less adventurous was Ernest Gardiner. When adventuring was done he finally settled down at 25 West Castle Street.

Warrant Officer (511) Ernest William Gardiner – 4th KSLI

Ern Gardiner was an enterprising man, not exactly tinker, tailor soldier, sailor – but he was, at one time or another, tailor, soldier, harbour master, and miner.

Born in 1876, his early life was spent in Friar's Street. His father was landlord of the Old Friar's Inn, and a coal merchant. Richard Gardiner died young, his widow, Sarah took on the licence of the pub and remarried. Ernest's step-father maintained the engine at the Fire Station in the High Street.

Coal merchant, publican, fireman, none of these trades appealed to Ern Gardiner, he was apprenticed to a tailor in the town. He liked to dress smartly, he was six feet tall, and in the uniform of the Shropshire Rifle Volunteers he must have looked every inch a soldier.

To gain more experience as a tailor he moved to London, took lodgings in Islington and worked as a 'cutter'. Returning to Bridgnorth, he set up business as a Master Tailor in West Castle Street and married.

In the outside world there was disquiet, rivalry between the European nations grew. The Royal Navy launched more dreadnought battle ships to match those of the German High Seas Fleet. Volunteer soldiers began training to a more professional standard, in Britain the Territorial Force was created and Major William Westcott welcomed him back in 1908. By the outbreak of war he was ready for action although he was by then thirty-eight years old.

Marian Gardiner and her baby boy, James, waved goodbye as Ernest marched away with the 4th Battalion to take ship to the Far East. When or where would they meet again?

Arriving in Singapore Sergeant Gardiner played a part in supressing the mutiny of a local infantry regiment, before 'A' and 'D' Company sailed on the Hong Kong to take up garrison duties. No one would describe life in Hong Kong as dull, it was vibrant full of enterprising business men. Ernest Gardiner understood this. He was now a man with authority, the senior non-commissioned officer, a Warrant Officer. There were married quarters for the privileged few.

In January 1917 the War Office decided that the 25th Middlesex Regiment would take over the duties of 4th KSLI in Singapore and Hong Kong. After some delay, half the regiment arrived in Hong Kong to replace two Companies of the KSLI.

The Shropshire lads said their farewells, and boarded the *Ingoma*, happy that they were on their way home, at last. The voyage back, to home waters, took over three months, nervous times for the waiting families. Mrs Charlie Smith wrote to the regimental depot at Shrewsbury – where were her brothers, Dick and Ernie Gardiner, both of 'D' Company, she wanted to know? Ernie was still in Hong Kong, he had decided to stay.

Ernest Gardiner had celebrated his fortieth birthday in the Far East, he was therefore too old for active service. A year earlier he had been offered a position with the China Mining and Smelting Company. They were mining lead and silver at Lin-Ma Hang, a village in the New Territories.

When medals were sent out, to those who had served in the Great War, Ernest's were posted to Holt's Wharf, Shanghai. The whole family moved from Hong Kong to Shanghai, where Marian and her children, James, Winifred and Joyce, enjoyed a privileged life style. Ernest was

Takes Some Handling

Wharfinger – an outdated title for the Harbour Master.

The whole family sailed, first class, from Shanghai to the port of London in 1927. Ernest gave their address as c/o Mrs Austin of 'Ridesdale' Bridgnorth. It was then perhaps that he invested in a three-storey house in West Castle Street, number 25. They returned to the Far East.

Over the next decade the family prospered, James went into the shipping business at Tientsin, an important trading port in China. Several European nations had concession on the river and built warehouses, town houses, clubs and even churches in the architectural styles of their home countries. In 1937 the Japanese invaded China and the comfortable lifestyle of the Tientsin traders came to an end.

Trouble was brewing in Europe. James made a move, he joined his mother in Hong Kong. They boarded SS *Tatua Maru* in the harbour, Marian claimed to be 'an hotel owner' on the ship's manifest, they arrived in San Francisco on the 25th of May 1939. Marian crossed the United States and in June sailed from New York to Southampton. She travelled alone, tourist class, on the *Queen Mary*, gave an address in Southsea, and her occupation as 'housewife'.

The Second World War broke out within two months of Marian's arrival in England. The south coast was going to be a dangerous place. Ernest was by then well over sixty. Where better to sit out this war than at the gates of the Castle Gardens in Bridgnorth?

At the same time, the Harrisons were even further removed from the war in Europe, William in the West Indies, Alan in the South Pacific

ALAN HENRY HARRISON – NEW ZEALAND LIGHT HORSE

In the early years of the last century the Harrisons appeared to have a comfortable life at the Manor House in Chelmarsh. William and Mary had the perfect family, three boys and a girl, three servants and good land to farm. Head of the household, William Harrison was by all accounts a difficult man to get on with and this may explain why three of his children chose to go to the Ends of the Earth. Samoa is literally on the other side of the world.

Alan Harrison stepped ashore on this Pacific island in 1912 to take up a position as plantation manager at Puipa'a. This was certainly a big step, Samoa was then a German possession. Alan (he preferred to be called Jack) could not have known that within eighteen months troops from New Zealand would be landing to 'liberate' the islands.

The British government recognised that Samoa could have been used as a base for German warships operating in the Pacific and asked Australian and New Zealand forces to invade, they did so without a shot being fired. 'Jack' Harrison became part of the British administration until duty called and he joined the New Zealand forces.

A farm boy, he was at home in the saddle and rode with the New Zealand Light Horse. It was a dusty ride back to England, first he had to face the Turks in Palestine. In October 1917 New Zealand cavalry captured four machine guns and over a hundred prisoners. They charged into the Turkish defences on the road to Beersheba with just a bayonet in one hand; the trooper's rifles were slung across their backs. The Australians went on to take Beersheba. This action was probably the last great cavalry charge in history.

Jack's brief war was over, he had been wounded low down in the back and was shipped to England to recover. The greenery of the Severn Valley must have seemed strange after the dust of the desert in the Middle East, and the bright blue of sea and sky seen from the shores of a Pacific island.

Perhaps to disguise it, maybe to draw attention to it, we do not know; Jack had a tattoo placed over the scar on his back.

Five years after Jack Harrison left Samoa to join the 'Light Horse' he returned to Samoa as Resident Commissioner at Savaii. A tourist resort has since been built there and comments on Trip Advisor refer to Savaii as 'Paradise'.

A countryman at heart Jack was not comfortable behind a desk, after two years in Paradise he moved to Australia, took up share farming in New South Wales and married Esther Coffey. The family moved to Canberra and Jack set up a trucking business. He had survived the war with 'just a scratch' but one day in the workshop, while changing a tyre, the rim of the wheel cut into his leg. It 'wasn't much' but gangrene set in and he lost his leg. The Harrisons were an extraordinary family, accident prone. William had walked into a piece of shrapnel in France and Hilda had walked out of the family home in Chelmarsh.

SERGEANT WILLIAM HARRISON – ROYAL FUSILIERS AND GLOUCESTER REGIMENT

William had joined the Royal Fusiliers and was wounded in February

1916, he recovered and transferred to the Gloucester Regiment. His luck did not change, he was 'dangerously wounded by shrapnel' later in the year in the final skirmishes of the Battle of the Somme. Sergeant William Harrison was treated first in a Military Hospital in Boulogne and then came home for further treatment. He never fully recovered.

There was more trouble for the Harrisons on the home front. Hilda Harrison was battling with her father. He did not believe that Joe Ingram was a suitable man to marry his daughter. High spirited, like her brothers, she climbed out of a window and ran away to marry Mr Ingram. It did not last, William Harrison paid him off and the couple were divorced. Hilda was not allowed back in the house.

A second marriage to Basil Ryan was more successful, the couple moved to Canada where Hilda spent the rest of her life. She died in 1970. Basil flew back to England with her ashes to be placed in the family grave at Atcham, the final reconciliation with her father.

William, 'dangerously wounded on The Somme', was unhappy to see that his name appeared on the war memorial at Glazeley. He did not die in war nor did several others whose names were also carved alongside his. He believed that only those who had given their lives should be honoured with a memorial.

He never fully recovered from his wounds. Perhaps persuaded by his younger brother, Jack, that a warmer climate would help he sailed to Dominica in the West Indies, and found work as an administrator. He came home to die in the 1950s.

Tropical islands in the West Indies or the South Pacific have the ideal climate for rest and recuperation, why then would Bernard Chadwick choose to spend the best part of twenty years in The White Man's Grave?

CAPTAIN BERNARD PERCIVAL CHADWICK – SHROPSHIRE YEOMANRY
ROYAL FIELD ARTILLERY

Among the Old Boys 'serving with the colours' in 1915 was Bernard Chadwick, a Private in the Shropshire Yeomanry. Compared with some he was an 'old man', he was twenty-six. Maturity and education gave him promotion. He transferred to the Royal Field Artillery as a Second Lieutenant, by the end of the war he had been promoted to Captain. He stayed with the Army for two more years and then joined the Civil Service and was posted overseas.

Bernard had taken risks during the war but when he accepted the appointment, as engineer in the Public Works Department in Nigeria, he was again in some danger. The whole of West Africa was an unhealthy place, some Europeans died within weeks of their arrival.

The sun burned down from above, they protected themselves with pith helmets. Poisonous snakes slithered underfoot, strong leather boots were recommended. In fact only a small proportion of these reptiles were deadly. The real danger came from tiny insects, the tick that carried typhus, and the Anopheles mosquito that spread malaria. Quinine was the recommended antidote for malaria, taken in large quantities. Daily doses of gin and tonic in the expatriates clubs did produce a few alcoholics but saved them from malaria.

Bernard made several trips from Lagos to Liverpool during the nineteen twenties and thirties, sometimes accompanied by his wife, Dorothy. The social life of the expatriate revolved around The Club. In the cool of the evening the wives might play bridge or mah-jong, while the men propped up the bar and talked about the events of the day. Occasionally, they dressed up in the uniform of the European Reserve

Saying Goodbye

Force and repeated wartime stories. It was gin and tonics all round and 'one for the road'.

Back in their bungalow in the evening Captain Chadwick and Mrs Chadwick tucked themselves into bed and tucked the mosquito net under the mattress. They spent over ten years together, in The White Man's Grave.

Finally, in 1937 they boarded ship at Port Harcourt, on the Niger Delta. This was a hot, swampy place, home to a countless number of evil little insects. The tide rose, the *Apapa* cast off from the quay and a sea breeze swept the mosquitos away.

Bernard Chadwick sometimes gave his address in England as Wylde Green, Birmingham. Dorothy's home was Old Hall, Bishop's Castle. Bernard was too old to take part in the Second World War. A sensible place to live during that time would have been in the Shropshire countryside, ten miles from the Welsh border, where there were no bombs and few mosquitos.

With the exception of bees, most insects were a nuisance, especially around cattle and horses. Victor Dayus knew all about that.

The Thiepval Memorial to the Missing of the Somme was unveiled in 1932. It bears the names of seventy-two thousand men who have no known grave.

LIEUTENANT CHARLES VICTOR DAYUS – 9TH BATTALION ESSEX REGIMENT
The Army Medical Board described the wound he received at Monchey-le Preux in 1917...

> *...struck by a bullet in the right shoulder below the clavicle and passed through making an exit over the scapula...*

The Department of Health concluded that his GSW (Gunshot Wound) had contributed to his death. His age must also have been taken into account, Victor Dayus was eighty-seven years old when he died. If others of his generation, school friends and fellow boarders, had been so lucky they too may have enjoyed long and productive lives.

The careers of many of the boys he knew were laid out for them, farmers' sons would follow their father, a place would be found in the family business for chemists, wine merchants and builders, and so it was

© BES Library

for Charlie Dayus. Great grandfather, grandfather and father were all veterinary surgeons.

Greeting his father in the evening he would know the nature of the animals he had treated that day, cattle and horse, sheep and pig, they all had their own distinctive smell.

Charles began his studies at the Royal Veterinary College in October 1914 and passed his first professional exams the following year. Many Bridgnorth boys were already in uniform, Charles joined a reserve battalion of the Coldstream Guards as a Private (155279). He applied for a commission and began his training with the Officer Cadet Corps of Balliol College.

Training complete Charles, joined the Essex Regiment as a 2nd Lieutenant in February 1917. His tour of duty in France was brief.

The battalion arrived at Le Havre on 13th of April. The very next day the Royal Newfoundland Regiment and the 1st Battalion Essex Regiment advanced on the German lines, their objective was Monchey-le-Preux. Twenty Canadians fought their way into the village. After four hours of fighting a wounded man reported to battalion headquarters that all the troops involved, Canadians and British, had been either killed or captured.

It was then the turn of the 9th Battalion of the Essex Regiment to show what they were made of. In May Lieutenant Dayus took up his duties on the front line. On the 17th of July they attacked over the same ground as the 1st Battalion.

Anyone of a superstitious nature would have avoided going into battle alongside John Deathridge. Private Deathridge was among forty men of the Essex Regiment who died on the 17th of July, the day Charles Dayus was wounded. Carried from the battlefield and treated at a base hospital he was moved to the coast and sailed back to Southampton on *H M Hospital Ship Aberdonian.*

Safely Home

All Charles had to show for three months service in France was a scar on the shoulder and a scar on his back. He never returned. In October the following year he was released from the army and awarded the Silver War Badge, 'for services rendered'.

He returned to his studies and qualified as a veterinary surgeon in 1921 and joined his father's practice. He was back in familiar territory, the fields and farms and the hills of South Shropshire. After two years new pastures beckoned.

The *Ascanius*, steamed away from her berth at Liverpool, to begin her voyage to Sydney. There were all sorts on the passenger lists, architects and accountants, farmers and physicians, a solitary schoolmistress and just one veterinary surgeon. Charles sailed on from Sydney, across the Tasman Sea to Auckland to begin his work with the New Zealand Department of Agriculture.

Over the next twenty years he made a name for himself as a regular contributor to the New Zealand Journal of Agriculture. He was also a noted sportsman. Grammar School boys were all expected to take part in sporting activities and that included swimming. The waters of the Severn, above Southwell's carpet factory, was where many learned their first strokes.

The Waikato River is the longest in New Zealand, in parts not unlike the Severn, perhaps a little warmer. Charles was tempted, one fine day he took the plunge and swam downstream for twenty miles to establish a record.

'CV', as he was known to his friends, did visit England at the beginning of the Second World War. He was granted a commission as a Captain in the New Zealand Veterinary Corps, and in 1952 he was appointed adviser at the New Zealand High Commission in London. He interviewed young vets planning to emigrate. He was sympathetic, he recognised in them the same adventurous spirit he had shown in his youth.

Following his retirement he returned to New Zealand and settled for a time at Timaru, a most attractive town on the coast of South Island with distant views of snowclad mountains. However, the call of 'the old country' was too strong and 'CV' came home to England.

In later life he must have wondered how different it might have been for other 'old boys' had they not been asked to play a part in the Great War. Charles Dayus was an active man, a sportsman in his youth, with wide interests, photography and the theatre in particular. He had time for reflection during the twenty years of his retirement, on his childhood at Coton House in the Corvedale, his boyhood as a boarder, the battleground east of Arras and the beautiful landscapes of New Zealand.

He could still remember his old school and most of the scholars and boarders, Rudolf Dawes, Cookson and Spurway in particular. He could recall the clatter they made when they were sent up the stairs to their rooms at the end of the day. 'CV' was eighty-seven when he died, his had been a full and active life. Not all his old friends had been so fortunate, to survive and see the world.

Chapter 24

History Repeated

Hundreds of local lads passed through the gates of Prees Heath Camp in the first six months of 1919. It was here that they received their discharge papers, and accepted them happily.

The war was over but there was still a need for an army of occupation. Youngsters who had seen little or no active service were not released. There was also the matter of the troubles in Afghanistan, this was soon resolved. The troubles in Ireland were not so easily overcome.

The servicemen who seemed most reluctant to return to civilian life were the airmen. The thrill of flying was addictive, Milner Deighton couldn't give it up.

He found the perfect pastime to carry on flying with an element of danger in every flight. He raised funds for wounded comrades by performing with Bertram Mill's Flying Circus. One daring display was filmed when Milner flew his Sopwith Camel over Margate. A journalist, writing an article for Autocar, could not contain his enthusiasm.

> *I have never beheld so dazzling display as that of Captain Deighton for he passed from one feat to another with such rapidity that the eye could scarcely follow him. The machine, a Sopwith Camel, similarly darted about at very high speed, at all angles, just like a dragonfly, and even improved upon natural flight by careering along upside down.*

Milner was reluctant to give up this sort of excitement, but eventually when he took over responsibility for the family firm, he was finally grounded.

It would certainly have been best if Alexander Boon and his squadron had stayed on the ground on a rainy day in August 1927.

FLYING OFFICER ALEXANDER GOODISON BOON – ROYAL SCOTS AND ROYAL AIR FORCE

John Goodison Boon was a surgeon and physician, and able to provide a very comfortable lifestyle for his wife, Olive, and sons Patrick and Alexander. Living at 'Whitehall' in Church Street Broseley they had three live-in servants to cook and clean, and look after them. Alexander had a 'private governess' to give him a basic education, before he was admitted to the Grammar School in 1915.

As a schoolboy he would have followed the wartime career of Milner Deighton with great interest, and this may have been reason enough to join the Royal Air Force in his early twenties.

Alexander missed the war, he was just too young. Nevertheless, he must have planned a military career. On leaving school, in 1919, he went straight to the Royal Military Academy, Sandhurst; he went on to be commissioned in the Royal Scots.

The Royal Scots and many infantry regiments of the British Army found themselves in a very unpleasant place in 1919 – Ireland. A rebellion had been put down in 1916, but trouble flared up once again three years later. The Irish Republican Army (IRA) was founded, and a guerrilla war, which they called the Irish War of Independence began. Men died, not on the scale of the Great War but died they did. The Royal Scots lost a handful of men, to pneumonia, suicide, and a few kidnapped and executed by the IRA. This unpleasant affair came to an end in 1921.

Alexander Boon's career progressed, he was an acting Captain when, in 1925, he was seconded to the Royal Air Force and joined No 13 Army Co-operation Squadron at Andover. He flew the Bristol Fighter that had performed well during the war, a two-seater with a Lewis gun mounted behind the pilot.

Alex's squadron was to be relocated to an airfield in Kent, and what should have been a routine operation proved to be a disaster. The weather on the morning of the 1st of August was appalling; undeterred, six aircraft took off in a torrent of rain. Almost immediately they were in trouble. An officer of the Royal Fusiliers, supervising a training exercise nearby, described what happened.

The machine was attempting to land. It appeared to be some 200 feet up. It stalled, turned to land, and then dropped like a stone, nose first, to the ground with a great crash.

Ambulances, from the nearby aerodrome at Farnborough, were on the scene in less than two minutes. Mr Hammond, a groundsman on the Aldershot golf course was already there.

I cut three straps round the waist of the aircraftsman, and helped to draw the man out of the wreckage.

Leading Aircraftsman Stan Vincent was dead. Flight Lieutenant Alex Boon died in the ambulance. Accidental death was the verdict at the Aldershot inquest.

Flying was then a dangerous occupation, this was the second fatal accident within a fortnight for 13 Squadron – unlucky for some. Those of a superstitious nature might also have noted that within a radius of three hundred yards from the spot on the golf course, where Alex Boon fell to the ground, there had been three other crashes in the previous twelve months.

Another Old Boy familiar with the Surrey countryside, and one who had also experienced the troubles in Ireland, was Ernest Corfield. He too was a Sandhurst graduate and a lucky man, to serve in both World Wars and survive.

Lieutenant Colonel Ernest John Moore Corfield – KSLI & Royal Army Ordnance Corps

Sir John Moore died a hero's death at Coruna in 1809. His military career had been long and distinguished. There is modest statue of him in the centre of Glasgow, his native city, but he was never as well known as Lord Nelson or the Duke of Wellington. He is best remembered by infantrymen who have benefited from his training methods. Barracks at Folkestone, Winchester and Shrewsbury bear his name.

This may have caused some embarrassment to 2nd Lieutenant Ernest John Moore Corfield when he arrived at the John Moore Barracks in Shrewsbury to join the county regiment. 'You've got something to live up to, Corfield,'

© BES Library

When choosing names for their first-born son did Thomas and Margaret Corfield expect him to become a great general, probably not? Tom Corfield, a farmer from Middleton Priors, married Margaret Anne Moore in 1897, Ernest was born in April the following year and was given his mother's surname to add to Ernest John.

To complete his education Ernest travelled daily from North Farm to Bridgnorth. He left with an Oxford Senior Certificate to become an elementary school teacher, he was seventeen. The following year he applied to Sandhurst and was commissioned in the county regiment just before Christmas 1917. In the New Year he was dispatched to Ireland to join the reserve battalion. He attended a course at the 'Gas School' and a 'Transport' course at Fermoy in preparation for service in France.

To remind him of the 'Duties of an Officer' he was given a pamphlet with extracts from an address given by a Senior Officer who was very clear on one thing.

Don't be an 'Old Woman' whatever else you may be! No troops ever possessed a discipline that was worth a damn who were commanded by weak, slow, irresolute Old Women".

Slightly more useful was another slim document for Ernest to refer to: *Questions a Platoon Commander Should Ask Himself before an Attack*. There were twenty-five questions to be answered, among them were:

8. Is my watch synchronised?

10. Have I told my Platoon Sergeant everything I can to enable him to carry on if I get knocked out?

15. Have I warned my men to shoot or bayonet anyone giving the order "Retire"?

18. Do I know what to do with prisoners?

Another question that he may have considered was 'What the hell am I doing here?'

For the 1st Battalion KSLI, March 1918 was a particularly humiliating month, 388 men and fourteen officer were taken prisoner. The captured men were marched away from the front at Noreuil to Marc. One party marched fifty kilometres without food.

To bring the Battalion up to strength officers were replaced and 427 'other ranks' drafted in.

2nd Lieutenants Taffs, Bodman and E J M Corfield arrived in April. Taffs and Bodman were experience soldiers, both promoted from the ranks, good men to have at your side when facing battle for the first time.

The Battalion held the front line in trenches near Zillebeke Lake, any rainfall turned the whole area into a sea of mud. They were under constant bombardment, even in the reserve trenches. Gas shells caused at least eighty casualties. Some men had been in France only a matter of weeks. They were withdrawn to School Camp on the 7th of June, nerves were frayed, and everyone needed a rest.

Ernest Corfield and his men marched off to Cornette for musketry practice. The rest period lasted just two weeks and much of that was spent tramping from one camp to another, Proven Camp, Ramsford Camp and the aptly named Dirty Bucket Camp, an unpleasant spot overlooked by German artillery on Kemmel Hill.

July was spent here, in the southern neck of the Ypres salient, making preparations to recapture the Kemmel Hill. A German prisoner who surrendered to 'A' Company admitted that morale was low in their ranks; they were 'tails down'. The presence of fresh American troops was being felt. A company of New Yorkers was attached to the 1st KSLI to gain battlefield experience. Rumours of a German attack persisted and the Royal Artillery increased their shelling, German retaliation caused more casualties. They were replaced by a fresh draft of close to a hundred men. There was little change in the routine of trench life throughout July. The Battalion spent the first ten days of September at Heilly practising for open warfare, anticipating the final breakthrough. There was a general feeling that victory was in sight.

The Hindenburg Line, the last and strongest of the German army's defences, consisted of three well-defended trench systems. The Australians had won back the ground lost to the Germans earlier in the year and were now preparing to attack Holnon Wood. This was where, men of Kent, (The Buffs), Yorkshiremen, Lancashire lads and The Shropshires stood together facing the 'Quadrilateral', a position of such strength that the German officers of the garrison regarded it as impregnable.

The attack began at 5.20 am on the 18th of September. Conditions could hardly have been worse, black cloud and heavy rain all night, thick mist in the morning. The entire brigade became hopelessly mixed. Despite this they advanced nearly two miles but came to a halt in front of the fortified village of Fresnoy-le-Petit. The French brigade on their left were less successful. The Battalion 'dug in' and awaited orders, communications had broken down. They spent a miserable night in the open. The following day they were sent in to attack the village once again. 'B' Company fought their way in and were cut off, resisting capture until dusk when the survivors joined up with 'D' Company. All the officers involved were casualties, 2nd Lieutenant Corfield was one of the wounded. This was the end of the war for Ernest.

A week later the garrison of the 'Quadrilateral' surrendered, and within two months fighting on the Western Front ceased.

Victory was declared, but that did not mean that all the troubles were over for the British Army. Troops were dispatched to Northern Russian to face the Red Army. Others were sent to Afghanistan.

Ernest returned to Ireland, to barracks at Fermoy. Service in Ireland at the time was an unhappy experience for all, particularly ordinary soldiers who did not concern themselves with politics. Irishmen had fought well in France and now they were considered the enemy. After two grim years of guerrilla warfare the Irish were granted their independence. The weary British troops could go home.

The Kings Shropshire Light Infantry was the last British battalion to leave Dublin Castle in 1921. They withdrew to the Curragh Camp outside the capital. Lieutenant Corfield, now serving with the 2nd KSLI, had a responsibility for ordnance, the supply and maintenance of weaponry.

In May 1922 the Battalion prepared to leave. General O'Connell, commander of the Irish Free State Army arrived to witness the withdrawal of the British Army and the takeover by the Irish Army. The union flag flew on a flagpole on top of a water tower within the Curragh Camp. This was a very impressive structure, postcard pictures taken from the top showed the layout of the camp and the surrounding countryside. Boys in the barracks wrote a final message home.

Not a nice place, Mum

View of Curragh Camp, looking South East from Tower

The union flag was lowered on the morning of 16th of May 1922, and carefully folded. Then with equal care, as was traditional in the British Army at the time, they cut down the flag pole. This meant that when the Irish Tricolour was raised at noon the flagpole had to be held up by Irish troops. This did not make for a dignified ceremony.

Hang On a Minute, I'm Making History

No one was sorry that it was over. Lieutenant Corfield and his Company sailed home to Liverpool. At the Curragh Ernest's commanding officer had applied for war medals on his behalf, they were sent to 36 North Side, Clapham Common, London SW4. Ernest was now transferred to the Army Reserve.

No sooner was he released by the army than he signed the church register in Neath when he married Elsie Mills, a watch-repairer's daughter.

These were difficult times for anyone looking for work, one thing was certain Ernest was not a watch-repairer and he did not go back to the farm. He might have been a schoolmaster but it seems he became an estate agent.

The couple spent the early years of married life in Wandsworth and moved to Cheam in the 1930s when Ernest took over the business of 'Howards of Sutton' (Surrey.) It was the time of the Depression and trade was slow. Buying and selling, manufacturing, farming, the whole economy of Britain was suffering.

Tom Corfield, Ernest's father was then farming at Astley Abbots, this was not particularly profitable and when Ernest visited them in 1934 he promised some help. He wrote just before Christmas to say that his business, selling houses, was so bad that he could only afford to send a cheque for £5.

This was the least of his worries, Elsie had not been well and when the matter was investigated it was revealed that she had a condition that meant she would never have children, or as Ernest put it in his letter, '...you cannot look in this direction for any grandchildren I'm afraid'. Tom and Margaret responded by sending a parcel with two ducks, some apples and a bunch of sage. This was well received and brought good cheer at Christmas.

Business picked up in the spring and must have prospered in the years that followed. If Ernest and Elsie lacked a family life at least they had a social life. A dedicated freemason, Brother Corfield was the Worshipful Master of the Star of India Lodge. He hosted a lavish 'Ladies Festival' in the Connaught Rooms in February 1938. There was fine food, dancing and entertainment. Lillian Keyes a well-known soprano sang and Arthur Askey a popular comedian told jokes, suitable for ladies, on this occasion. This was something to enjoy at a time when there were rumours of another war.

Captain Corfield was recalled for service in June 1939 and mobilised the day after war broke out.

No longer an infantryman, he transferred to the Royal Army Ordnance Corps and seconded to the Indian Army. This meant separation for Ernest and Elsie, a sad period in their lives, but at least Ernest was far removed from the battlefields of Europe.

The life of a military man in Peshawar was routine, training, inspecting, corresponding, issuing and carrying out orders. There was just occasionally a social event to break the monotony, an invitation to an 'At Home' from the Governor General of the North West Frontier Province or an invitation to dinner with His Highness the Maharaja of Bavorda. These were rare events, mostly Ernest dined in the officers' mess at the garrison, at 'The Club' in Peshawar or alone in his bungalow with just his 'bearer', Ghulan Nabi, in attendance.

The threat to India came from the Japanese. Their advance had been halted in the East, in Burma. If they had broken through, as they had in Malaya, this would have changed the course of the war. It was the responsibility of the Ordnance Corps to supply the shells and bullets, the ammunition that would sustain troops in the front line. Major Corfield fulfilled his duties, and by the end of the war he had been promoted to Lieutenant Colonel.

Ernest John Moore Corfield was finally released from service in June 1949. Elsie and Ernest lived comfortably in Victoria Gardens, Neath, for over twenty years. Ernest had very satisfying work as area organiser for the Royal National Institute for the Blind. His dear wife died in 1974 and the following year he returned to Bridgnorth. 'A real gentleman, greatly respected', he settled in the town and renewed friendships.

Selby Piper and Ernie Corfield had much in common, same school, same regiment, and service in both wars, and in distant parts of the empire.

William and Marie Piper started a family in 1890, and within five years they had three boys. Within ten years they had moved on, from 38 West Castle Street to a 'modern' house, 9 Victoria Road. William Piper's work as a carpet designer made this move possible. Harold Selby Piper chose the same trade as his father but he was not fully committed. He spent sixteen years in the army and claimed to have celebrated Christmas on four continents.

By contrast, Ralph Piper left school went into Lloyd's bank in Bridgnorth, moved to Ironbridge as the manager and retired to Whitchurch; he hardly left the county.

'Edgy', William Egell Piper landed at Boulogne in November 1915, with the Royal Warwickshire Regiment, and spent three uncomfortable years in Europe. Of the three, the career of Harold Selby Piper was the most remarkable.

MAJOR HAROLD SELBY PIPER – KSLI – INDIAN ARMY & PIONEER CORPS

Selby Piper shared the fortunes and misfortunes of 'F' Company (Bridgnorth) of the 1st /4th King's Shropshire Light Infantry for six years. He was nineteen when he enlisted as a Territorial in 1912.

The Drill Hall in St Mary's Street was more like a social club than a military training establishment. As the nation rumbled to war the training did become more serious, especially at the annual camp. Selby spent a fortnight at Hereford the year he joined. The experience was repeated at Pembroke the following year, but cut short at Aberystwyth in 1914. They arrived on the 1st of August and were mobilised for war three days later.

Expecting to take on the Germans the Battalion volunteered 'en masse' for overseas service. Overseas it was. On board SS Deseado they sailed the North Atlantic Ocean, the Mediterranean Sea, the Red Sea, and the Indian Ocean. They docked in Bombay, crossed India by train and sailed on from Calcutta, across the Bay of Bengal to Rangoon. The barracks were close to the Shwedagon pagoda. It was true to say that no one in Private Piper's Company had ever seen anything like it.

The Shropshires were not on a sight-seeing tour, they had hardly arrived when they were called on to quell a mutiny. The 129th Baluchi Regiment did not share their enthusiasm for military service. Order was quickly restored after a 'show of strength' at the forts along the Irrawaddy.

The first Christmas away from home was celebrated in Burma. No sooner was that over than they were called out to deal with another mutiny, this time in Singapore. Steam Ship *Edavana* landed them at the docks and they engaged with the mutineers immediately. This time it was 5th Bengali Light Infantry that were revolting, and this was an altogether more serious affair. It was a month before all the ringleaders were rounded up. The KSLI carried out some ofthe executions. There were other minor incidents but nothing more serious.

The Battalion settled down to the routine of life in barracks and training exercises in 'the bush'.

A notable break for Selby Piper came in July 1915, and it earned him promotion. Corporal Piper was the only man who spoke colloquial German. Perhaps he had anticipated the war, and done some homework.

The German light cruiser *SS Emden* had caused a lot of trouble, she had sunk fifteen merchant ships, a Russian cruiser and a French destroyer. This trail of destruction was brought to an end by *HMAS Sydney*. German survivors of the encounter in the Cocos Islands, were made prisoners of war, and held in Singapore before being shipped to Australia. Captain Haslewood and Corporal Piper led the escort party. Selby found this a difficult assignment, nerve-wracking

The men of the Emden always seemed on the verge of making trouble.

There was trouble ahead for Selby Piper.

Eventually the 4th Battalion were relieved by the Middlesex Regiment, and they began to make their way back to home waters. On the way they stopped in Ceylon for training and in South Africa and Sierra Leone to pick up a stomach bug. They boarded *RMS Walmer Castle* at Freetown and docked at Plymouth on 27th July 1917.

Everyone was looking forward to home leave after nearly three years on the other side of the world. It was not to be. The Battalion disembarked, and the next morning taken by train to Southampton. Stores and baggage were loaded onto yet another ship that sailed to France immediately. At 3 o'clock in the afternoon they reached Le Havre, still dressed in their tropical kit.

With all speed they were re-equipped, re-armed and given training in wiring, bombing, and how to cope with gas attacks. The Shropshire's joined the Royal Navy Division on the front line. The men were now granted home leave in batches of twenty. For some this would be their last home leave.

They return to France to prepare for battle. In small batches, the troops from the tropics were treated to 'trench familiarisation', which meant spending forty-eight hours in a damp, miserable and dangerous place. They then returned to billets at Maroeuil. Even here there was still the sound of guns in action, and disturbing shell holes in the walls of their sleeping quarters.

They were a disciplined force, this was what they had trained for. When Sergeant Piper and his Company went into action during the Battle of Passchendaele 'they moved forward as accurately as on parade'. Over twenty men died and a hundred were wounded.

In December 1917, Selby mentions in his diary Metz-en-Couture, where the Battalion spent a quiet Christmas. The season of goodwill ended abruptly before the New Year, when a German artillery bombardment destroyed the Battalion communication system completely, and trenches held by a neighbouring regiment were invaded. The enemy was driven out by 'D' Company, led by a young officer who had only just joined them. He lost his life, he was recommended for the Victoria

Cross – several of his men received awards for gallantry.

The Battalion moved off Welch Ridge to rest, and Sergeant Piper took the train to the coast and returned to England. The 'paperwork' had finally caught up with him. In 1914 he had applied for a commission, but he had moved about so much that his documents, lost in the system, had taken nearly three years to catch up with him.

During his period of training at the Whittington Barracks Selby had time to consider his next move. The Hindenburg Line was broken, the Germans were in retreat and the war would soon be over. Selby received his commission in October 1918. 2nd Lieutenant Piper needed to test his newly-acquired leadership skills. He was one of the volunteers who was posted to the Indian Army Reserve of Officers, and set off for the East without delay.

He crossed France by train in the company of 250 young officers all seeking adventure. There was some excitement as they approached the Italian border, they were about to enter a tunnel. Of course Selby had seen a railway tunnel before, there was one under Bridgnorth town on the line to Shrewsbury. It was dark and smoky, but after about a minute the train would emerge, and when the steam cleared from the carriage windows green fields and the River Severn came into view. The Mon Cenis Tunnel was thirteen kilometres long, an engineering marvel. Passengers entering the tunnel must have wondered if they would ever see daylight again. The lively young officers probably cheered.

They certainly cheered on the way to Taranto when they heard that the Armistice had been signed and the war in Europe was over. In fact they became a bit too excited in the view of a senior officer. He ordered the train to stop at the next station so that he could give them 'a talking to', a lecture on the sort of behaviour expected of an officer. He got off the train marched up and down the platform. To get everyone's attention he blew a whistle, the engine driver thought it was the signal to leave. More cheers from the train as it chugged away, leaving the fuming officer at the station platform!

There was another reason to celebrate at Port Tewfig, on the Gulf of Suez, it was Christmas. This was the second time Selby had passed through the Suez Canal and sailed into the Indian Ocean.

Karachi, Bahawalpur and the rail track to Rawalpindi, this was all new territory. Lieutenant Piper was attached to the 112th Infantry, they manned the Bannu Frontier Fort and it wasn't easy to get to. Down the Indus valley by train to Mari Indus, cross the river by ferry, carry stores in convoy with 'pony tongas' (pony and trap) 40 miles through mountain passes to Dardoni.

A rocky road

Given some training here in the art of mountain warfare, they went on to supply troops on the border with Afghanistan, anticipating an invasion.

War was declared, the forts at Dardoni and Miramshah were besieged for three weeks. Contact with the relief column was possible by radio. A personal 'wireless' message arrived for Selby Piper. His old employer, William Southwell, had successfully applied for his release from the Army, he was urgently needed in the design department of the carpet factory in Bridgnorth. There is no record of his reply. The relief column arrived and the Afgan War came to an end in August 1919.

Selby did not go back to the design department immediately, he remained in India for the next two years, by which time he had been promoted to Major. Awaiting transport home he was posted to Deolali, he was there for six months. This transit camp became a joke, but it wasn't funny. The boredom and frustration men suffered here had a deep psychological effect on some, they caught 'doolally tap' (tap, Urdu for fever), they lost their minds.

Major Piper did not 'go doolally', after a six-month wait he boarded *SS Naldera* and sailed home. He reported to the India Office in London and they presented him with four medals, including one for his efforts on the Afghan border.

At the time Major Piper gave a contact address in London, although he had returned to his pre-war position as a carpet designer. His interest in Essex Road, Acton may have been eighteen year old Constance Norton. Harold Selby Piper was eleven years her senior and it took a little while for Constance to be persuaded that he was the right man. They were married in 1928.

The following year they emigrated to America and set up home in a suburb of New York. In the US census of 1930 Selby was described as a designer in a Rug Mill, Southwell's Carpet Factory sounded so much better. The Pipers spent five years in the United States, visited Canada and crossed the Atlantic twice before deciding that life in a quiet market

Harold Selby Piper ID

town was better than a city full of skyscrapers. The peace was disrupted once again by German aggression.

At the outbreak of the Second World War Selby volunteered immediately, for 'any kind of Military Service'. Although he was forty-seven years old he was accepted, and after a refresher course posted to Scotland to command a company of the Pioneer Corps. These troops did the 'donkey work'; digging trenches, road work, burying the dead. Many 'colonial' troops were recruited to carry out these tasks. To command them a hundred British officers were dispatched to South Africa.

Selby arrived in Basutoland in 1940 and set up a training camp at Maseru. His Basuto Pioneers were the first Company to be sent to the Middle East, to Palestine. Trouble between Jews and Arabs had flared up before the war, this complicated the situation. Lieutenant Piper and his Basutos did not concern themselves with international politics, they had work to do – in the sulphur mines of Gaza, building a railway to Beirut, and manning coastal defences at Haifa.

Victory in 1945 meant that Selby could become a tourist, and visit the cedar forests of Lebanon and the Roman temple at Baal, before he sailed home to Constance, to England and finally back to the design department.

There were familiar faces in Southwell's factory, Fred Head, George Gower, Len Parton. They had all served together with Selby Piper in the Great War.

There were reunion dinners from time to time, tales of youth were repeated, until one by one the old soldiers faded away. Selby was ninety-one when he passed away. He will always be remembered because his widow gave the diaries and documents he had collected over the years to be preserved in the county archives. Details of the lives of others may never be known. Where was Geoffrey Peck in the 1930s?

Lieutenant Commander Geoffrey Awdry Peck – Royal Navy

Geoffrey Peck served in both World Wars and as a harbour master on a Pacific island. He loved the sea, but the sea could be cruel.

The treatment of Cadets preparing to enter the Royal Navy was harsh, the best possible training for those intending to lead rough men on rough seas. *HMS Conway*, a three-masted wooden sailing ship, moored on the Mersey, was Geoffrey's classroom. He went from school, to sea, to war.

By the end of the Great War he had served in the North Atlantic on ships protecting the supply lines of Britain. They escorted convoys, laid mines, fired torpedoes, and chased U-boats.

One of Geoffrey Peck's last duties was to lead a boarding party to take control of a Danish vessel, with a cargo of cryolite. This mineral, mined in Greenland, was vital for the production of aluminium and could not be allowed to fall into the hands of the Germans.

This sort of experience should have laid the foundations for a successful career. Vice Admiral Stanley thought he was 'an excellent young officer who shows great promise'. Commander Farquharson said he was 'a very keen and zealous officer, handles men well.'

Not everyone agreed. The final entries on his record noted that he had 'incurred grave displeasure' when he was found to have 'misused a travel warrant'. Perhaps he had made an unauthorised visit to his parents in Bridgnorth or to Greta Sansom in Berkshire.

Greta was five years his senior and should have been a steadying influence, they were married at Wargrave parish church in 1920. The next comment on his naval record said 'needs careful handling', good advice for his next Captain or for his new wife.

Ships were being decommissioned, men discharged and officers transferred to the reserve. It was time to move on. Geoffrey applied to the Board of Trade for a 'masters' ticket' and he was issued with the Masters' Certificate for Foreign-going Ships.

In 1922 he was on his way, sailing to the South Pacific on the 'Berengaria', not as master but as a passenger. Lieutenant Peck now called himself a diplomat.

Life for Colonial Administrators anywhere in the world was very agreeable and particularly comfortable in Fiji. There were palm-fringed beaches and warm sea breezes, and good company in the evening.

The Grand Pacific Hotel in Suva was built to attract world travellers, and local residents might also socialise there. Geoffrey could spend the evenings in the billiard room while Greta chatted with the wives on the terrace. On formal occasions Geoffrey would put on uniform, dress up in tropical whites and sport his war medals.

He was comfortable in uniform and wrote to the Admiralty to request permission to accept the appointment of Harbourmaster at Levuka. The setting was idyllic, among coconut and mango trees with the forested slopes of an extinct volcano in the background, a white coral beach and the blue Pacific all around.

All good things have to come to an end; Greta and Diana, their two year old daughter, sailed home on the *Jervis Bay* from Melbourne to Hull. Geoffrey retuned alone, in a 2nd class cabin, on *RMS Rangitata* from Wellington to Southampton. The family was reunited in East Castle Street.

It is not clear what Greta, Diana and Geoffrey did during the 1930s. He may have returned to the Colonial Service, to Africa most likely. What is certain is that he returned to the Navy in 1939.

With the rank of Lieutenant Commander he took up his duties at Pembroke Dock in 1940, tucked away in an inlet on the Welsh coast, but not out of harm's way. Luftwaffe bombers swarmed in, blew up oil tanks, and created the biggest blaze since the Great Fire of London.

Geoffrey was posted to *Collinwood*, a training establishment near Gosport. His sailing days were over, he was twice admitted to hospital, suffering 'congenital neuralgia' and 'duodenal ulcer, chronic'. His active service ended in Malta at St *Angello*.

All shore bases were called 'stone frigates' and this one really was. Built in the Middle Ages it had withstood many assaults. Defended by the Royal Marines and their three Bofors guns the fort suffered 69 direct hits during the Second World War.

When the war was over if Lieutenant Commander Peck wanted to exchange 'yarns of sea' with old friends he could join them at HMS President, not an ocean-going vessel, not a stone frigate, but a suite of rooms in the Port of London Building, close to the Tower of London.

The Peck's last voyage many have been on the *Durban Castle*. Greta and Geoffrey stepped on board at Mombasa, sailed south along the coast of Africa, it was a leisurely voyage. They called at Cape Town. Las Palmas, in the Canary Islands was their last port of call before docking at the Port of London. It was all very familiar, The Tower, HMS President, Trinity Square Gardens and The Memorial to the thirty-six thousand Merchant Seaman lost during both wars.

Geoffrey and Greta retired to a cottage on The Close next to Salisbury Cathedral, thirty miles from the Bristol Channel.

Awdry Peck, Geoffrey's father, retired naval surgeon, was eighty-nine when he died, his son was eighty-one. Living dangerously as a youth

383

seems to have been a recipe for long life. Victor Dawes must have done something dangerous to deserve a Military Cross.

MAJOR RUDOLF VICTOR DAWES MC – ROYAL ARTILLERY

Retired headmaster Henry Dawes must have been pleased and proud that his son had chosen to follow his example and become a schoolmaster. Between the wars his career progressed, and in 1938 he was appointed headmaster of East Grinstead Grammar School.

The following year, like Ernest Corfield, Selby Piper and Geoffrey Peck, he too volunteered to serve in the Second World War. To confirm his appointment as a Major in the Royal Artillery his name appeared in the London Gazette. It appeared again in 1948 when he was awarded the King Haakon VII Freedom Medal. What did he do to deserve it, did he help the Resistance Movement in Norway in some way, who knows?

Chapter 25

A Fitting Tribute

Every community, every town, village, club, and school, lost young men, and every community was determined that the sacrifice they had made would never be forgotten. Within a month of the end of the war the governors of the Grammar School set up a committee to create their own memorial. Everyone concerned had a personal interest.

James Wightman and Harold Dove were both schoolmasters, they were released from duty at the same time and both became soldiers. Harold Dove died on the battlefield. Jimmy Wightman was given the task of constructing a Memorial Board and painting on it the names of the fallen, including Harold Dove, and his own brother Charlie Wightman.

His work was completed in 1921 and placed in the entrance hall of the school. At the same time a more ambitious project was underway. Plans for a Memorial Library and Dining Room were drawn up. A committee to raise funds and to oversee the work was established, and the obvious choice for chairman was a military man, Lieutentant Colonel John Cunliffe, of Bradeney House.

Controlling the finances was the headmaster, the Reverend Henry Dawes. The mayor of Bridgnorth, Tom Whitefoot was on the committee – his son had served with the Canadian Medical Corps and was one who had witnessed the senseless slaughter. The third member of the committee was William Southwell, chairman of the governors and manging director of the carpet factory – his son Arthur had been killed in action in 1916.

It was agreed that the building work should be carried out by T E Lay and Sons. This was work Tom Lay, and his son Ted, could take some pride in. Ted had lost many good friends. For the best part of ten years he employ all his skill as a builder to create a lasting memorial to them. He knew he was lucky to be alive.

On the 1st of July 1916, the first day of The Battle of the Somme, thousands were killed and wounded, Private Ted Lay was wounded, Private Charlie Wightman died.

Construction complete, arrangements were made for the opening ceremony in July 1930. Tom Lay and his son made sure that everything was spick and span within the building before any guest went through the door.

The opening ceremony of the Memorial Library was Henry Dawes's last duty for the school. He was the last minister of the church to be appointed as headmaster.

Over two hundred guests assembled in the school hall. The service of remembrance began, led by the Reverend Dawes. The opening hymn was announced, there was polite coughing before all gave full voice to...

Oh God our help in ages past, our hope for years to come...

The congregation knew it by heart, one line had particular meaning that day,

...time like an ever rolling stream bears all her sons away...

Then followed a carefully chosen reading, (Ecclesiastes XLIV 1-10), that begins 'Let us now praise famous men".

It was read by Arthur Dyer, he had served with the county regiment on the Somme, and his brother had died there. School assemblies were nothing new to him. His career as a schoolmaster had progressed since the end of the war, he had just been appointed headmaster of Thame Grammar School.

Although the congregation was attentive they could not digest every word, certain phrases were particularly appropriate –

...these were men furnished with ability, living peaceably... men renowned for their power, but these were merciful men...and some there be that have no memorial, who perished as though they had never been. Their bodies are buried in peace but their name liveth forever more.

In his closing remarks the Reverend Dawes recalled once again, with pride, brave deeds of boys he had known and who had brought honour to the school. Those attending the ceremony that day hardly needed reminding, they were of that generation and familiar with the faces and actions of these Old Boys they had known so well.

Slowly, thoughtfully, the congregation moved from the hall to witness the opening ceremony.

Major Sydney Westrop was the most decorated Old Boy, he had been awarded the Distinguished Service Order and the Military Cross, for 'conspicuous gallantry and devotion to duty'. He was entrusted with the key to the library door.

He spoke, not of his own war record but of the loss to the community, and in particular of the loss of two school captains, Percy Nevett and Bernard Cookson who had both died in battle.

He quoted lines from In Flanders Fields by John McCrae, now part of every Remembrance Service.

...Short days ago we lived, felt dawn, saw sunset glow,
Loved and were loved, and now we lie in Flanders Fields...

The door unlocked, he handed the key to Sir Offley Wakeman, chairman of the county council. Serving as a Captain with the Grenadier Guards he had been wounded on the Western Front.

Roll of Honour

IN MEMORY OF THE FORTY-THREE OLD BRIDGNORTHIANS WHO GAVE THEIR LIVES FOR THEIR COUNTRY FROM 1914 TO 1918			
J.H.P BEAMAN	A.L.GEORGE	M.JONES.	L.C. SMITH.
A.E.BOUCHER.	H.W GIBBS	R.H.KELLY.	D.SPURWAY.
R.BOURNE.	H.GLENN.	C.J.W MACMICHAEL.	W.J.STEWARD.
E.F BURTON.	R.GREGORY.	J.MARSTON.	A.W.STOKES.
H.B.COOKSON	V.J.GRIFFITHS	W.P.NEVETT.	R.VAUGHAN.
J.L.DAIN.	G.HASELER.	W.ORMESHER.	R.H.WALKER.
H.DICKINSON	F HEAD.	H.C.PRICE.	C.N.WIGHTMAN
H.F DOVE.	J.W.HINCKESMAN.	T.H.ROBINS.	O.WILLIAMS.
H.F DYER.	R.B.HINCKESMAN.	O.SCHOOLCRAFT.	A.W.WILSON.
F L.FINDON	A.J.JOHNSON	W.S.SKELCHER.	T.R.WILSON.
R.B FINDON	H.M.JONES	R.M.R.THURSFIELD.	
SO THEY PASSED OVER AND ALL THE TRUMPETS SOUNDED ON THE OTHER SIDE.			

He promptly handed on the key to Alderman Lee George. He had lost a son.

Alan George, wounded by a shell at the Battle of Hazebrouck had died in April 1918; his father spoke briefly of the sacrifice the boys of Bridgnorth had made.

The doors were opened and those near the front could see the stairs leading to the library. Below a bright new stained glass window and behind a simple curtain was the plaque that honoured the fallen.

A couple stepped forward, the lady carrying a wreath. Her husband addressed the crowd, he had a 'presence' and spoke with authority. The names of the fallen were read. They could not have chosen a better man to perform the unveiling. Cedric Hardwicke was one of the leading Shakespearian actors of the time, and he was about to make a name for himself in Hollywood.

Helena Hardwicke laid the wreath. There was a minute's silence.

Guests were invited in, to view the dining room and kitchen on the ground floor and the library above. In the corner of the library, the names of the fallen appeared again on a wooden plaque, surrounded by their regimental badges. It is no longer there and some wooden carvings have also been lost – a pelican feeding her young with her own blood, symbolising sacrifice – a carrier pigeon with a message – and a mouse which had saved many from poisoned gas.

This was not a generation that chose to go to war, but when called upon to do so left the comfort and security of home and fought to preserve freedom. Those who served in the Second World War and all the conflicts since have acted in exactly the same way. There is nothing to suppose that students attending school today would act differently. Let us hope they are not called upon to do so.

Permission given by Nathan Jones and Geogina Ballantyne

Acknowledgements

The list is long of those who helped me compile this tribute to the Old Boys of Bridgnorth Grammar School. Certainly top of the list is my wife, Pat, who has been supportive throughout, despite the fact that military history is not her favourite subject.

Next on the list must be Jane Peeler, Bridgnorth Endowed School librarian. The material she so carefully preserved, school magazines and photographs, were invaluable. Her enthusiasm was infectious, when I dithered she put me back on track.

My task was made easier by the support of many in the community.

Mr Chris Aked, for instance, who gave me a tour of his home – the Old School House where I could look out over the Severn Valley, the same view the boys had from their dormitory. I was welcomed into the homes of many town resident and walked through the doorways that Old Boys passed through at end of their final leave. In the surrounding district farmers and landowners allowed me to wander across fields were young men had exercised ponies and turned them into war horses before they rode off with the Shropshire Yeomanry in 1914.

The list goes on, and I apologise to anyone I have missed, there have been so many, among them:

Roger and Anabel Bayliss, Sutton Maddock
John and Trish Beaman
Richard Cottam
Gerald and Linda Clarke
Margaret Crawford-Clarke
Pat Debes

David Deighton
Clive Gwilt
The Hockenhull family
Lord Gavin Hamilton
Vicki Norman
Karen North of 'Fairfield', Oldbury
Lyn Parnaby
The Ryder Family
Martin Steward
Gillian Waugh-Pead
Simon and Anabel Wadlow, of the Croft

Documents and photographs loaned to me by these individuals are reproduced with their consent.

Many professional bodies also gave advice and valuable information.

Bridgnorth Library – Emma Spencer and her staff
Claverley Local History Group - Sue Burns
Shropshire County Archives – Sarah Davis
Shropshire Regimental Museum – Christine Bernayth
Royal Warwickshire Regimental Museum – David Baynham

I am particularly grateful to Rob Weston of The Severn Arms, Bridgnorth for the loan of several books that I used as reference

I also frequently referred to Greg Lewin's website to check the accuracy of some of my own research.

Further afield, the staff of the National Archives at Kew have been most helpful. Also the Commonwealth War Graves Commission

These were impersonal bodies, but they have always welcomed my enquiries, particularly Catherine Long and Neera Puttapipat at the Imperial War Museum.

Finally, and how could I forget, my sincere thanks go to SilverWood Books. Their expertise has made this possible. None of the errors are theirs – they are all mine. They have been so patient and understanding. I cannot thank them enough.